Stylin' with CSS:
A Designer's Guide
Second Edition

CHARLES WYKE-SMITH

New
Riders

Stylin' with CSS: A Designer's Guide, Second Edition
Charles Wyke-Smith

New Riders
1249 Eighth Street
Berkeley, CA 94710
510/524-2178
510/524-2221 (fax)

Find us on the Web at: www.newriders.com
To report errors, please send a note to errata@peachpit.com

New Riders is an imprint of Peachpit, a division of Pearson Education

Project Editor: Michael J. Nolan
Development Editor: Marta Justak
Production Editor: Hilal Sala
Proofreader: Doug Adrianson
Indexer: Julie Bess
Compositor: David Van Ness
Cover design: Aren Howell
Cover image: Veer
Interior design: Mimi Heft

ISBN 13: 978-0-321-52556-7
ISBN 10:   0-321-52556-6

9 8 7 6 5 4 3 2

Printed and bound in the United States of America

For Jemma and Lucy

Acknowledgements

A book like this is never a solo effort and thanks go to publisher Nancy Ruenzel at Peachpit for encouraging me to write this second edition, Editor-in-Chief Nancy Davis for her insightful advice and good humor, and to Michael Nolan, New Riders' Acquisition Editor for once again setting everything in motion. On the production team, I want to thank my development editor, Marta Justak, for her input and direction as we thrashed the book into shape; production editor, Hilal Sala, for her grace and constant encouragement; David Van Ness, the compositor, for his care in laying out the pages, and Doug Adrianson for his detailed proofing. A special thanks goes to my technical reviewer, Virginia DeBolt, for her skilled review of my code and the related text.

Thanks next to all the readers of the first edition who wrote to me with ideas and feedback. I hope that I understood and have delivered on what you were looking for, and do keep on writing to me with your suggestions and sending me the URLs of your sites.

At Benefitfocus.com where I work, I want to thank my boss, VP of Enterprise Product Strategy Nancy Sansom, for giving me the flexibility I needed to write this book, for her constant energy and guidance in my work, and for giving me the opportunity to work for a really amazing company. I also want to thank Benefitfocus' CEO, Shawn Jenkins, and COO, Jerry Lepore, for their support and leadership, and for building and running the best organization I have ever worked in.

A big shout-out goes to the talented and creative members of the User Experience Group team who I am privileged to manage and learn from—they are Brad Bonham, Darin Cavenaugh, Daniel Nadeau, Michael Rosier, Mike Attisano, Leah Giorlando, Tony Malatanos, and Matt Megrue. I also really enjoy the challenge of being part of the Product Strategy team, which includes the inventive minds of Raymond Minnis, Nathan Reel, John "Coach" Wilson, Kinsey Rawe, and Mike Fullan. Let's next mention some other people who make working at Benefitfocus fun and exciting: Nina Sossamon-Pogue, Andrew Alberico, Elena Tudor, Will Deupree, Manon Husman, Kelli Hicks, Tracey Snyder, Annmarie Fini, Michelle Pagel, Nate DaPore, Randy Chitwood, Glenn Miller, Heather Norton, Rebecca Laney, Paul Sparrow, Robert Moss, Don Taylor, and Jonathan Chandler—I appreciate your inspiration, friendship, and support every day.

I'll save the last and biggest thank you for my wife, Beth. She really stepped up to help me with this book and her graphic design and writing skills are on every single page. She checked my grammar, clarified my explanations, and re-punctuated my paragraph-length run-on sentences that I like so much. She also laid out the diagrams, designed the *Stylin' with CSS* Web site that is featured in Chapter 7 (I wouldn't have made my photo so big, but otherwise, nice job, Sweetie!), and generally ensured that complete and coherent chapters went to the editor the first time. This book is whatever it is in large part due to her unceasing attention to detail and constructive suggestions for improvements. Thanks, my love.

Finally, to my two lovely daughters, Jemma and Lucy, I want to say you both have been incredibly patient and understanding while your daddy has been writing, and now we can go and get ice cream again on Saturday mornings!

—Charles Wyke-Smith
Charleston, South Carolina, November 14, 2007

About the Author

Charles Wyke-Smith has been creating Web sites since 1994 and is currently Director of User Experience at Benefitfocus.com (www.benfitfocus.com), a South Carolina software company that provides online benefits enrollment for over 40 million people through the nation's major healthcare insurance companies, and that also develops consumer healthcare Web sites, including ICyou.com and iHealthfocus.com.

In 1986, he started PRINTZ Electronic Design, which was the first all-computerized design house in San Francisco. Charles has worked as a Web design consultant for such companies as Wells Fargo, ESPN Videogames, and the University of California, San Francisco. An accomplished speaker and instructor, he has taught multimedia and interface design and spoken at many industry conferences.

Charles lives in Charleston, SC, with his wife, Beth, and two daughters. In his spare time, he composes and records music in his home studio.

Contents

Introduction

It's hard to believe it's been over three years since I wrote the first edition of *Stylin' with CSS*. In the intervening time, I have been involved in the development of numerous Web sites and have fine-tuned the way I use CSS in the process. I intended to make a few small adjustments to this book for the second edition to cover IE7 and generally bring it up to date, but I ended up making numerous improvements to the first three chapters and completely rewriting the rest of the book. What should have taken weeks took almost a year.

The changes I have made reflect the inevitable improvement to the skills of anyone who works constantly with CSS, and these changes also more deeply address two skills that all programmers need to master: to avoid rewriting code that they have previously written elsewhere, and to learn to write code in the most economical way possible. Ways in which you can achieve these two worthy goals in your own work are presented throughout this new edition of the book.

Reuse and DRY

The first goal, **re-use of code**, is a theme that I explore in several chapters. I show techniques that let me create building blocks of functionality, whether that is the skeleton framework of a page layout or a nicely styled list of links, and store them as CSS classes that can be quickly attached to my markup and modified for the specific use. I've started to add these building blocks to a code library I call *Stylib* that contains all kinds of interface elements, organized as CSS code with its associated XHTML markup. I have included this library with the downloadable code examples for the book on the Web site, www.stylinwithcss.com. It's at an early stage but already contains many useful components that have saved me hours of development work, and I hope will do the same for you. I will continue to publish new code for this library and make it available for download.

The other goal, **economy of code**, is another theme that runs through this new edition. For example, by adding a style at the highest possible level in the document hierarchy, that style can then influence numerous elements. I often see CSS style sheets that declare the same font-family on every heading and paragraph, but adding that font-family to the top-level body tag means you only write and maintain that style in one place. The underlying concept is a programming maxim known as DRY, meaning *Don't Repeat Yourself.* We will look at many other examples like this in the chapters ahead.

Master the Key Techniques

I've also come to realize that truly understanding just a few important CSS techniques can turn a struggling newbie into a competent CSS journeyman. These techniques include correctly using the positioning and display properties, and understanding how floating and clearing really work. I have dedicated Chapter 4 to explaining these aspects of CSS and showing simple examples that illustrate how to apply them in practice. Anyone who has dabbled in CSS and wants to take their skills to the next level may find this chapter to be very enlightening—I certainly hope so.

Use the Right Tools

So before we launch into to the book proper, I want to explain how to get set up to work so that you can in the shortest possible time achieve page layouts that will work across the largest number of browsers.

You need a good code editor to write your code, and an FTP client to move your files to the Web server. Adobe Dreamweaver (about $400) integrates both of these and is my programming tool of choice. The code view is very helpful, color coding the different elements of your code, indicating syntax errors, and guessing what you are typing so you can auto-complete many common code elements after typing the first couple of letters. The design view, which attempts to render the page like a browser, is also useful if only because you can click any displayed element and immediately be jumped to related part of the code in the code view. There are also many low- and no-price editors and FTP clients out there that offer similar features if you don't want to make the investment in Dreamweaver. However, what ultimately matters is not what tools you use to write and upload your code, but what your Web pages look like in the user's browser.

Only Four Browsers Matter

You may be surprised when I tell you that there are only four browsers you really need to care about testing your work in:

- Firefox

- Safari

- Internet Explorer 7

- Internet Explorer 6

That is because these four browsers account for over 95 percent of all Web users, with none of the others having more than about a 2 percent market share (source: my averaging of Wikipedia's listing of many browser statistics sites at http://en.wikipedia.org/wiki/Usage_share_of_web_browsers).

One of these four browsers is IE6 which, despite its rendering bugs and poor support for many newer CSS properties, is currently still a dominant browser, although slowly (too slowly) falling out of use. The other three browsers are all what are commonly known as *SCBs*, which stands for Standards Compliant Browsers. This means they closely comply with the browser standards recommended by the World Wide Web Consortium. They all quite accurately render virtually all of CSS2 and many CSS3 properties. (CSS2 and CSS3 can be thought of as versions of CSS and you will learn more about them as we proceed.) Generally, there is little difference between them in the way that they render valid CSS-styled XHTML.

You could include Netscape in the above list, even though at best its market share is in single digits, but because Netscape and Firefox are both built on the Mozilla rendering engine, if your page works in Firefox, you're almost sure to see the same result on Netscape. So really, testing and tweaking to the point where you get a satisfactory result on just the four browsers listed above enables you to be confident that virtually everyone will see your site as you intended. I don't even bother testing in IE5.5 any more; it has less than half a percent usage now, and anyone who is running an eight-year-old browser probably has bigger technical problems than how your site renders.

My advice is definitely not to use IE6 as a development browser, but to develop using one of the three SCBs above, and then test and make any adjustments for IE6 only after your page is in advanced state on your SCB of choice. Actually, I'll go further, and say that I strongly advise you to view your pages during development using the Firefox browser. I say this because I find that overall Firefox is the most standards-compliant of all the SCBs. Also, you can install the Web Developer Toolbar add-on on Firefox, which allows you to: easily validate your XHTML and CSS without uploading to a server; turn style sheets on and off; view the outlines of the XHTML elements on your page so you can accurately see if the elements are laying out on the page as you intend; and use its numerous other useful and time-saving tools. Quite simply, if you don't have the Web Developer Toolbar installed you are probably wasting a lot of development time. Also add the Firebug add-on for some handy code debugging tools, and you are ready to work like a pro. Firefox and these two add-ons can be downloaded for free at www.getfirefox.com.

Download My Code, Don't Retype It

Finally, in a book like this, there are bound to be some errors, although a concerted effort has been made to review this book in great detail before it went to press. However, the code is all mine, and while I have tested every line of it, I ask you to do two things. First, if you want to use code shown in the book, don't copy it from the pages. Besides being a waste of time as all the code can be downloaded in seconds from the book's Web site, www.stylinwithcss.com, I will also fix any errors that are found and update the downloadable files.

... and Don't Forget to Write

Second, if you do find errors, please use the email form on the *Stylin' with CSS* site to let me know and I will publish them on the site. I also welcome your comments and suggestions, so do take a minute to drop me a line after you get through with the book. I will try to reply to everyone who writes, and I'll certainly also try to answer any questions you may have. I have limited time to help solve specific code problems, but if you really want to send me CSS to look at, please embed it in the head of the XHTML document and put any images on your own server with absolute URLs to them; then email the XHTML document to me and I can just pop the page open and take a quick look.

Finally, thanks for buying this book. I hope it's a huge help to you.

KEY TO ICONS USED IN THE BOOK:

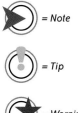 = Note

= Tip

 = Warning

CHAPTER 1

XHTML:
Giving Structure to Content

STYLIN' WITH CSS is all about building standards-compliant Web sites in the most efficient, streamlined way possible, while making those sites accessible to the widest audience and easy to update. Web standards are simply a set of recommendations by the World Wide Web Consortium. If all browser manufacturers and all Web programmers followed them, so the theory goes, all Web pages would look and behave the same in every browser. Nice idea, but hard to realize.

When I wrote the first edition of *Stylin'* in late 2004, the Web standards movement was gaining massive momentum. Today, most new Web sites are being programmed to meet Web standards, and the Web is a better place because of it.

The Web standards advocates who drove this movement have made the Web a better and more predictable place. They worked with browser manufacturers to ensure that new browsers interpret the three primary interface programming languages (XHTML, CSS, and JavaScript) in the ways recommended by the W3C, instead of each one using custom tags and features in the self-interest of competitive advantage.

Web Standards

By following best Web standards practices, Web developers like you and me can be very close to achieving a consistent display and performance of our sites for all our users. For example, you might expect Microsoft Internet Explorer to be the best, most Web standards-compliant browser, yet despite its current dominance, that is still not the case.

Every so often I'll mention CSS2 or CSS3. These terms simply refer to a specific version of the CSS standard. As with any technology, CSS continues to be refined. CSS2 is now almost fully implemented in most browsers; CSS3 has been defined for some time, but is supported only partially by Firefox and Opera and barely at all by IE7. More on both later.

Several other browsers do a good job of interpreting CSS, according to the W3C recommendations; the latest versions of Firefox and Opera on PC, and Safari and Firefox on Macintosh, all render XHTML styled with CSS2 in a remarkably consistent manner, but Microsoft Internet Explorer 6 (IE6) has numerous unimplemented features and buggy implementations of others.

Microsoft Internet Explorer 7 (IE7), released in October 2006, is a big improvement with regard to Web standards over IE6, and I had hoped that there would be rapid switchover from IE6 to IE7. However, according to thecounter.com, IE6 was still used by about 50 percent of all Web surfers as of July 2007.

Even Today, IDWIMIE

Anyway, as a result of IE6's refusal to die a rapid death, I still sometimes have to mention a CCS feature and tell you IDWIMIE (pronounced id-wimmy)—It Doesn't Work In Microsoft Internet Explorer.

I'll always indicate if this applies only to IE6 or to both IE6 and 7.

For some of Internet Explorer's (and other older browsers) short-comings, there are workarounds known as *hacks*—the nonstandard use of CSS to fool particular browsers into seeing or ignoring certain styles. It's tedious and time-consuming to create hacks, but as long as IE6 is around, the hacks must continue.

For us Web site designers and the visitors to the sites we create, Web standards offer the prospect of sites displaying and behaving consistently in every browser, on every platform. We're not there yet, but the days of every browser supporting a different feature set, with all the resultant inconsistencies that can make cross-browser/cross-platform Web development slow and frustrating, are, it seems, almost over. Web standards are clearly here to stay.

Strictly speaking, XHTML and CSS aren't programming languages, but mechanisms for marking up and styling content respectively, so I am using the term "language" in a general way here.

This img tag also has two attributes for the image source and alternative text respectively—see the sidebar "What Are Attributes?" to learn more.

Content, Structure, and Presentation

So, following the W3C's Web standards recommendations, *Stylin'* shows you how to publish *content* by defining its structure with XHTML and then defining its *presentation* with CSS.

1. **Content** is the collective term for all the text, images, videos, sounds, animations, and files (such as PDF documents) that you want to deliver to your audience.

2. **XHTML** (e**X**tensible **H**yper**T**ext **M**arkup **L**anguage) enables you to define *what* each element of your content is. Is it a heading or a paragraph? Is it a list of items, a hyperlink, or an image? You determine this by adding XHTML *markup* to your content. Markup comprises tags (the tag name is enclosed in angle brackets < >) that identify each element of your content. You create an *XHTML element* (hereafter just called an *element*) by either surrounding a piece of content with an opening and a closing tag like this

   ```
   <p>This tag defines the text content as a paragraph</p>
   ```

   or, for content that is not text (an image, in this example), by using a single tag

   ```
   <img src="images/fido.gif" alt="a picture of my dog" />
   ```

   This chapter focuses on XHTML and how to use it, but the most important thing to know right now is this: XHTML defines a document's *structure*.

3. **CSS** (**C**ascading **S**tyle **S**heets) enable you to define *how* each marked-up element of your content is presented on the page. Is that paragraph's font Helvetica or Times? Is it bold or italicized? Is it indented or flush with the edge of the page? CSS controls the formatting and positioning of each of the content elements. To format the size of the text in a paragraph, I might write

   ```
   p {font-size: 12px;}
   ```

   which would make the text 12 pixels high. Almost this entire book is dedicated to teaching you CSS, but the most important thing to know right now is this: CSS defines a document's *presentation*.

What Are Attributes?

Attributes can be added to a tag and can help further define that tag. Each attribute comprises two parts: the attribute name and the attribute value, in the format `name="value"`. For example, this image tag

```
<img src="images/fido.gif" alt="a picture of my dog" />
```

has two attributes: the image source, which has the value `"images/fido.gif"` that defines its relative location on the server, and an alternative text description, which has the value `"a picture of my dog"` that appears on-screen if the image fails to load, or that could be read aloud by a screen reader. Both these attributes are part of the structure of the document.

Before Web standards, it was common practice to load up tags with additional presentational attributes, such as text sizes and colors. Now, we can move all presentational information into the style sheet and thereby greatly reduce the complexity of our markup and use only attributes that define document structure.

Providing a means of separating a document's structure from its presentation was the core objective in the development of Web standards, and it is key to development of content that is both portable (can be displayed on multiple devices) and durable (ready for the future).

The Top 10 Benefits of Standards-Based Coding

You may be wondering "Why should I bother to change the way I have been marking up pages for years?" Here are 10 great reasons to adopt standards-based coding practices:

1. **Deliver to multiple user agents.** The same piece of marked-up content is readily deliverable in a wide variety of user agents, the collective name for devices that can read XHTML, such as browsers, handhelds like smartphones, cell phones with browsers, and screen readers that read text for the sight impaired. You simply create a different style sheet for each device type, or let the XHTML display as is.

2. **Improve performance.** Pages are much lighter (smaller in file size) and therefore download faster, because your content only needs minimal structural markup. We can now replace all of the presentational markup we used to load into the tags in every page of a site with a single style sheet. As you will see, a single style sheet can define the presentation of an entire site, and the user's browser only needs to download it once.

3. **Serve all browsers.** With a little effort, you can have your pages degrade nicely in older browsers, so all users get the best experience possible with their available technology.

4. **Separate content and presentation.** You can modify, or entirely change, either the content or the presentation (read: design) of your site without affecting the other.

(continued on next page)

The Top 10 Benefits of Standards-Based Coding (continued)

5. **Build fluid pages.** It's easier to code for varying quantities of dynamic content within your pages. For example, it's much easier to create pages that can accommodate varying numbers of items in a given listing or menu of your e-commerce store.

6. **Confirm your code is correct.** Validation services for XHTML and CSS can be used during development to report instantly on errors in your coding. This provides faster debugging, and the assurance that a page is truly completed when it both displays correctly on-screen and passes validation.

7. **Streamline production.** Production is more efficient. It's too easy for you (the designer) to be sidetracked into content management, because you are the only person who knows where the content goes in the mass of presentational markup. You end up being the one to add it—a tedious job and probably not what you were hired to do. By adopting standards-based practices, you can provide simple markup rules to the content team and work in parallel on the presentational aspects, knowing their content and your design will marry seamlessly down the line.

8. **Distribute content more easily.** Distributing your content for third-party use is much easier because the content is separate from any specific presentation rules, and in many cases, simply not feasible otherwise.

9. **Make it accessible.** It's easier to make your site accessible and meet legal requirements, such as the Americans with Disabilities Act, Section 508, known colloquially as ADA 508.

10. **Do less work.** You write less code, and it's a whole lot quicker and easier to get the results you want and modify your work over time.

The Times They Are A-Changing

Web standards are now quite widely adopted. Designers are moving away from using tables to lay out their pages and using clean structural markup, free of nested tables, spacers, and numerous `<br>` (line breaks) and ` ` (non-breaking spaces). These techniques were used only to force everything into the right place and had no meaning with respect to the content.

Here's an example of the old way of doing things:

The Way We Were...

Take a look at this classic example of how Web sites were coded before Web standards became widely adopted. This is a snippet of markup from the Microsoft home page, July 1, 2004.

```
<table cellpadding="0" cellspacing="0" width="100%"
height="19" border="0" ID="Table5">

<tr>

<td nowrap="true" id="homePageLink"></td>
```

```
<td><span class="ltsep">|</span></td>

<td class="lt0" nowrap="true" onmouseenter="mhHover('localTo
olbar', 0*2+2, 'lt1')" onmouseleave="mhHover('localToolbar',
0*2+2, 'lt0')">

<a href="http://go.microsoft.com/?LinkID=508110">MSN Home</a>
</td>

<td><span class="ltsep">|</span></td>

<td class="lt0" nowrap="true" onmouseenter="mhHover('localTo
olbar', 1*2+2, 'lt1')" onmouseleave="mhHover('localToolbar',
1*2+2, 'lt0')">

<a href="http://go.microsoft.com/?linkid=317769">Subscribe</a>
</td>

<td><span class="ltsep">|</span></td>

<td class="lt0" nowrap="true" onmouseenter="mhHover('localTo
olbar', 2*2+2, 'lt1')" onmouseleave="mhHover('localToolbar',
2*2+2, 'lt0')">

<a href="http://go.microsoft.com/?linkid=317027">Manage Your
Profile</a></td>

<td width="100%"></td>

</tr>

</table>
```

All of this code produces just one row of buttons on this page
(**Figure 1.1**).

FIGURE 1.1 It takes nearly 1,000
characters of code to create the three
links above the picture.

The three links

The essential code is in green—247 characters out of 956, or less than 26 percent. The remaining 74 percent is just gooey chocolate sauce. Except for the `href` attributes, everything inside the tags is *presentation* and could all be ripped out and converted into a few brief definitions in a style sheet. The table is not used to display data; its purpose is solely to line everything up. The rest of the code is mostly concerned with making rollovers work. Each link requires the following information: a class to identify it to JavaScript, a forced `nowrap` attribute to keep the words on the link together, and two JavaScript function calls—yeah, on *every* link. (As an aside, rollovers are easy to create with CSS and require two simple CSS styles, as you will see later.) Note also that a table cell that contains a nested span with a class is required to display each tiny vertical line between the links.

Microsoft has recently made a decent effort to make its site more standards-compliant, but if your site's source (sauce?) code resembles the above, then read on. In the chapter on Interface Components, you will see how to create a similar navigation element with no more markup than a simple un-ordered list. After applying a few CSS rules, the result is a lightweight, easy-to-read, and most of all, semantically meaningful element that works on any XHTML-capable device, regardless of screen size, or even its capability to read CSS.

The Future Just Happened

Today, with so many browsers and other devices standardizing around XHTML and CSS, noncompliant Web sites are finding that it is difficult to deliver their existing content on these newer devices and browsers. Have you seen your home page on a handheld computer lately?

Although bringing your current Web site into the modern age may take a substantial amount of work, you can console yourself that by following the new Web standards, you can do it once and do it right. If you are starting a new site, you can do it right the first time.

In *Stylin'*, you will learn to future-proof your site by separating the content from the presentation. You do this by marking up your content with XHTML, and then, using a single line of code, you link these pages to a separate file called a *style sheet*, which contains the presentation rules that define how the markup should be displayed.

The power of this church-and-state separation is that you can create different style sheets for browsers, for handheld devices, for printing, for screen readers used by the visually impaired, and so

You can define which type of device a style sheet relates to using the link *tag's* media *attribute.*

on. Many of today's user agents (types of devices) look for their specific type of style sheet. For example, smartphones such as RIM's Blackberry and Palm's Treo look for a style sheet defined for use by a handheld device—and if it is present, use it, thus enabling you to provide a modified or entirely different presentation of the same XHTML on these small-screen devices.

Each style sheet causes the content to be presented in the best possible way for that use, but you only ever need *one* version of the XHTML content markup. As you will see, an XHTML page can automatically select the correct style sheet for each device or environment in which it is displayed. In this way, your write-once, use-many content becomes truly portable, flexible, and ready for whatever presentational requirements the future may bring its way. Note, however, that like any great vision of the future, there are still some current realities that we need to deal with.

XHTML and How To Write It

If you want more than this rather simplistic description of XML, check out the XML tutorial at the SpiderPro Web site (www.spiderpro.com/bu/buxmlm001.html).

Because CSS is a mechanism for styling XHTML, you can't start using CSS until you have a solid grounding in XHTML. And what, exactly, is XHTML? XHTML is a reformulation of HTML as XML—didja get that? Put (very) simply, XHTML is based on the free-form structure of XML, where tags can be named to actually describe the content they contain; for example, <starname>Madonna</starname>. This very powerful capability of XML means that in XHTML, where the tag set is already defined for you, there is both a set of custom tags for your XHTML content and a second document, known as a *DTD* (document type definition), to explain how to handle those tags to the device that is interpreting the XHTML. By becoming XML-compliant, XHTML has been able to transcend the limitations of HTML and can be expanded over time, and can be shared as real-time Web services between other data systems. The DOCTYPE tag at the start of every XHTML Web page makes this critical association between the markup and the DTD.

XML has been almost universally adopted in business, and the fact that the same X (for eXtensible) is now in XHTML emphasizes the unstoppable movement toward the separation of presentation and content.

The rest of this chapter is dedicated to the latest, completely reformulated, totally modern, and altogether more flexible version of HTML.

XHTML—The Rules

Correctly written XHTML markup gives you the best chance that your pages will display correctly in a broad variety of devices for years to come. The clean, easy-to-write, and flexible nature of XHTML produces code that loads fast, is easy to understand when editing, and prepares your content for use in a variety of applications.

You can easily determine if your site complies with Web standards—if your markup is *well-formed* with *valid* XHTML, and your style sheet is *valid* CSS.

Well-formed means that the XHTML is structured correctly according to the markup rules described in this chapter.

Valid means that that page only uses tags that are defined in the DTD (document type definition) that is associated with every modern Web page by the page's DOCTYPE tag (more on DOCTYPEs later). Certain tags that you may have been used to using in the past are now deprecated, meaning they still work but that a different, and usually more semantically correct, tag is now available for this purpose. To encourage you to use the newer tags, which unlike deprecated tags will still work in the future, deprecated tags are flagged as errors by the validator. You can check to see if your page meets these two criteria by uploading the page onto a Web server and then going to http://validator.w3.org and entering the page's URL.

Press Submit, and in a few seconds you are presented with either a detailed list of the page's errors or the very satisfying "This Page Is Valid XHTML 1.0 Strict!" message (**Figure 1.2**). CSS can be validated in the same way at http://jigsaw.w3.org/css-validator.

If you install the wonderful Developer's Toolbar into Firefox, you can easily validate pages on your local machine without uploading them to your web server. Download it from http://chrispederick.com/work/web-developer/

FIGURE 1.2 This nice message from the W3C validator almost guarantees that your page will display meaningfully on any XHTML-capable device.

![Screenshot of W3C Markup Validation Service showing "This Page Is Valid XHTML 1.0 Strict!" with Result: Passed validation, Address: http://www.stylinwithcss.com/chapter_1/code/sample_XHTML_markup_ch1.html, Modified: (undefined), Server: Apache, Size: (undefined), Content-Type: text/html, Encoding: iso-8859-1, Doctype: XHTML 1.0 Strict, Root Element: html, Root Namespace: http://www.w3.org/1999/xhtml]

Does My Page Have To Validate?

The W3C validator (jigsaw.w3c.com) exists to enable you to ensure your pages are *valid* (only use elements and attributes as defined by the DOCTYPE's DTD) and *well-formed* (tags are structured correctly). It's definitely good practice to attempt to write pages that pass validation, and some would say that your pages *must* pass validation. What's undeniable is that the validator can instantly find common errors in your code that might otherwise take you hours to find.

However, just because a page doesn't validate doesn't necessarily mean it won't display the way you intend in current Web browsers. What future devices or other non-browser devices might do with such a page is not so certain.

My recommendation is to validate every page you create and take heed of the errors the validator displays. Close any tags it determines are left open, for example, and recode tags that it determines are being incorrectly nested (such as block elements inside inline elements). In short, you do want to ensure that your page is *well-formed*. However, *valid* is another story.

For example, in order to use Peter-Paul Koch's excellent JavaScript code that reveals additional parts of a form as the user makes selections (see http://www.quirksmode.org/dom/usableforms.html), you must add a `rel` attribute to each of the divs that hold the elements to be revealed. `rel` tags are not valid attributes for divs, and the page no longer passes validation, but the document can still be well-formed, so I am OK with letting that error go in exchange for added functionality. Some purists insist that every page must pass validation, but if it fails because of minor "valid" errors like this and is still well-formed, I think it's OK to ignore that advice.

Looking forward to the email I'm going to get on this one...

Here's the complete (and mercifully, short) list of the coding requirements for XHTML compliance:

For a list of deprecated tags that you should abandon and replace with their XHTML equivalents, refer to the About.com Web site (http://web-design.about.com/od/htmltags/a/bltags_deprctag.htm).

1. **Declare a DOCTYPE.** The DOCTYPE goes before the opening `html` tag at the top of the page and tells the browser whether the page contains HTML, XHTML, or a mix of both, so that it can correctly interpret the markup. There are three main DOCTYPEs that let the browser know what kind of markup it is dealing with:

Strict: All markup is XHTML-compliant.

```
<!DOCTYPE html PUBLIC "-//W3C//DTD XHTML 1.0 Strict//EN"

  "http://www.w3.org/TR/xhtml1/DTD/xhtml1-strict.dtd">
```

There are other flavors of DOCTYPES, and you can read about them at http://www.oreillynet.com/pub/a/javascript/synd/2001/08/28/doctype.html?page=1.

Transitional: This states that the markup is a mix of XHTML and deprecated HTML. Many well-established sites are currently using this one, so their old HTML code can exist happily in the document alongside the XHTML they are now adding.

```
<!DOCTYPE HTML PUBLIC "-//W3C//DTD HTML 4.01
Transitional//EN"

"http://www.w3.org/TR/html4/loose.dtd">
```

If you copy a DOCTYPE or namespace from some other site, make sure that the URL is absolute (that is, it starts with http:// followed by a complete path to the document). Some sites (including W3C, of course) host their own DOCTYPE and namespace files, so they can use relative URLs to them. But if you use these URLs as is, with a different server that doesn't host these files, your pages may behave unpredictably because the URLs aren't pointing at anything.

You can learn more about Quirks mode at the Dive into Mark Web site (http://diveintomark.org/archives/ 2002/05/29/quirks_mode).

Because the DOCTYPE (and the XML namespace and content type discussed in items 2 and 3) are a pain to type, they are in the page templates on the Stylin' Web site (www.stylin-withcss.com). You can use these as a starting point for your own XHTML documents. Just pick whichever of the three (Strict, Transitional, or Frames) DOCTYPEs you want to use.

Frameset: This is the same as transitional but in this case frames, which are deprecated under XHTML, are OK, too.

```
<!DOCTYPE HTML PUBLIC "-//W3C//DTD HTML 4.01 Frameset//EN"
"http://www.w3.org/TR/html4/frameset.dtd">
```

It is important to specify a DOCTYPE. Browsers that don't see a DOCTYPE in the markup assume that the site page was coded for browsers developed long before Web standards. My recommendation is that if you are building a site from scratch, and can therefore avoid deprecated or abandoned tag attributes, such as FONT and COLOR, use the XHTML Strict DOCTYPE listed previously.

When encountering a page without a DOCTYPE, many browsers go into what is known as *Quirks mode,* a backwards-compatibility feature supported by Mozilla, Internet Explorer 6 for Windows, and Internet Explorer 5 for Macintosh.

In Quirks mode, the browser functions as if it has no knowledge of the modern DOM (document object model) and pretends it has never heard of Web standards. This ability to switch modes depending on the DOCTYPE, or lack thereof, enables browsers to do the best possible job of interpreting the code of both standards-compliant and noncompliant sites.

Note that for some weird reason, the DOCTYPE tag does not need to be closed with a slash and DOCTYPE is always in caps. This entirely contradicts XHTML rules 4 and 7 below. Go figure.

2. **Declare an XML namespace.** Note this line in your new html tag. Here's an example:

```
<html xmlns="http://www.w3.org/1999/xhtml" lang="en" xml:
lang="en">
```

When a browser is handling an XHTML page and wants to know what's in the DTD, which lists and defines all the valid XHTML tags, here's where it can find it: buried away on the servers of the WC3.

In short, the DOCTYPE and namespace declarations ensure that the browser interprets your XHTML code as you intended.

3. **Declare your content type.** The content type declaration goes in the head of your document, along with any other meta tags you may add. The most common is

```
<meta http-equiv="Content-type" content="text/html;
charset=iso-8859-1" />
```

This simply states what character coding was used for the document. ISO-8859-1 is the Latin character set, used by all standard flavors of English. If your next site is going to be in Cyrillic or Hebrew, you can find the appropriate content types on Microsoft's site (http://msdn.microsoft.com/workshop/author/ dhtml/reference/charsets/charset4.asp).

4.   **Close every tag, whether enclosing or nonenclosing.** Enclosing tags have content within them, like this

```
<p>This is a paragraph of text inside paragraph tags. To
be XHTML-compliant, it must, and in this case does, have
a closing tag.</p>
```

Nonenclosing tags do not go around text but still must be closed, using space-slash at the end, like this

```
<img src="images/siamese.jpg" alt="My cat" />
```

The space before the slash isn't required in modern browsers, but I always add it as it's easier to see that the tag is correctly closed.

5.   **All tags must be nested correctly.** If a tag opens before a preceding one closes, it must be closed before that preceding one closes. For example:

```
<p>It's <strong>very important</strong> to nest tags
correctly.</p>
```

Here, the `strong` tag is correctly placed inside the `<p>`; it closes before the containing p tag is closed. A tag enclosed inside another in this way is said to be *nested.*

This is wrongly nested

```
<p>The nesting of these tags is <strong>wrong.</p></
strong>
```

Multiple elements can be nested inside a containing element; a list nests multiple `li` elements inside a single `ul` or `ol` element, like this:

```
<ul>

   <li>Item 1</li>

   <li>Item 2</li>

   <li>Item 3</li>

</ul>
```

Because CSS relies on proper nesting in order to target styles to elements, you have to get this right. Use the W3C validator for confirmation that all tags are correctly nested and therefore your document is well-formed.

6. **Inline tags can't contain block level tags.** Block-level elements, such as p (paragraph) and div (division), automatically organize themselves one under the next down the page. If you have two paragraphs, the second paragraph appears by default under the previous one—no line breaks are required. By contrast, inline tags, such as a (anchor, a hyperlink) and em (emphasis, usually displayed as italics) occur in the normal flow of text, and don't force a new line.

We discuss block and inline elements in detail later in Chapter 4, but for now, just remember that if you nest a block element, such as a paragraph p, inside an inline element, such as a link a, your code won't validate.

Also, some block-level elements can't contain other block-level elements either; for instance, an h1-6 (heading) tag can't contain a paragraph. Besides using validation, you can let common sense be your guide to avoid these problems. You wouldn't put an entire paragraph inside a paragraph heading when you are writing on paper or in Word, so don't do illogical things like that in your XHTML either, and you won't go far wrong.

7. **Write tags entirely in lowercase.** Self-explanatory—no capital letters at all. I've always done this myself, but if you haven't, the days of P are over. Now it has to be p.

8. **Attributes must have values and must be quoted.** Some tags' attributes don't need values in HTML, but in XHTML, all attributes must have values. For example, if you previously used the select tag to create a pop-up menu in an HTML form, and wanted to have one menu choice selected by default when the page loaded, you might have written something like this

```
<SELECT NAME=ANIMALS>

<OPTION VALUE=Cats>Cats</OPTION>

<OPTION VALUE=Dogs SELECTED>Dogs</OPTION>

</SELECT>
```

which would have given you a drop-down menu with Dogs displayed by default.

The equivalent valid XHTML is this

The use of a as the tag name for a link comes from the fact that a link that jumps to another location within the same page is know as an anchor. The same tag can be used to jump to a different page; an a tag used for this purpose is now universally referred to as a link. Of course, there is an XHTML link tag, which is used to associate a style sheet with a page, so don't get confused here. Remember, a "hyperlink" that the user clicks to jump to a new location is technically known as an anchor and always uses the a tag, even though everyone refers to this mechanism as a link.

```
<select name="animals">
<option value="cats">Cats</option>
<option value="dogs" selected="selected">Dogs</option>
</select>
```

Note that in this revised version, all the tag and attribute names are in lowercase and all the attribute values are in quotes.

9.   **Use the encoded equivalents for a left angle bracket and ampersand within content.** When XHTML encounters a left angle-bracket, < (also known as the less-than symbol), it quite reasonably assumes you are starting a tag. But what if you actually want that symbol to appear in your content? The answer is to encode it using an entity. An entity is a short string of characters that represents a single character; an entity causes XHTML to interpret and display the character correctly and not to confuse it with markup. The entity for the left angle-bracket/less-than symbol is <—remember lt stands for less than.

Entities not only help avoid parsing errors like the one just mentioned, but they also enable certain symbols to be displayed at all, such as © for the copyright symbol (©). Every symbolic entity begins with an ampersand (&) and ends with a semicolon (;). Because of this, XHTML regards ampersands in your code as the start of entities, so you must also encode ampersands as entities when you want them to appear in your content; the ampersand entity is &.

A good rule of thumb is that if a character you want to use is not printed on the keys of your keyboard (such as é, ®, ©, or £), you need to use an entity in your markup.

There are some 50,000 entities in total, which encompass the character sets of most of the world's major languages, but you can find a shorter list of the commonly used entities at the Web Design Group site (www.htmlhelp.com/reference/html40/entities).

And those are the rules of XHTML markup. They are relatively simple, but you must follow them exactly if you want your pages to validate (and you do).

An XHTML Template

There are certain tags that must be in your Web page for it to be valid XHTML. As you learned from items 1, 2, and 3 above, you need to tell the browser whether your page is pure XHTML or also contains deprecated tags, and what character encoding the page uses. No matter what content your page displays, these tags need to be present. You also need tags to indicate the head and body areas of the page. Dreamweaver will generate a "page template" containing all the required elements when you select New from the File menu—ready for you to add your page content. You can preset which DOCTYPE appears at the top by selecting: Edit > Preferences: New Document: Default Document Type (DTD) in your Preferences.

To show you what this template looks like, here's the required code for a valid and well-formed page that uses the Strict XHTML 1.0 DOCTYPE:

```
<!DOCTYPE html PUBLIC "-//W3C//DTD XHTML 1.0 Strict//EN"
"http://www.w3.org/TR/xhtml1/DTD/xhtml1-strict.dtd">
<!--the DOCTYPE-->

<html xmlns="http://www.w3.org/1999/xhtml">

<head>

<meta http-equiv="Content-Type" content="text/html;
charset=iso-8859-1" />

<title>XHTML 1.0 Strict template</title>

</head>

<body>

        <!--the content of your page goes here-->

</body>

</html>
```

To use this template, add the code for your page's content. You would also want to change the text between the title tags to something that describes the content of your page for both screen readers and search engines. See the sidebar "About Title Tags."

When I use the term "page template" in this book, I am simply referring to a block of code such as the one shown to the right that forms the basis of an XHTML-compliant page, and not the notion of page templates that contain the nonchanging parts of page layouts as used by Dreamweaver and content management systems.

This template is in the Stylin' site download package. For more HTML and XHTML templates, see the Web Standards site (www.webstandards. org/learn/templates/index.html).

About Title Tags

It's easy to miss the title of a page because it is displayed at the very top of the browser window, but title tags carry a lot of weight with search engines. The pages that get listed on page one of Google's results, for example, almost always have some or all of your search terms present in their titles, which are also displayed as the titles of each of the results. Make sure that your page title contains keywords that your users might use to search with and is written so that it entices clicks when it appears in search results. Don't waste your title tag with the useless and all-too-common "Welcome to our Home Page."

Marking Up Your Content

Adopting Web standards means working in new ways. Start the development process by thinking about the structure of the content—what it means—rather than its presentation—what it looks like. That said, it's absurd to think you would begin programming without some sense of how the final page is gong to look when finished. I'll usually whip up (i.e., obsess over for days) an Adobe Fireworks comp to get an approval of the design from the client before I start, and I'll use that comp as a guide to what content needs to be in the markup. When actually marking up the page elements (as headings, paragraphs, images, etc.), so that I have something to style with my CSS, my focus is on "what is the most meaningful tag I can wrap around each piece of content?"

Once we cover the workings of CSS in the next chapter, then we can start looking at markup in terms of both using the right tag on each content element *and* ensuring that the elements are organized in a way that makes it easy to target them with your CSS rules.

Right now, we are going to focus on the individual XHTML tags and their semantic meaning, so that you can consider any piece of content that will appear on your page and select the most appropriate tag to mark it up. As we do this, we can also think about the concept of document flow.

Document Flow—Block and Inline Elements

I mentioned previously that most XHTML tags fall into two broad categories in respect to the way they display on the page: block and inline. Block level elements such as headings `<h1>` through `<h6>` and paragraphs `<p>` will obligingly stack down the page with no line breaks required. They even have preset margins to create space between them. Inline elements have no such margins, and sit side by side across the page, only wrapping to the next line if there is not enough room for them to sit next to each other.

A SIMPLE EXAMPLE OF XHTML MARKUP

In this first simple example of an XHTML page, the screenshot shows not only the stacking effect of block level elements, but also that inline elements, in this case `<a>` (a link) and `<strong>` (usually displays bold), can appear within block level elements and don't create new lines (**Figure 1.3** on the next page).

```
<!DOCTYPE html PUBLIC "-//W3C//DTD XHTML 1.0 Strict//EN"
"http://www.w3.org/TR/xhtml1/DTD/xhtml1-strict.dtd">

<html xmlns="http://www.w3.org/1999/xhtml">

<head>

<meta http-equiv="Content-Type" content="text/html;
charset=iso-8859-1" />

<title>Block and inline XHTML elements</title>

</head>

<body>

<h1>Here's a level 1 heading</h1>

<h2>Here's a level 2 heading</h2>

<p>This paragraph is very short and contains very little
text.</p>

<p>This paragraph is longer and contains not only
<strong>bold text</strong> but also <a href="#">a link</a>
that doesn't really link to anything.</p>

</body>

</html>
```

FIGURE 1.3 Example of the document flow of block and inline elements.

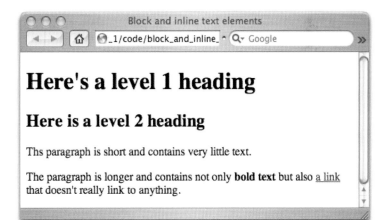

This example also illustrates XHTML's default document flow, which refers to the way the browser lays out block and inline elements. Document flow ensures meaningful layout of correctly marked-up content that has no author styling associated with it. As you will see later, there are all kinds of ways to use CSS to reorganize the default document flow into a variety of layouts—multiple columns, for example—without having to pollute the markup with presentational tags and attributes.

THE BROWSER'S INTERNAL STYLE SHEET

One interesting thing to note here is that each element by default has certain styles associated with it. As the screenshot shows, h1 headings are already styled to be larger type than h2 headings, and paragraph text is styled to be smaller than both of them. This is because a browser has a built-in style sheet that sets each element's default font size, color (type is black, links are blue, for example), display setting (block or inline), and usually many other settings, too.

When you use CSS to style an element, you are actually overriding the default settings for that element as set in the browser's style sheet. This makes the job easier, as you only need to change the styles that aren't already to your liking. However, if the browser doesn't read your style sheet for some reason, these default styles are your fallback, so it's worth making sure that your marked-up, but unstyled, page displays meaningfully in the browser before you start on the CSS. If it's well-formed XHTML, the default document flow pretty much guarantees it will.

A MORE STRUCTURED XHTML PAGE

Here's a more extensive example (**Figure 1.4**) of a marked-up page that uses some common XHTML tags and also organizes the tags into logical groups using div tags based on their purpose in the page. We will look at more XHTML tags as we go on. I don't want to get into a full-blown rundown of each XHTML tag and its associated attributes here, as it would be a book in its own right, but I will show you examples of many different tags and their uses throughout this book.

For a quick reference of XHTML tags and attributes, take a look at a listing at the Cookwood site (run by another Peachpit author, Elizabeth Castro, whose books I highly recommend) at http://www.cookwood. com/html/extras/xhtml_ref.html.

Highlighted code is the XHTML template shown earlier in the chapter..

```
<!DOCTYPE html PUBLIC "-//W3C//DTD XHTML 1.0 Strict//EN"

  "http://www.w3.org/TR/xhtml1/DTD/xhtml1-strict.dtd">

<html xmlns="http://www.w3.org/1999/xhtml" lang="en" xml:
lang="en">

<head>

<title>A Sample XHTML Document</title>

<meta http-equiv="Content-type" content="text/html;
charset=iso-8859-1" />
```

```
<meta http-equiv="Content-Language" content="en-us" />

</head>

<body>

<!--header-->

<div id="header">

<img src="images/stylin_logo1.gif" width="150" height="80"
alt="Stylin logo" />

   <h3>a New Riders book by Charles Wyke-Smith</h3>

</div>

<!--end header-->

<!--main content-->

<div id="contentarea">

   <h1>Welcome to XHTML</h1>

   <p>Good XHTML markup makes your content portable,
   accessible and future-proof. Creating XHTML-compliant pages
   requires following a few simple rules. Also, XHTML code
   can be easily validated online so you can ensure your code
   is correctly written.</p>

   <p>Here are the key requirements for successful validation
   of your XHTML code.</p>

   <ol>

      <li>Declare a DOCTYPE</li>

      <li>Declare an XML namespace</li>

      <li>Declare your content type</li>

      <li>Close every tag, enclosing or non-enclosing</li>

      <li>All tags must be nested correctly</li>

      <li>Inline tags can't contain block level tags</li>

      <li>Write tags in lowercase</li>

      <li>Attributes must have values and must be quoted</li>

      <li>Use encoded equivalents for left brace and
      ampersand</li>

   </ol>
```

```
    <a href="more.htm">more about these requirements</a> </div>

    <!--end main content-->

<!--navigation-->

<div id="navigation">

    <p>Here are some useful links from the Web site of the
    <acronym title="Word Wide Web Consortium">W<sup>3</sup>C
    </acronym> (World Wide Web Consortium), the guiding body of
    the Web's development.</p>

    <ul>

      <li><a href="http://validator.w3.org">W3C's XHTML
      validator</a></li>

      <li><a href="http://jigsaw.w3.org/css-validator/">W3C's
      CSS validator</a></li>

      <li><a href="http://www.w3.org/MarkUp/">XHTML Resources
      </a></li>

      <li><a href="http://www.w3.org/Style/CSS/">CSS
      Resources</a></li>

    </ul>

</div>

<!--end navigation-->

<!--footer-->

<div id="footer">

  <p>&copy; 2007 Charles Wyke-Smith.</p>

</div>

<!--end footer-->

</body>

</html>
```

FIGURE 1.4 This is the above code rendered in the Firefox browser with the default browser styles. It's not beautiful, but it is useable.

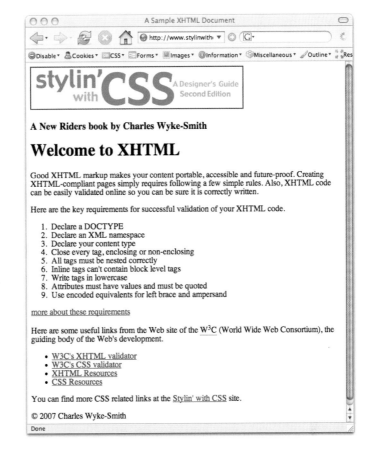

The default blue border around the header graphic indicates that the image is clickable (the img tag is enclosed in an a tag), and this rather ugly border can easily be removed with CSS, as we will see later.

Class attributes are similar to IDs in as much as they can be used to identify groups of tags, but while a class can appear many times within a page, an ID can appear only once. We will learn about the correct uses of classes and IDs in the next chapter. Also see the sidebar "Naming Classes and IDs."

This page nicely illustrates the inherently structured document flow produced by correctly marked-up elements. You can see from the code that the markup has been divided with (aptly named) divs into four logical groups: header, content, navigation, and footer. The id attribute of these divs allows us to give each group a name that is unique to that page.

While it's helpful that these div IDs let us see at a glance where we are within the document structure, the primary purpose of organizing our tags within divs with IDs is to enable us to target sets of CSS rules at a specific group of tags, rather than the entire document. An element type, such as p, can be styled one way within one div and another way within another div. Let's start understanding how this works by looking at *document hierarchy*.

Naming Classes and IDs

IDs and class attributes are identifiers you can add to your tags. You can add a class or an ID attribute to any tag, although most commonly, you add them to block-level elements. IDs and classes help you accurately target your CSS to a specific element or set of elements. I get into the uses for (and differences between) IDs and classes later, but for now, it's helpful to know that an attribute value must be a single word, although you can make compound words that the browser sees as single words using underscores, such as `class="navigation_links"`.

Because the browser can misinterpret attribute names made of bizarre strings of characters, my advice is to start the word with a letter, not a number or a symbol. Because the only purpose of a class or ID is to give an element a name that you can reference in your style sheet (or JavaScript code), the value can be a word of your own choosing. That said, it's good practice to name classes and IDs something meaningful such as `class="navigationbar"` rather than `class="deadrat"`. Although the deadrat class might provide a moment of levity during a grueling programming session, the humor may be lost on you when you are editing your code at some point in the future. Don't save time with abbreviated names either; call the ID `"footer"` rather than `"fr"` or you are apt to waste your time (or someone else's) later trying to figure out what you meant. Do yourself a favor and take the time to give classes and IDs unambiguous and descriptive names.

Document Hierarchy: Meet the XHTML Family

Document hierarchy is the final XHTML concept we'll look at before we start looking at CSS. The document hierarchy is like a family tree or an organizational chart that is based on the nesting of a page's XHTML tags. A good way to learn to understand this concept is to take a snip of the body section of the markup we just discussed and strip out the content so that you can see the organization of the tags better. Here's the stripped-down header

```
<body>

  <div id="header">

    <img />

    <h3> </h3>

  </div>

<!-- remaining tags removed here for clarity -->

</body>
```

Dreamweaver's Code View will automatically indent nested tags as shown above (Commands > Apply Source Formatting) to help you see the hierarchy more clearly.

Now you can clearly see the relationships of the tags. For example, in the markup, you can see that the body tag contains (or nests) all the other tags. You can also see that the div tag (with the ID of "header") contains two tags: an image tag and a head 3 tag.

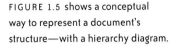

FIGURE 1.5 shows a conceptual way to represent a document's structure—with a hierarchy diagram.

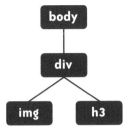

When examining this hierarchical view (**Figure 1.5**), we can say that both the img tag and the h3 tag are the *children* of the div tag, because it is the containing element of both. In turn, the div tag is the *parent* tag of both of them, and the img tag and the h3 tag are *siblings* of one another because they both have the same parent tag. Finally, the body tag is an *ancestor* tag of the img and h3 tags, because they are indirectly descended from it. In the same way, the img and h3 tags (and the div, for that matter) are *descendants* of the body tag. To quote Sly Stone: "It's a family affair…"

In CSS, you write a kind of shorthand based on these relationships, for example

```
div#header img {some CSS styling in here}
```

Such a CSS rule only targets img tags inside of (descended from) the div with the ID of "header" (the # is the CSS symbol for an ID). Other img tags in the page are unaffected by this rule because they aren't contained within the "header" div. In this way, you can add a border around just this image or set its margin to move it away from surrounding elements.

We will get into learning to write CSS rules like this in greater detail in the next chapter, but the important concept to understand is that every element within the body of your document is a descendant of the body tag, and, depending on its location in the markup, the element could be an ancestor, a parent, a child, or a sibling of other tags in the document hierarchy.

By creating rules that use (and often combine) references to IDs, classes, and the hierarchy structure, you have means by which you can accurately dictate which CSS rules affect which XHTML elements, and this is exactly what you will learn to do next.

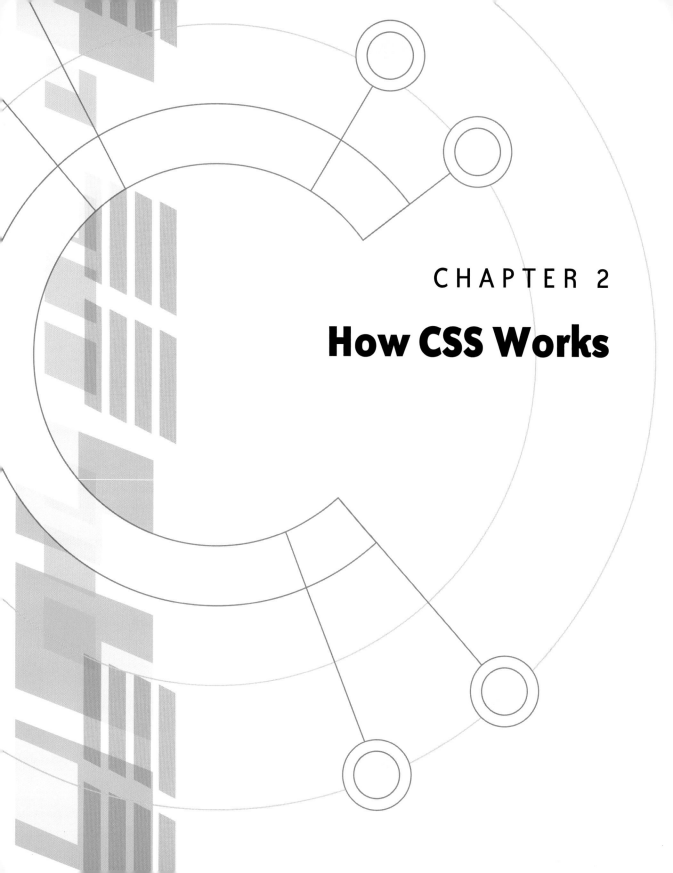

CHAPTER 2

How CSS Works

IN THE PREVIOUS CHAPTER, I showed you how XHTML markup provides a structural hierarchy to your document. We saw that elements have a basic set of styles applied to them by the browser, and that each element is either displayed as a block (stacked) or inline (side-by-side) element. If correctly marked up, the document will then automatically lay out in a useable way down the page—an effect know as document flow. However, "useable" doesn't mean "beautiful," so CSS enables creative people like you to change the browser's default styles and apply additional styles to create a more functional and aesthetically pleasing result for your visitors. This chapter will teach you the mechanics of CSS, and by the end of this chapter, you'll be ready to create your own styles for the piece of sample XHTML markup we studied in Chapter 1.

The Three Ways to Style Your Document

There are three ways to add CSS to your Web pages: *inline, embedded,* and *linked* from a separate CSS style sheet. The only one that really makes any sense in terms of developing Web sites is to link your XHTML pages to a CSS style sheet, but we will examine the other two as well, as they can be useful while creating your pages.

A style sheet can be linked to an infinite number of XHTML pages, which helps ensure a consistent look from page to page and allows edits made to a style to be instantly reflected across an entire site.

Inline Styles

Inline styles (also known as *local styles*) are added to a tag using the XHTML `style` attribute, like this

```
<p>This paragraph simply takes on the browser's default
paragraph style.</p>

<p style="font-size: 25pt; font-weight:bold; font-style:
italic; color:red;">By adding inline CSS styling to this
paragraph, we can override the default styles.</p>

<p>And now we are back to a regular default paragraph without
any inline styles.</p>
```

which looks like this (see **Figure 2.1**)

FIGURE 2.1 Inline styles are only applied to the tag to which they are attached.

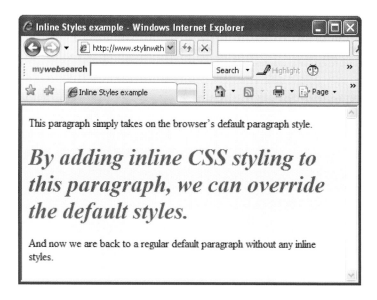

Here are some things you need to know about inline styles:

- Their scope is very restricted. An inline style only affects the tag to which it is attached.

- The practice of using inline styles is simply another way of putting presentational markup directly on the tags, as we did in days of yore. Adding inline styles everywhere is as bad for the portability and editability of your markup as adding deprecated HTML attributes, such as FONT. Inline styles should be generally avoided.

- On those rare occasions when you need to override a style in just one specific instance and there is no better way to do it, you can create an inline style and not feel too guilty about it. That said, you could almost always avoid using inline styles by adding a unique ID or class to the tag in question and then writing a corresponding style in your style sheet.

- Using an inline style is a good way to try out a style before you move it into the style sheet (see "Linked Styles" on the next page). Just remember to clear out the `style` attribute entirely once you achieve the effect you want and then cut and paste just the style itself into the style sheet. If you have it in the markup, that inline style will always override whatever change you try to make to that particular tag from the style sheet, and you can spend hours trying to fix the style sheet when the problem is, in fact, hidden in the markup.

- Inline styles override the same styles you define with embedded styles (described next), which override global styles you define in style sheets. (See "The Cascade" later in this chapter for details on this.)

Embedded Styles

You can place a group of CSS styles in the head of your XHTML document. These are known as *embedded styles* (or *page styles*) because they are part of the page (or embedded in it). Embedded styles work like this:

```
<head>

<title>Embedded Styles example</title>

<meta http-equiv="Content-type" content="text/html;
charset=iso-8859-1" />

<meta http-equiv="Content-Language" content="en-us" />
```

```
<style type="text/css">

h1 {font-size: 16px;}
p {color:blue;}

</style>
</head>
```

The style tag tells the browser it is about to encounter code other than XHTML; the tag's attribute states that the code is CSS.

Here's what you need to know about embedded (or page) styles:

- The scope of embedded styles is limited to the page that contains the styles.

- If you are only publishing a single page with these particular styles, you can embed the styles in the head of the document, although you are not truly separating the styles from the content; they are still in the same document. You will become familiar with embedded styles as you follow along with the hands-on single-page examples in this chapter.

- If you are working up multiple styles for a complex layout such as a form, sometimes it's easier to write the styles as embedded styles in the head of the document so that you don't have to constantly switch between the markup and the style sheet. Then, once everything is working, you can move the styles into the main style sheet and replace the styles in the header with a link to the style sheet.

- Page styles override style sheet styles, but they lose out to attributes you define in inline styles.

- If you are sending an XHTML page to someone for a critique, it's considerate to embed the CSS styles in the page, so the reviewer only has to open the page and everything works; however, for a Web site of any scale, there is really only one way to manage the CSS and that is in a style sheet that can be linked to all of the site's pages.

Linked Styles

Ideally, you place styles in a separate document (a style sheet) that links to multiple pages so that the styles have global (site-wide) scope. The styles defined in this style sheet can then affect every page of your site, not just a single page or a single tag. This is the only method of the three that truly separates the presentational styles from the structural markup. If you centralize all your CSS styles in a style sheet in this way, Web site design and editing become much easier.

For example, if you need to make changes that affect the whole site ("The client wants all the paragraph text to be blue, not black."), doing so can be as quick and painless as modifying one CSS style. This is certainly much easier than the pre-CSS task of modifying every FONT attribute of every paragraph tag in every page of the site.

You can link your style sheet to as many XHTML pages as you want with a single line of code in the head of each XHTML page:

```
<link href="my_style_sheet.css" media="screen"
rel="stylesheet" type="text/css" />
```

Then the styles are applied to each page's markup as the page loads.

Note that, in the above `link` tag, the `media` attribute is defined as `"screen"`, meaning the style sheet is designed for the screen, which currently means Web browsers. (Certain user agents look for particular media attributes that best suit their display capabilities; possibilities here include: all, projection, handheld, print and aural. See a full list on the W3 Schools site (www.w3schools.com/css/css_mediatypes.asp).

A browser reads a style sheet where the `link` tag media attribute is `all` or `screen`. But by adding a second `link` tag with the `media` attribute of `"print"`, you can offer a second style sheet that the browser will use when printing. A style sheet for printing might hide navigational and other elements that don't make sense when the content goes to paper.

If you create a second style sheet for printing, its link tag might look like this

```
<link href="my_style_sheet_print.css" media="print"
rel="stylesheet" type="text/css" />
```

So now that you know what style sheets are, let's look at how you write style sheet rules, and how concepts like Inheritance, Specificity, and the Cascade control how these rules affect your markup.

Don't use spaces in file names. They end up being replaced by the %20 string, which really obfuscates your file names for the user. I use underscores instead of spaces—then the whole file name string is one long word to the browser and can easily be selected by clicking it.

Anatomy of a CSS Rule

While a p tag in the XHTML markup is enclosed in angle brackets, in the CSS style, you just write the tag name without the angle brackets.

Let's start learning about how CSS is written by looking at a simple CSS rule. For example, here's a rule that makes all text in all paragraphs of your document red

```
p {color:red;}
```

So if you have this XHTML markup

```
<p>This text is very important</p>
```

then it will be red.

A CSS rule is made up of two parts: the *selector*, which states which tag the rule selects, (or, as I like to say, which rule the selector *targets*)—in this case, a paragraph—and the *declaration*, which states what happens when the rule is applied—in this case, the text displays in red. The declaration itself is made up of two elements: a *property*, which states what is to be affected—here, the color of the text—and a *value*, which states what the property is set to—here, red. It's worth taking a good look at this diagram (**Figure 2.2**) so that you are absolutely clear on these four terms; I'll be using them extensively as we move forward.

FIGURE 2.2 There are two main elements of a CSS rule—a selector and a declaration. The declaration is made up of two subelements—a property and a value.

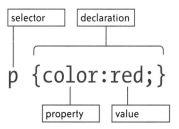

Writing CSS Rules

CSS demands absolute accuracy; a missing semicolon can cause CSS to ignore an entire rule.

You may be wondering what other values properties such as font size and color may have. For example, you might want to know if you can specify a color using RGB (red, green, blue) instead of a color name. (The answer is yes, you can.) For now, just hang in there while I focus on showing you how selectors work. Then, later in this chapter, I'll show you the declaration part of the rules.

This basic structure of the selector and the declaration can be extended in three ways:

Multiple declarations can be contained within a rule.

```
p {color:red; font-size:12px; line-height:15px;}
```

Now our paragraph text is red, 12 pixels high, and the lines are 15 pixels apart. (Pixels are, of course, the tiny dots that make up your screen display.)

Note that each declaration ends with a semicolon to separate it from the next. The last semicolon before the closing curly bracket is optional, but I always add it so that I can tack on more declarations later without having to remember it.

Multiple selectors can be grouped. If, say, you want text for tags h1 through h6 to be blue and bold, you might laboriously type this

```
h1 {color:blue; font-weight:bold;}
```

```
h2 {color:blue; font-weight:bold;}
```

```
h3 {color:blue; font-weight:bold;}
```

and so on. But you can avoid this kind of repetition by grouping selectors in a single rule like this

```
h1, h2, h3, h4, h5, h6 {color:blue; font-weight:bold;}
```

Just be sure to put a comma after each selector except the last. The spaces are optional, but they make the code easier to read.

Multiple rules can be applied to the same selector. If, having written the previous rule, you decide that you also want just the h3 tag to be italicized, you can write a second rule for h3, like this

```
h1, h2, h3, h4, h5, h6 {color:blue; font-weight:bold;}
```

```
h3 {font-style: italic;}
```

Targeting Tags Within the Document Hierarchy

If you have forgotten what the document hierarchy is since the end of the last chapter, you might want to reread "Document Hierarchy: Meet the XHTML Family" in Chapter 1 now so that I can avoid the redundancy of repeating myself repeatedly and redundantly.

Using Contextual Selectors

If you write a rule where you simply use the tag name as the selector, then every tag of that type is targeted. For example, by writing

```
p {color:red;}
```

every paragraph would have red text.

But what if you only want one particular paragraph to be red? To target tags more selectively, you use contextual selectors. Here's an example

```
div p {color:red;}
```

Now only paragraphs within div tags would be red.

As you can see in the example above, contextual selectors use more than one tag name (in this case, div and p) in the selector. The tag closest to the declaration (in this case the p tag) is the tag you are targeting. The other tag or tags state the containing ancestor tag(s) in which the target tag must be contained for it to be affected by the rule. Let's look at this idea in detail.

We'll work with this bit of sample markup

```
<h1>Contextual selectors are <em>very</em> selective.</h1>

<p>This example shows how to target a <em>specific</em> tag

using the document hierarchy.</p>

<p>Tags only need to be descendants <span>in the <em>order
stated</em> in the selector</span>; other tags can be in
between and the selector still works.</p>
```

If you are new to XHTML, note that span *is a neutral container like* div *that has no default attributes: in other words,* span *has no effect on your markup until you explicitly style it. It's useful for marking up elements in your markup that have some meaning to you not defined by XHTML; however, if your document finds itself in an environment where it cannot use your style sheet, the spans will have no effect on the presentation. Unlike* div, *which is a block element and forces a new line,* span *is an inline element, so it does not force a new line. By default,* strong *results in bold text, and* em *(emphasis) results in italics; but of course, you can use CSS to restyle them if you wish.*

Note that the first paragraph contains an em element; the second paragraph's em element is nested inside a span tag. **Figure 2.3** shows how this code looks with just the browser's default styling.

FIGURE 2.3 Here, only the browser's default styles are applied.

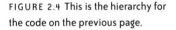

FIGURE 2.3 Here, only the browser's default styles are applied.

Figure 2.4 shows the markup's hierarchy.

FIGURE 2.4 This is the hierarchy for the code on the previous page.

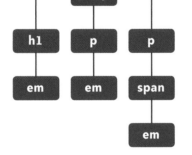

This hierarchy diagram illustrates which tag is nested inside which. If you write this style

```
em {color:green;}
```

for the markup on the previous page by adding it between the style tags in the head of your document, all the text in em tags would turn green (**Figure 2.5** on the next page).

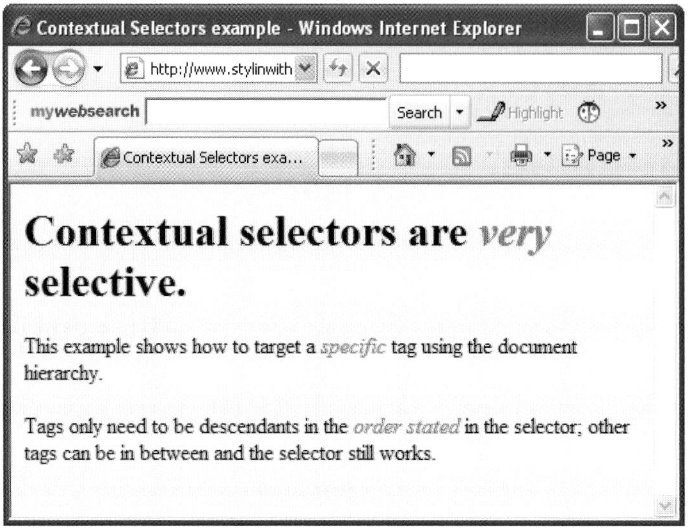

FIGURE 2.5 In this example, all text within em tags is green.

FIGURE 2.5 In this example, all text within em tags is green.

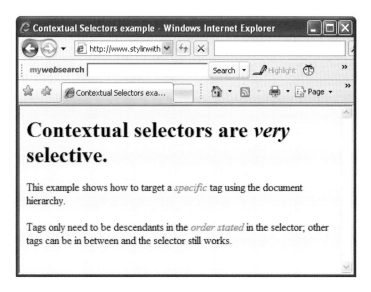

But what if you want to be more selective? Let's say you only want the em text within the paragraphs to be green. If this is the case, you would write a rule like this

```
p em {color:green;}
```

which would result in **Figure 2.6**.

FIGURE 2.6 By adding a contextual selector, you cause the rule to affect only paragraphs, not the heading.

Because you preceded the em with a p in the selector, only em tags within p tags are now targeted by the rule; the em tag in the h2 tag is no longer affected. Note that, unlike the group selectors you saw earlier, contextual selectors have spaces, not commas, between the selectors.

Remember, rules with contextual selectors are applied only to the last tag listed, and then only if the selectors that precede it appear in this same order *somewhere* in the hierarchy above it. It doesn't matter how many tags appear in between.

Because of this, the em tag within the span tag is affected by this rule. Even though it is not an immediate child of the p tag, the rule still applies, because it is a descendant of the p tag. Here's an example of how you can state multiple tags in the selector to make the targeting even more specific

```
p span em {color:green;}
```

This results in **Figure 2.7**.

FIGURE 2.7 With three elements in the selector, you can get very specific about which text will be green.

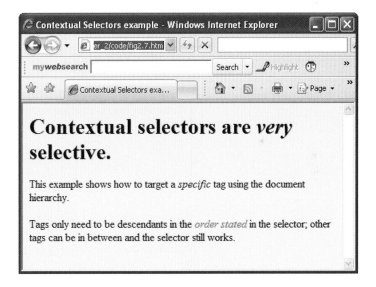

Your rule now states that only an em within a span within a p tag is selected; you set a very specific context in which the rule works, and only one tag meets this criterion. In a contextual selector like this, you can list as many selectors as you need to ensure that the tag you want to modify is targeted.

However, things get more difficult if you want to target the word "specific" only; as you saw in **Figure 2.5**, the rule p em {color: green;} selects the em tags inside both the paragraphs, and you simply can't target just this particular tag with a standard contextual selector. What you need here is a *child selector*.

The > symbol is used between the two selectors to mean "child of."

Working with Child Selectors

In Chapter 1, I mentioned that a child tag is a direct descendant of an enclosing tag. If you want to write a rule so that the tag you're targeting *has* to be a child of a particular tag, then you can do that too, using the > symbol, like this

```
p > em {color:green;}
```

Now you have successfully targeted the word "specific" without affecting the other em text, because "specific" is contained in an em tag that is a child of the p tag, but the words "order stated" are not (**Figure 2.8**).

FIGURE 2.8 A child selector provides the required context to select the word "specific" in this markup.

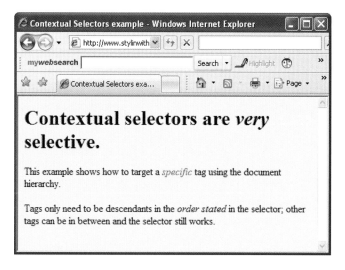

Before you drop this book in your haste to start using child selectors in your CSS, it's important to know that, at the time of writing, IDWIMIE6; Internet Explorer for Windows 6 simply ignores them (although Internet Explorer 7 for Windows does implement them). However, there are work-arounds if you find yourself in situations where only a child selector will do. As you will see shortly, classes and IDs let you target any individual tag you want, but to use them, you'll need a little extra markup.

So until Internet Explorer 6 becomes insignificant in usage, you'll mainly use child selectors to create variations in your style sheet to work around Internet Explorer's various nonstandards-compliant quirks, or in ways that cause IE6 to display a different but still acceptable result. We will use them in this way in later chapters.

Adding Classes and IDs

So far you've seen that when you have a rule with a selector that simply states a tag name such as p or h1, the rule is applied to every instance of that tag. You've also seen that to be more specific in the selection process, you can use contextual selectors to specify tags within which target tags must be contained.

However, you can also target specific areas of your document by adding IDs and class attributes to the tags in your XHTML markup. IDs and classes give you a second approach to styling your document—one that can operate without regard for the document hierarchy.

SIMPLE USE OF A CLASS

Here's a piece of markup that illustrates how you might use a class

```
<h1 class="specialtext">This is a heading with the <span>same
class</span> as the second paragraph</h1>

<p>This tag has no class.</p>

<p class="specialtext"> When a tag has a class attribute, we
can target it <span>regardless</span> of its position in the
hierarchy.</p>
```

When you write a class selector, start it with a . (period). Do not put a space between the period and the selector.

Note that I've added the class attribute specialtext to two of these tags. Let's now apply these styles to this markup where specialtext is formatted as bold (**Figure 2.9**).

```
p {font-family: Helvetica, sans-serif;}

.specialtext {font-weight:bold;}
```

FIGURE 2.9 Here I use a class selector to bold two different tags.

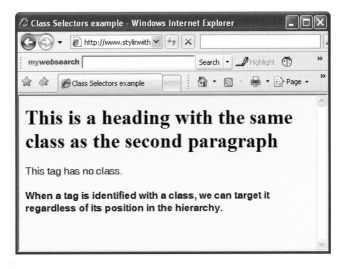

These rules result in both paragraphs displaying in the Helvetica font (or the browser's generic sans-serif font if Helvetica is not available) and the paragraph with the `specialtext` class displaying in Helvetica bold. The text in the h1 tag remains in the browser's default font (usually Times), but it is bold because it also has the `specialtext` class. Note that the span, a tag that has no default attributes, doesn't affect anything because I didn't explicitly style it.

CONTEXTUAL CLASS SELECTORS

If you only want to target one paragraph with the class, you create a selector that combines the tag name and the class, like this (**Figure 2.10**)

```
p {font-family: Helvetica, sans-serif;}

.specialtext {font-weight:bold;}

p.specialtext {color:red;}
```

FIGURE 2.10 By combining a tag name and class name, you make the selector more specific.

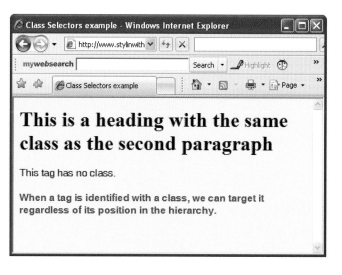

This is another kind of contextual selector because the class must be in the context of a paragraph for the rule to be applied.

You can go one step further and write the following (**Figure 2.11**)

```
p {font-family: Helvetica, sans-serif;}

.specialtext {font-weight:bold;}

p.specialtext {color:red;}

p.specialtext span {font-style:italic;}
```

FIGURE 2.11 By adding a second selector, you can be very specific about which tag is styled.

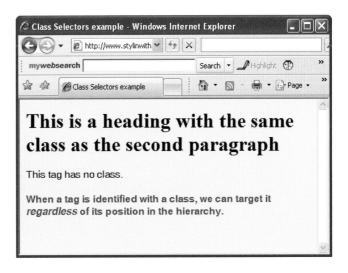

Now the word "regardless" is bold *and* italicized because it is in a span tag that is in a paragraph with the specialtext class, as the rule specifies. If you also want this rule to target the span in the h1 tag, you can modify it in one of two ways. The easiest way is not to associate the class with any specific tag (**Figure 2.12**).

```
.specialtext span {font-style:italic;}
```

FIGURE 2.12 With a less specific selector, the headline's span text is also selected.

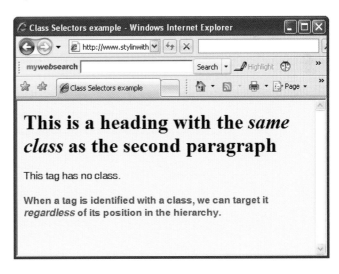

The words "same class" in the headline are now also italicized. By deleting the p from the start of the selector, you remove the requirement for the class to be attached to any specific tag, so now both span tags are targeted. The rule states that the span tag can be a descendant of *any* tag with the specialtext class because no tag is specified.

The benefit of this approach is that you can use a class without regard for the tag to which it belongs, so you are escaping the inherent constraints of the hierarchy when you do this.

The downside is that other tags that you don't intend to style might also be affected because this modified rule is less specific than it was. So, say you later added a span inside another tag that also had the specialtext class, such as this one:

```
<div class="specialtext">In this div, the span tag <span>may
or may not</span> be styled.</div>
```

The text within the span would be italicized also, which may or may not be the desired effect (**Figure 2.13**).

FIGURE 2.13 The less specific the selector, the more likely other tags will be inadvertently targeted.

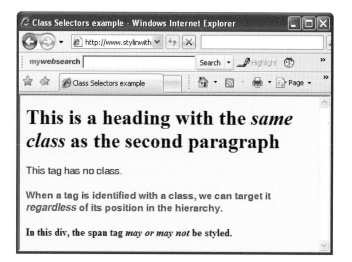

If you don't want to style this new div's span, you can adopt a second, more focused, group selector approach, like this (**Figure 2.14**)

```
p.specialtext span, h1.specialtext span {font-style:italic;}
```

Now only the two tags in question are targeted and your new tag is not affected. Your grouped rules don't target that span because it's descended from a div, whereas if you use the more simple and less specific .specialtext span approach, it is targeted.

Although this may seem like a lot to think about when you are styling a four-line example like this, when you are working on a style sheet that might be dozens or hundreds of lines long, you need to keep these considerations in mind, as we do in later chapters.

FIGURE 2.14 By using two grouped rules, you focus your targeting to specific tags.

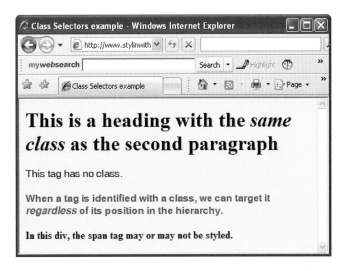

MULTIPLE CLASSES

One final note on classes is that you can apply multiple classes to a single tag, like this

```
<div class="specialtext featured">In this div, the span tag
<span>may or may not</span> be styled.</div>
```

You can see that both the specialtext and the featured class names go in the same set of quotes with a space between them, which looks a little strange at first, but please refer any questions about this to the W3C. You will see uses for multiple classes in examples in later chapters.

Introducing IDs

IDs are written in a similar way to classes, except you use a # (hash symbol) to indicate them in your CSS instead of the class's . (period)

If a paragraph is marked up with an ID, like this

```
<p id="specialtext">This is the special text</p>
```

then the corresponding contextual selector looks like this

```
p#specialtext {some CSS rules here}
```

Other than this, IDs work in the same way as classes, and everything in our previous discussion of classes applies equally to IDs. So what's the difference?

The Difference Between IDs and Classes

So far, I have shown aspects of classes and IDs that might make them seem to be interchangeable—we have used them both to identify a specific tag within our markup. However, an ID is more powerful than a class, rather like the queen is more powerful than a pawn in a game of chess. (You will see just how true this is when you look at the concept of rule specificity in the "The Cascade" section later in this chapter.) This is because, according to the rules of XHTML, only a single instance of a particular ID (such as `id="mainmenu"`) can be in a page, but a class (such as `class="strongparagraph"`) can appear many times.

So, if you want to identify a unique piece of your page's markup, such as the main navigation menu to which you want to target a special set of CSS rules, you might use an ID on a `div` (division element) that encloses the menu's elements.

To identify a number of special paragraphs in a page that all require the same variation of styling from the basic paragraph, you would use a class.

As an aside, you also use an ID to enable JavaScript to be targeted at a tag (for example, to activate a DHTML animation when the user mouses over a link). You JavaScript jocks might like to know that the `id` attribute replaces the deprecated `name` attribute (which the XHTML validator flags as invalid) for this purpose. It's especially important that you make sure JavaScript-related IDs appear only once in a page, or the JavaScript may behave unpredictably.

Don't Go Crazy with Classes

Generally, you should use IDs and classes sparingly; the right kind of use is putting them on the divs that contain the main sections of your markup, and then accessing the tags within them with contextual selectors that begin with the ID or class's name.

What you want to avoid is what Jeffrey Zeldman describes as "classitis—the measles of markup," where you add a unique class or ID to just about every tag in your markup and then write a rule for each one. This is only one step removed from loading up your markup with FONT tags and other extraneous markup. The good doctor Zeldman has cured me and many others of this nasty affliction. If you are already in the habit of slapping classes on every tag, as most of us do when we enthusiastically jump into CSS, take a look at the markup sample in Chapter 1 in light of what you just read in this chapter. You'll see that you can target styles at every tag quite easily without adding any more IDs or classes.

If you use IDs to identify only the main sections of your markup—and use those classes for occasional tags that can't be specifically targeted with contextual tag-based selectors—you won't go far wrong. This approach has the added benefit of making your style sheet simpler too.

In summary, you can use multiple `id` attributes in a page, but each one must have a unique value (name) to identify it. You can apply a particular class name to as many tags as needed.

Specialized Selectors

Although not an official CSS category, these "specialized" selectors let you target markup in ways different from the selectors we have seen so far. With the exception of the * (star) selector, the following selectors effectively examine the markup and apply themselves if certain conditions are true—for example, if one particular type of tag follows another type of tag sequentially. These selectors offer some powerful capabilities, but are not well supported by older browsers, especially IE, including IE6. IE7, however, is much improved in this regard. If you want to test any browser's capability to support pseudo-classes, I have put up a test page at www.stylinwithcss.com/chapter_2/code/pseudo_tests.htm. This page will allow you to see at a glance how well the browser you are using supports these "specialized" selectors.

THE UNIVERSAL SELECTOR

The * universal selector (commonly known as the star selector) means "anything," so if you use

```
* {color:green;}
```

in your style sheet, all type will be green, except where you specify it to be different in other rules. Another interesting use for this selector is as the inverse of the child selector—a not-a-child selector, if you will.

```
p * em {font-weight:bold;}
```

Here, any `em` tag that is at least a grandchild of the `p` tag, but not a child, is selected; it doesn't matter what the em's parent tag is. (The star selector is supported by all browsers, old and new.)

THE ADJACENT SIBLING SELECTOR

This rule selects a tag that follows a specific sibling tag (sibling tags are at the same level in the markup hierarchy—that is, they share the same parent tag). Here's an example

```
h1 + p {font-variant:small-caps}
```

Applying this rule to this markup

```
<div>

  <h1>All about siblings selectors</h1>

  <p>There must be at least two selectors, with a + sign
  before the last one.</p>

  <p>The targeted selector will only be affected if it is a
  sibling to, and preceded by, the one before the + sign.</p>

</div>
```

results in what is shown in **Figure 2.15**, because only the first paragraph is preceded by a sibling h1 tag.

FIGURE 2.15 Sibling selectors work based on the preceding tag in the markup, and both must be nested at the same level. This is one of the trickier selectors to understand.

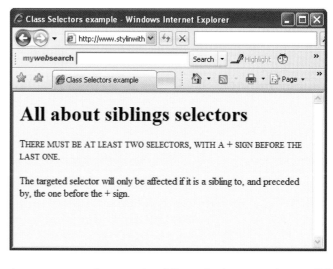

As you can see, the p tag that follows the h1 meets the condition of the rule, so it is in small caps. The second p tag, which is not adjacent to the h1, is unaffected. This is a good way to have the first item in a list be bold, for example (ul + li {font-weight:bold;}). (Adjacent sibling selectors work in SCBs and IE 7, but not IE6).

ATTRIBUTE SELECTORS

Attribute selectors use the attributes of the tag. This is another way to target different CSS at similar elements; as long as there is some difference between attributes on the tags you are trying to target, you can apply different rules to those tags. However, this interesting capability is of limited use, since neither IE 6 nor even the new, improved IE 7 supports them. So for now, we can only use attribute selectors to enhance the experience of viewers with SCBs.

This rule

```
img[title] {border: 2px solid blue;}
```

causes any img with a title attribute, like this

```
<img src="../images/Windsor-castle_walls.jpg" title="Windsor-
castle walls" alt="Windsor-castle walls" />
```

The text of these image alt tag examples is deliberately very brief for the sake of clarity. From an accessibility point of view, however, always write alt text that is meaningful for a user who can't see the image.

to have a blue, two-pixel border around it; it doesn't matter what the value of the title attribute is, just that there is one. You might use such a style to indicate to the user that if he points at this image, a tooltip (pop-up text generated by the title attribute) displays. It's common practice to duplicate the alt and title attribute values—the <alt> tag text displays if the image does not load, or can be read by a screen reader, and the title causes a tooltip to appear if the user points at the image.

You can also be specific about what the attribute's value should be. For example, the rule

```
img[alt="Dartmoor-view of countryside"] {border:3px green
solid;}
```

only puts the border around the image if the image's alt attribute is "Dartmoor-view of countryside"; in other words, if the image markup looks something like this

```
<img src="../images/dartmoor-view.jpg" title="Dartmoor-view
of countryside" alt="Dartmoor-view of countryside" />
```

This selector is made more useful by the fact that it lets you specify just the first characters of the attribute value, but the "common" part of the attribute must be separated from the "different" part of the attribute with a hyphen. So, if you have carefully written your img tags with attributes like these (note the hyphens)

```
<img src="../images/dartmoor-cottage.jpg" title="Dartmoor-
small cottage" alt="Dartmoor-small cottage" />
```

```
<img src="../images/dartmoor-view.jpg" title="Dartmoor-view
of countryside" alt="Dartmoor-view of countryside" />
```

then you can select them by adding the pipe symbol (usually typed with Shift-\) into your rule, like this

```
img[alt|="Dartmoor"] {border:3px blue solid;}
```

By the way, this rule would also select this example

```
<img src="../images/dartmoor-view.jpg" title="Dartmoor "
alt="Dartmoor " />
```

even though this example's alt tag doesn't have the hyphenated extension to the value.

Figure 2.16 is a screenshot in Firefox displaying these code examples.

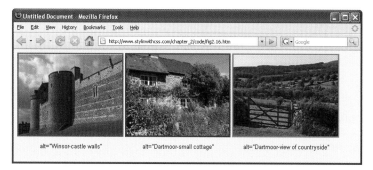

FIGURE 2.16 Firefox correctly displays attribute selectors. The title tags of the images are the same as the alt tags shown in the screenshot…

FIGURE 2.16A. …but IE 7 has no attribute selector capabilities.

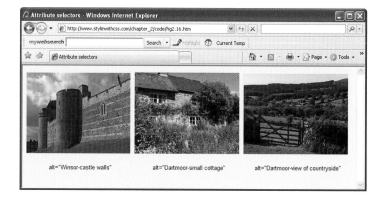

Summary of Selectors

So far, you've seen that you can target CSS rules in several ways: by using tag selectors, by using class and ID selectors, by using selectors that are a combination of both, and even by selecting based on the attributes that are attached to the tag.

One common aspect of these selectors is that they all are targeting *something* in the markup—a tag name, a class, an ID, an attribute, or an attribute value. But what happens if you want some kind of styling to happen when *some event* occurs, such as the user pointing at a link? In short, you want a way to apply rules based on events. And after all this buildup, you know I'm going to tell you there's a way to do that.

Pseudo-Classes

You can find the `hover.htc` file in the Javascript folder of the Stylib CSS library download at www.stylinwithcss.com/stylib.

The distinctive `:` (colon) in the selector screams (well, indicates) "I am pseudo-class!"

Named for the fact that they are classes that aren't actually attached to tags in the markup, pseudo-classes cause rules to be applied to the markup when certain events occur. The most common event that occurs is that the user points at or clicks on something. With the newer browsers (sadly, not Internet Explorer 6 or earlier; at least not without adding the special JavaScript function, `hover.htc`), it's easy to make any on-screen object respond to a rollover, which is the act of moving the pointer over something, also known as *hovering*. For example, the `:hover` pseudo-class can cause a border to appear around an image when the mouse rolls over the image.

Anchor Link Pseudo-Classes

Pseudo-classes are most commonly used with hyperlinks (a tags), enabling things like a change in their color or causing their underlining to be removed when rolled over.

There are four pseudo-classes for anchor links, since links always are in one of these four states:

- **Link.** The link is just sitting there looking like a link and waiting for someone to click on it.

- **Visited**. The user has clicked on the link at some point in the past.

- **Hover**. The link is currently being pointed at (rolled over).

- **Active**. The link is currently being clicked.

Here are the corresponding pseudo-class selectors for these states (using the a selector with some sample declarations):

```
a:link {color:black;}

a:visited {color:gray;}

a:hover {text-decoration:none;}

a:active {color:navy;}
```

First, let's save the debate about appropriate link colors and behavior for later and simply observe that, according to the declarations above, links are initially black (and underlined by default). When the mouse rolls over them (the hover state), the underlining is removed, and they stay black, because no color is defined here for the hover state. When the user holds the mouse down on the link (the active state), it turns navy, and forever after (or more accurately, until the browser's history of the visit to the link's URL expires or is deleted by the user), the link displays in gray. When using these pseudo-class selectors, you have complete control over the look and behavior of the four states of links.

And that's all very nice, but the real power comes when you start using these anchor link pseudo-classes as part of contextual selectors. Then you can create different looks and behaviors for various groups of links in your design—navigation, footers, sidebars, and links in text, for example. We'll explore using these pseudo-classes for styling of links and other things to the point of tedium (or perhaps, ecstasy) later in the book, but for now, let's note the following and then move on:

You don't have to define all four of these states. If you just want to define a link and a hover state, that's fine. Sometimes it doesn't make sense to have links show as having been visited.

A browser may skip some of these rules if you don't state them in the order shown above: link, visited, hover, active. The mnemonic "LoVe-HA!" is an easy, if cynical, way to remember this.

You can use *any* element with these pseudo-classes, not just `a`, to create all kinds of rollover effects. For example

```
p:hover {background-color:gray;}
```

This code will, well, I don't think I even need to tell someone as smart as you what is apt to happen to your paragraph when you roll over it.

Link (a) pseudo-classes are supported by all browsers tested for this book—IE5 and later. As mentioned before, be aware that IE6 does not support hovers on anything except links without a special JavaScript file called `hover.htc` being linked as an Internet Explorer behavior to the page. IE7 *does* support hover on any element, but only in pages with the Strict DOCTYPE. All a bit confusing, but we will see how to make hover work on any element in any of our tested browsers in a later chapter.

Other Useful Pseudo-Classes

The purpose of pseudo-classes is to simulate classes being added to your markup when certain conditions occur. Not only can they be used to provide a response to user actions such as pointing and clicking, but they can also be applied based on certain conditions being true in your markup.

:FIRST-CHILD

Where x is a tag name

`x:first-child`

This pseudo-class selects the first-child element with the name x. For example, if this rule

`div.weather strong:first-child {color:red;}`

is applied to this markup

`<div class="weather">`

`It's <strong>very</strong> hot and <strong>incredibly</strong> humid.`

`</div>`

then `very` is red and `incredibly` is not.

See **Figure 2.17**.

(SCBs and IE7 support :firstchild.)

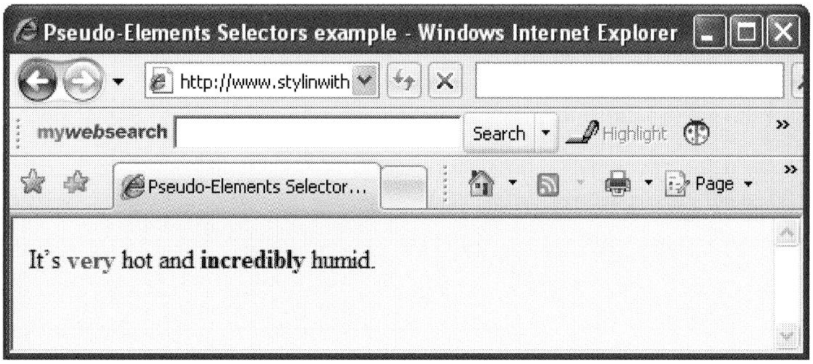

FIGURE 2.17 First-child selectors enable you to target the first tag of a particular type with a set of tags.

:FOCUS

Where x is a tag name

`x:focus`

An element such as a text field of a form is said to have focus when the user clicks it; that's where the characters appear when the user types. For instance, the code

```
input:focus {border: 1px solid blue;}
```

puts a blue border around such a field when the user clicks it. (IE6, IE7 and Safari do not support :focus.)

Pseudo-Elements

Pseudo-elements provide the effect of extra markup elements magically appearing in your document, although you don't actually add any extra markup. Here are some examples.

This pseudo-class

| Where x is a tag name |——⎰ x:first-letter

For example:

```
p:first-letter {font-size:300%; float:left;}
```

enables you, for example, to create a large drop-cap effect at the start of a paragraph.

This pseudo-class

| Where x is a tag name |——⎰ x:first-line

enables you to style the first line of (usually) a paragraph of text. For example,

```
p:first-line{font-variant:small-caps;}
```

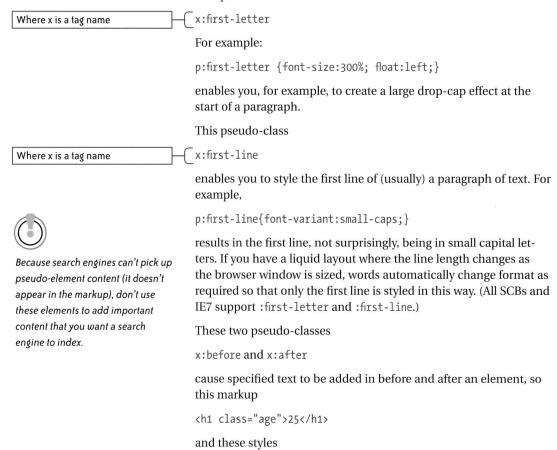

Because search engines can't pick up pseudo-element content (it doesn't appear in the markup), don't use these elements to add important content that you want a search engine to index.

results in the first line, not surprisingly, being in small capital letters. If you have a liquid layout where the line length changes as the browser window is sized, words automatically change format as required so that only the first line is styled in this way. (All SCBs and IE7 support :first-letter and :first-line.)

These two pseudo-classes

```
x:before and x:after
```

cause specified text to be added in before and after an element, so this markup

```
<h1 class="age">25</h1>
```

and these styles

```
h1.age:before {content:"Age: "}
```

```
h1.age:after {content:" years old."}
```

Don't make critical features of your site dependent on pseudo-classes and pseudo-elements because they are not supported by IE6 and only partially supported by IE7 (and these two browsers are currently used by about 70 percent of your visitors). Instead, use these selectors to enhance the user experience in browsers that support them—for example, use the `:focus` *selector to add a strong border around the form field in which a user is currently typing. Users that don't get this enhancement still have an acceptable experience.*

result in text that reads "Age: 25 years old." Note that the spaces added inside the quoted content strings ensure proper spacing in the resultant output. These two selectors are especially useful when the tag's content is being generated as a result of a database query; if all the result contains is the number, then these selectors allow you to provide that data point with some meaningful context when you display it for the user. (IE7 does not support `:before` and `:after`.)

CSS3

Most modern browsers support CSS2, which defined a slew of new features that were added to the initial CSS recommendations in the mid-nineties. CSS3 is the latest upgrade to CSS. Actually, it's been around since about 2000, and the specification was refined over the next five years, but browser developers have been very slow in adopting CSS3.

The objective of CSS3 is to move yet more presentational control of documents to CSS and further emulate the sophisticated controls that are available to our print design colleagues through programs such as Adobe InDesign and QuarkXPress.

The CSS3 spec is so extensive that it has been divided into several modules, which include a Color Module, Backgrounds and Borders, and Multi-Column Layout. You can go to http://www.css3.info to learn all about the various CSS3 modules.

What I will say is that when I wrote the original version of *Stylin'* some three years ago, the CSS3 specification was pretty much where it is today, and the fact remains that in virtually all browsers, it is very poorly supported. Attribute selectors are the only part of it that has really made inroads, and although useful, they represent a small part of the entire specification.

Is CSS3 so incredibly difficult to implement? Even though it seems that the whole notion of Web 2.0 is visually encapsulated by boxes with rounded corners, rounded corners on XHTML elements are a part of the CSS3 specification that only Mozilla can render using its special "-moz" selectors. A common work-around technique has been to wrap lots of spans around an element, each containing rounded-corner background graphics, to achieve this effect. We will look at more simple ways to create rounded corners without resorting to graphics later in the book.

There are four other pseudo-classes. The first is `:lang`, *which is applied to elements with a specific language code, and the other three are* `:left`, `:right`, *and* `:first`, *which apply to paged media (print) rather than content displayed in browsers. They are little used and unevenly or not at all supported by browsers, so I am not covering them here.*

Inheritance

Just like the money you hope you'll get from rich Uncle Dick, inheritance in CSS involves passing something down from ancestors to descendants: the values of CSS properties. You may remember from our discussion on the document hierarchy in Chapter 1 that the body tag is the great-ancestor of them all—all CSS-targeted tags in your markup descend from it. So thanks to the power of CSS inheritance, if you style the body tag like this

```
body {font-family: verdana, helvetica, sans-serif; color:
blue;}
```

then the text of every text element in your entire document inherits these styles and displays in blue Verdana (or in one of the other choices if Verdana is not available), no matter how far down the hierarchy it is. The efficiency is obvious; rather than specify the desired font for every tag, you set it once in this way as the primary font for the entire site. Then you only need font-family properties for tags that need to be in a different font.

For now, simply remember that styles that relate to text and its color and size are inherited by the descendant elements. Styles that relate to the appearance of boxes created by styling divs, paragraphs, and other elements, such as borders, padding, margins, and background colors, are not inherited.

Many CSS properties are inherited in this way, most notably text attributes. However, many CSS properties are *not* inherited because inheritance doesn't make sense for them. These properties primarily relate to the positioning and display of box elements, such as borders, margins, and padding. For example, imagine that you want to create a sidebar with text in it. You might do this by writing a div (which you can think of as a rectangular box), which has a list of links inside it, and styling the div with a border, say a two-pixel red line. However, it makes no sense for every one of those list items within the div to automatically get a border too. And they won't— border properties are not inherited. When we look at the box model in Chapter 4, we'll look at inheritance in greater detail.

Also, you must be careful when working with relative sizes such as percentages and ems; if you style a tag's text to be 80 percent and it's descended from a tag whose text is also sized at 80 percent, its text size will be 64 percent (80 percent of 80 percent), which is probably not the effect you want. In Chapter 3, I'll cover the pros and cons of absolute and relative text sizing.

In the examples that follow, we will be examining the effect that inheritance has on your styles as you write them, and how to make the most of inherited styles so that you write the minimum amount of CSS necessary to achieve the desired result.

The Cascade

OK, now we have enough information to have a meaningful discussion about one of the toughest aspects of CSS to get your head around—the Cascade. If this section gets to be too much, skip ahead and read the "Charlie's Simple Cascade Summary" sidebar later in this chapter. This sidebar is a simplified, if slightly less accurate, version that will serve you until you have done some CCS coding and really need the details.

As its name suggests, the Cascade in Cascading Style Sheets involves styles falling down from one level of the hierarchy of your document to the next, and its function is to let the browser decide which of the many possible sources of a particular property for a particular tag is the one to use.

The Cascade is a powerful mechanism. Understanding it helps you write CSS in the most economical and easily editable way and enables you to create documents that are viewed as you mean them to be seen, while leaving appropriate control of aspects of the document's display, such as overall font sizes, with users who have special needs.

Sources of Styles

Styles can come from many places. First, it's not hard to accept that there must be a *browser style sheet* (the default style sheet) hidden away inside the browser, because every tag manifests styles without you writing any. For example, h1 tags create large bold type, em tags create italicized type, and lists are indented and have bullets for each item, all automatically. You don't style anything to make this formatting happen.

If you have Firefox installed on your computer, search for the file html.css, and you can then see the Firefox default browser style sheet. Modify it at your peril.

Then there is the *user style sheet*. The user can create a style sheet, too, although very few do. This capability is handy, for example, for the visually impaired, since they can increase the baseline size of text or force text to be in colors that they can discern one from another. You can add a user style sheet to Internet Explorer for Windows (6 or 7) by selecting Tools > Internet options and clicking the Accessibility button. This capability, for example, enables visually impaired users to add a style like

```
body {font-size:200%;}
```

that doubles the size of all text—inheritance at work again. This is why it is important to specify text in relative sizes, such as ems, rather than fixed sizes, such as points, so you don't override such changes. We will discuss this interesting topic more in Chapter 3.

Then there are *author style sheets,* which are written by you, the author. We have already discussed the sources of these: linked style sheets, embedded styles at the top of pages, and inline styles that are attached to tags.

Here's the order in which the browser looks at, or cascades through, the various locations:

- Default browser style sheet
- User style sheet
- Author style sheet
- Author embedded styles
- Author inline styles

The browser updates its settings for each tag's property values (if defined) as it encounters them while looking sequentially in each location. They are defined in the default browser style sheet, and the browser updates any that are also defined in the other locations. If, for example, the author style sheet style defines the <p> tag's font-family to be Helvetica but the <p> tag is also specified to be Verdana in an embedded (page) style, the paragraph will be displayed in Verdana—the embedded styles are read after the author style sheet. However, if there is no style for paragraphs in the user or author style sheet, they will display in Times, because that's the style defined in all browser default style sheets.

That's the basic idea of how the Cascade works, but in fact, there are several rules that control the Cascade.

The Cascade Rules

In addition to the order in which styles are applied, you should know several rules about how the Cascade works.

Cascade Rule 1: Find all declarations that apply to each element and property. As it loads each page, the browser looks at every tag in the page to see if a rule matches it.

The Cascade defines the order in which the styles available to a document are read and updated.

Get more info on the Cascade at the W3C site (www.w3.org/TR/CSS2/cascade.html).

Cascade Rule 2: Sort by order and weight. The browser sequentially checks each of the five sources, setting any matched properties as it goes. If a matched property is defined again further down the sequence, the browser updates the value and does this repeatedly, if necessary, until all five possible locations of properties for each tag in that page have been checked. Whatever a particular property is set to at the end of this process, that's how it is displayed.

In **Table 2.1**, we look at this process for a page with numerous p tags. Let's assume, for the sake of the example, that two of those p tags have inline styles that define their color as red. In this case, every p tag text is blue, except for ones with the inline color attribute—these are red.

TABLE 2.1 Cascade Example

LOCATION	TAG	PROPERTY	VALUE
Default style sheet	P	color	black
User style sheet			
Author style sheet	P	color	blue
Author embedded styles			
Author inline styles	P	color	red

Of course, things aren't quite that simple. There is also the *weight* of the declaration. You can define a rule as important, like this

Note the exclamation point

```
p {color:red !important; font-size:12pt;}
```

The word !important follows a space after the style you want to make important but before the ; (semicolon) separator.

This style defines the text's red color as important, and therefore, it displays this way, even if it is declared as a different color further down the Cascade. Think hard and long before you force a particular style on the user with !important rule definition, because you may be messing up someone's personal style sheet, which may be set that way for a very good reason; be sure that it truly is important for such a style to dominate over any other possible style for that tag.

Charlie's Simple Cascade Summary

You need to remember just three things in this simplified version of the Cascade rules. These are true for virtually every case.

Rule 1: Selectors with IDs override selectors with classes; these, in turn, override selectors with only tags.

Rule 2: If the same property for the same tag is defined in more than one location in the Cascade, inline styles override embedded styles, which override style sheet styles. Rule 2 loses out to Rule 1, though—if the selector is more specific, it overrides, wherever it is.

Rule 3: Defined styles override inherited styles, regardless of specificity. A little explanation is required for Rule 3. This markup

```
<div id="cascadedemo">

<p id="inheritancefact">Inheritance is <em>weak</em> in the Cascade</p>

</div>
```

and this rule, which has a high specificity,

`2-0-4` — `html body div#cascadedemo p#inheritancefact {color:blue:}`

results in all the text, including the word *weak*, being blue because the em inherits the color from its parent, the p tag.

As soon as we add this rule for the em, even though it has very low specificity

`0-0-1` — `em {color:red}`

the em text is red. The inherited style is overridden by the defined style for the em, regardless of the high specificity of the rule for the containing paragraph.

There, three simple cascade rules. That was much easier, wasn't it?

Cascade Rule 3: Sort by specificity. Besides being very hard to pronounce, specificity determines just how specific a rule is. I tried to get you started on this idea by using the word specific in exactly this way many times while we were discussing selectors. As you saw, if a style sheet contains this rule

```
p {font-size:12px;}
```

and this rule

```
p.largetext {font-size:16px;}
```

then this markup

```
<p class="largetext">A bit of text</p>
```

displays text 16 pixels high because the second rule is more specific—it overrides the first rule. This may seem intuitively obvious, but what happens to that bit of markup if you use these styles instead?

```
p {font-size:12px;}
```

```
.largetext {font-size:16px;}
```

Both these rules match the tag, but the class overrides, and the text is 16 pixels. Here's why: the numeric specificity of the tag selector is 1, but the class has a specificity of 1-0. Here's how to calculate the specificity of any selector. There is a simple scoring system for each style that you plug into a three-value layout like this:

A - B - C

The dashes are separators, not subtraction signs. Here's how the scoring works:

1. Add one to A for each ID in the selector.

2. Add one to B for each class in the selector.

3. Add one to C for each element name (tag name).

4. Read the result as a three-digit number. (It's not *really* a three-digit number; it's just that in most cases, reading the result as a three-digit number works. Just understand that you can end up with something like 0-1-12, and 0-2-0 is still more specific.)

So let's look at the specificity of these examples

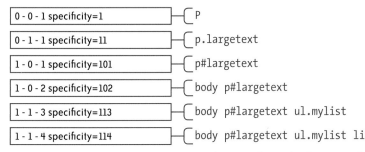

0 - 0 - 1 specificity=1	P
0 - 1 - 1 specificity=11	p.largetext
1 - 0 - 1 specificity=101	p#largetext
1 - 0 - 2 specificity=102	body p#largetext
1 - 1 - 3 specificity=113	body p#largetext ul.mylist
1 - 1 - 4 specificity=114	body p#largetext ul.mylist li

Each example is a higher specificity than the previous one.

Cascade Rule 4: Sort by order. If two rules have exactly the same weight, the one furthest down the Cascade overrides.

And that, dear reader, is the Cascade and, yes, it *is* somewhat hard to understand, especially if you have not yet had much experience with CSS, but my simplified version of the Cascade rules (see the sidebar earlier in this chapter) applies in about 98 percent of cases. If you find that something isn't behaving the way you want when you're using this simplified version, refer to the above rules.

Specificity is more important than order, so a more specific rule high up the Cascade overrides a less specific one further down.

Rule Declarations

So far I've focused on how you use CSS rule selectors to target tags, but you haven't yet looked much at the other half of a CSS rule, the declaration. I've used numerous different declarations to illustrate the selector examples but have only explained them minimally. Now it's time to look at declarations in detail.

The diagram showing the structure of a CSS rule earlier in this chapter (Figure 2.2) shows that a declaration is made of two parts: a property and a value. The *property* states what aspect of the element is affected (its color, its height, and so on) and the *value* states what that property is set to (green, 12px, and so on).

Every element has a number of properties that can be set using CSS; these differ from element to element. You can set the `font-size` property for text, but not for an image, for example. In each subsequent chapter of this book, I use real-world examples to show you the properties you can set for different elements and the values you can set for those properties. Because there are only a few different types of CSS rule values, let's look at them now.

Values fall into three main types:

Words. For example, in `font-weight:bold`, `bold` is a type of value.

Numerical values. Numerical values are usually followed by a unit type. For example, in `font-size:12px`, 12 is the numerical value and `px` is the unit type—pixels in this example.

Color values. Color values are written as `color:#336699`, where the color in this example is defined with a hexadecimal value.

There's not much I can tell you about word values that would make sense until you start using them, because they are specific to each element. Numerical and color values, however, can only be expressed in certain ways.

Numerical Values

You use numerical values to describe the length (and I use "length" generically to mean height, width, thickness, and so on) of all kinds of elements. These values fall into two main groups: absolute and relative.

Absolute values (**Table 2.2**) describe a length in the real world (for example, 6 inches), as compared to a relative measurement, which is simply a relationship with some other measurable thing (when you say "twice as long" that's a measure relative to something else).

TABLE 2.2 Absolute Values

ABSOLUTE VALUE	UNIT ABBREVIATION	EXAMPLE
Inches	in	height:6in
Centimeters	cm	height:40cm
Millimeters	mm	height:500mm
Points	pt	height:60pt
Picas	pc	height:90pc
Pixels	px	height:72px

*Examples are not equivalent lengths.

When writing CSS that relates to fixed-sized elements such as images, I use only pixels. It's up to you, but pixels are also the only absolute unit that I use throughout this book, except in print style sheets—because paper is measured in inches, it makes sense to design print layouts with the same units.

Although the absolute units are pretty self-explanatory, the relative units (**Table 2.3**) warrant a little more explanation.

Em and ex are both measurements of type size. The em is derived from the width of the characters in a font, so its size varies, depending on which font you are using. Ex is the equivalent of the x-height of the given font (so named because it is the height of a lower-case x—in other words, the center bit without the ascenders and descenders that appear on characters such as p and d).

TABLE 2.3 Relative Values

RELATIVE VALUE	UNIT ABBREVIATION	EXAMPLE
Em	em	height:1.2em
Ex	ex	height:6ex
Percentage	%	height:120%

Percentages are useful for setting the width of containing elements, such as divs, to the proportion of the browser width, which is the one way to create "liquid" designs that smoothly change size as the user resizes the browser window. Using percentages is also the right way to get proportional *leading* (pronounced like lead, the metal), which is the distance between the baseline of one line of text and the next in a multiple-line text block such as a paragraph. You will learn more about leading in Chapter 3.

Why You Should Use Ems to Specify Type Sizes

There are two important benefits to using a relative sizing method like ems to specify your font sizes:

- You can use inheritance to your advantage by declaring the body element to have a size of 1em, and this becomes a sizing baseline because it causes all other element's text to size relative to it. Because your content text always goes inside other elements, such as p and h4, you then simply write rules that state that the p tag is .8em, and that text links are .7em, for example. In this way, you establish proportional relationships between all the text elements of your design.

  Note that in Internet Explorer 6, when you set an em size for the body, paragraphs size in proportion automatically, but h1 thru h6 don't; you have to explicitly set some relative size for them (such as 1.1em for h1, .9em for h2, and so on), otherwise they remain fixed at their default sizes.

  If you later decide to increase the overall size of the text in your site, you can go back to the body tag and set its size to, say, 1.2em. Magically, all your text increases in size proportionally by the same amount (a fifth larger, in this case) because all the other tags inherit their size from the body tag.

- If you don't define font sizes with relative units, you effectively disable the font sizing capabilities available in the View menu of Internet Explorer (although other browsers can resize absolute font-size units), and therefore disenfranchise visually impaired users who rely on that capability to get your content to a size where they can read it. You need to check frequently during development to make sure that upping the font size in this way doesn't break your page's structure.

For these two reasons, I advise you to *set all font sizes in ems* rather than in absolute units, such as pixels. If you are designing a row of tabs in a fixed horizontal space, the layout has the potential to break if the text gets resized. If you're careful, however, and design with this possibility in mind, you can develop such components of your design so that they can accommodate larger type when the size is changed by the user.

Color Values

You can use several value types to specify color. Use whichever one of the following you prefer.

Hexadecimal (#RRGGBB and #RGB). If you already know languages like C++, PHP, or JavaScript, then you are familiar with hexadecimal (hex) notation for color. The format is this

#RRGGBB

In this six-character value, the first two characters define red, the next two green, and the next two blue. Computers use units of two to count, rather than base 10 like us mortals, and that's why hex is base 16 (2 to the power of 4), using the 16 numbers/letters 0–9 and A–F. A thru F effectively function as 10 through 15. Because color is represented by a pair of these base 16 numbers, there are 256 (16 × 16) possible values for each color, or 16,777,216 combinations (256 × 256 × 256) of colors. You definitely get the most color options by using hexadecimal, although you can get by with far less. You'd be hard pressed (to say nothing of your monitor) to discern the difference between two immediately adjacent hex colors. Don't forget the # (hash) symbol in front of the value.

So, for example, pure red is #FF0000, pure green is #00FF00, and pure blue is #0000FF.

You can also use the following shorthand hex format

#RGB

If you select a color where each pair has the same two letters, such as #FF3322 (a strong red), you can abbreviate it to #F32.

Percentages RGB (R%, G% B%). This is notation that uses a percentage of each color like this

R%, G%, B%

Acceptable values are 0% to 100%. Although this only yields a piddling one million color combinations (100 × 100 × 100), that's more than enough for most of us. Also, it's much easier to make a guess at the color you want in RGB compared with hex notation.

So, for example, 100%, 0%, 0% is max red, 0%, 100%, 0% is max green, and 46%, 76%, 80% is close to that dusky green-blue color I demonstrated in hex above.

Color Name (red). As you have seen from all the preceding color examples in the selector discussions, you can simply specify a color

Most hex colors aren't easy to guess at a glance; for example, #7CA9BE is a dusky green-blue color. But if you just look at the first value in each RGB pair, 7, A, and B in this case, then you can see that red is slightly below half of 16, the maximum value, and green and blue are higher and about the same value. With this information, it's easier to make an informed guess as to what the color is.

by name, or keyword, to use the official term. However, there are limitations. There is no W3C specification to say exactly how the browser should render a color like olive or lime; basically, every browser manufacturer assigns its own (presumably hex) values to each color keyword. Also, only 16 colors are in the W3C spec, and, therefore, you can be sure to find only these 16 in every browser. Here they are, in alphabetical order

aqua, black, blue, fuchsia, gray, green, lime, maroon, navy, olive, purple, red, silver, teal, white, yellow

Most modern browsers offer many more colors (usually 140), but if you want to specify colors by name, you can only absolutely rely on these 16.

I usually use hex colors because I program, and that's how you do it in the murky world of coding. To save you from struggling to mix up colors yourself, visit http://www.bookmarkbliss.com/tools/book-mark-bliss-10-tools-to-help-you-select-a-web-20-color-palette/, which has fun tools to help you choose color palettes. Also, see the sidebar "You Don't Have to Limit Yourself to Web-Safe Colors".

Now that you have a basic understanding of how CSS works, let's next look at how to style text

You Don't Have to Limit Yourself to Web-Safe Colors

If you use Adobe Dreamweaver or other Web development tools, you are used to picking colors from a Web-safe palette. This is a set of 216 colors that only an engineer would have come up with, comprising mostly bright and saturated colors, with limited choices in dark and pale colors. These colors, you may (not) be interested to know, comprise twin hex pairs like this, #3399CC or #FF99CC, and only use the values 0, 3, 6, 9, C, and F. So any color you can come up with that meets these criteria is Web-safe. These colors are a large subset of the 256 colors (40 are reserved for the system) that a monitor driven by an 8-bit VGA card can display (remember 8-bit?), so for years, we were told not to use any others. As of July 2007, fewer than .01 percent (source: http://www.thecounter.com/stats/2007/July/colors.php) of the world's surfers still use 8-bit color, so you can confidently use any color in your designs that you can create with the methods listed in this chapter.

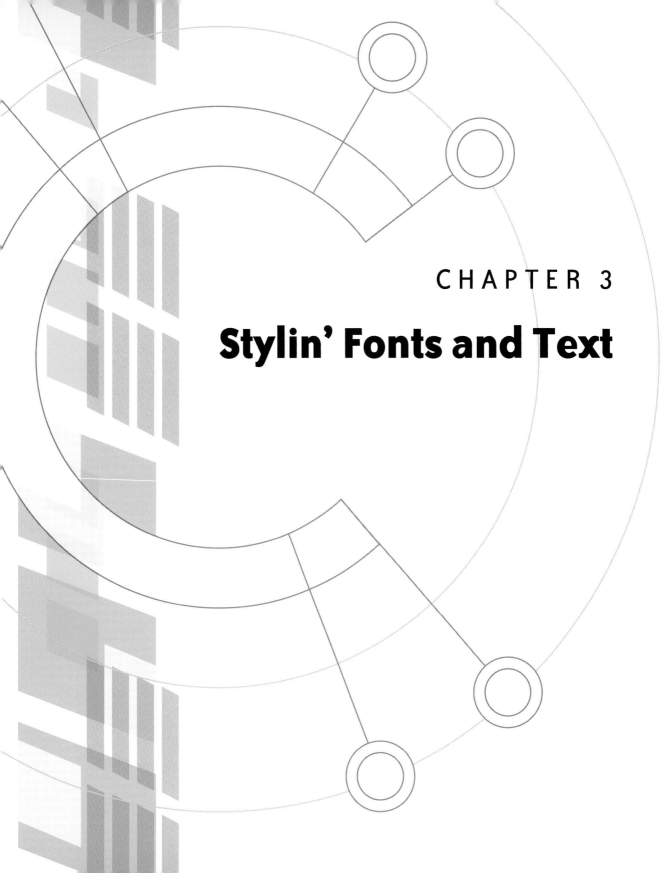

CHAPTER 3

Stylin' Fonts and Text

MUCH OF WEB DESIGN is dealing with text—in paragraphs, headlines, lists, menus, and forms. As a result, the CSS properties shown in this chapter are essential to making the difference between a site that looks thrown together and one that looks like it has the professional touch. More than any other factor, type makes the clearest visual statement about the quality of your site's offerings. Graphics are the icing on the cake; typography is where good design begins.

If the chapter title has you wondering "Aren't fonts and text the same thing?", the answer is "No," and here's why.

Fonts are the different kinds of typefaces. Each font is a set of letters, numbers, and symbols with a unique visual appearance. All fonts belong to large *collections,* which describe their general look, such as serif, sans-serif, or monospace. Font collections are made up of *families,* such as Times and Helvetica. A font family in turn can be broken down into font *faces,* which are variations on the basic family, such as Times Roman, Times Bold, Helvetica Condensed, Bodoni Italic, and so on.

Text simply describes a block of type, like this sentence or the heading of a chapter, regardless of the font in which it is set.

CSS has a set of properties relating to fonts and a set of properties relating to text. *Font properties* relate to the size and appearance of collections of type. What is its family (Times or Helvetica, for example)? What size is it? Is it bold or italic? *Text properties* relate to the font's treatment. What is its line height and letter spacing? Is it underlined or indented? And so on.

Here's a way I think about this perhaps seemingly subtle distinction. You can apply font styles, such as bold and italic, to a single character, but text properties, such as line height and text indent, only make sense in the context of a block of text, such as a headline or a paragraph.

Let's start with fonts.

Specifying Fonts in CSS

In this section, you'll learn how to use CSS to specify fonts. You can use any acceptable length units, both absolute and relative, to specify font sizes, but it's best to use a relative measurement such as ems. Relative type sizing allows the user to easily scale the type to other sizes by selecting an overall size from the Text Size setting (or similarly worded option) in the View menu of the browser, or less commonly, by adding a user style sheet.

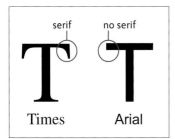

serif   no serif

Times   Arial

FIGURE 3.1 Serif fonts have notice-able details at the ends of the char-acter strokes. Sans-serif fonts do not have these details.

Both serif and sans-serif fonts are proportionally spaced, which means each character only takes up the space required for it, so an "i" takes up less space than an "m."

My general advice is to stick to serif, sans-serif, and monospace font col-lections. If you want to use cursive or fantasy, proceed with caution and test, test, test.

Introducing Font Collections

Example: `body {font-family: sans-serif;}`

Values: `serif, sans-serif, monospace, fantasy, cursive`

The simplest way to specify fonts in CSS is by using the five generic collection names—serif, sans-serif, monospace, fantasy, and cursive. These generic names cause the user agent (browser, smartphone, mobile phone, and so on) to serve up one of these font types. Generic collection names represent the lowest level of support for font styling, and as you will see in a moment, CSS offers some better options than these.

Serif fonts, as shown in **Figure 3.1**, are so named because of the little details, known as serifs, at the ends of the character strokes. These are particularly noticeable in the uppercase letters. Examples of serif fonts include Times New Roman, Georgia, and Palatino. The text of this sentence is set in a serif font.

Sans-serif fonts do not have any details at the ends of the charac-ter strokes. They have a more plain appearance than serif fonts. Examples of sans-serif fonts include Trebuchet MS, Arial, and Verdana. The headings in this book are set in a sans-serif font.

Monospace fonts such as Courier and Monotype give equal spacing to every letter ("i" has the same amount of space as "m") and are typically used for code blocks in computer-related books (this book is no exception), or to simulate the look of a typewriter, whatever that is.

Cursive fonts look like cursive handwriting, although much neater than my own. Examples include Comic Sans MS and Brush Script. Cursive fonts often have very thin strokes, which don't display well on-screen, and therefore aren't used much on the Web. If you use a cursive font, check it in various browsers, because every browser seems to use a different font for cursive.

Fantasy fonts are ones that don't fit in the other categories. The main fantasy here is the hope that this might be a useful way to specify a font. It's almost impossible to predict what font might be served up as a fantasy font from browser to browser, and therefore, it's best if you avoid fantasy fonts. Also, "fantasy" isn't really an accepted font collection name in the way that cursive and serif are. I have only seen this used as a collection name in CSS, but perhaps I don't get out enough.

A Serif headline
Serif paragraph text.

A Sans-Serif headline
Sans-Serif paragraph text.

A Monospace headline
Monospace paragraph text.

A Cursive headline
Cursive paragraph text.

A Fantasy headline
Fantasy paragraph text.

FIGURE 3.2 Generic font families as displayed by Safari Mac 2.0.4.

A Serif headline
Serif paragraph text.

A Sans-Serif headline
Sans-Serif paragraph text.

A Monospace headline
Monospace paragraph text.

A Cursive headline
Cursive paragraph text.

A Fantasy headline
Fantasy paragraph text.

FIGURE 3.3 Generic font families, as displayed by Firefox Mac 1.0.4.

A Serif headline
Serif paragraph text.

A Sans-Serif headline
Sans-Serif paragraph text.

A Monospace headline
Monospace paragraph text.

A Cursive headline
Cursive paragraph text.

A FANTASY HEADLINE
FANTASY PARAGRAPH TEXT.

FIGURE 3.4 Generic font families, as displayed by Internet Explorer 6 for Windows. They look virtually identical on IE7.

A Serif headline
Serif paragraph text.

A Sans-Serif headline
Sans-Serif paragraph text.

A Monospace headline
Monospace paragraph text.

A Cursive headline
Cursive paragraph text.

A Fantasy headline
Fantasy paragraph text.

FIGURE 3.5 Generic font families, as displayed by Firefox Windows 2.0.4.

If you want to specify a generic font, you write a declaration like this

```
body {font-family:sans-serif;}
```

In this case, the browser dishes up Helvetica or Arial or whatever sans-serif font is set as its default *and* is also on the viewer's computer (**Figures 3.2–3.5**). It's the most basic way to specify a font. But you can be more specific and declare a font family by name; usually, that's what you want to do.

Sans-Serif Fonts Are Better for the Web

Look at the big, text-heavy sites on the Web, such as CNN, MSNBC, or Amazon. See how just about all of them use sans-serif fonts? The small details of serif fonts provide useful additional visual information when you're reading print, but the inherently low-resolution world of the screen does not render serifs well, especially at smaller font sizes.

If you are new to Web design, I recommend using sans-serif fonts, at least while you gain some experience using serif fonts. Sans-serif fonts look crisper and more professional. Simply changing from the default Times served up by virtually all browsers to a sans-serif font is the easiest and most effective single thing you can do to make your site look more professional.

Exploring Font Families

In the world of print, you can use just about any font family you want. You purchase and install the font on your computer if it's not already there, and you use it in the design of your document. When your design is complete, you output your document in PDF format so that the fonts are converted to vectors (outlines), and you're done. In print, you can work with any of the thousands of available fonts because you have control over them all the way to the printing press.

On the Web, you simply don't have this freedom of choice as far as fonts are concerned. This is one of the most disappointing aspects of the Web for transitioning print designers—*you must trust that viewers have the fonts in which you want your document to be displayed installed on their computers.* Fonts aren't part of the browser; they are served up for all applications on a computer from the system software where they reside. Furthermore, it is impossible to know what flavor of any given font (Times, Times Regular, or Times Roman, for example) users might have on their computers.

WEB FONT SELECTION CHART		
	Georgia	
Serif fonts	Palatino	
	Times New Roman	
	Arial	
	Arial Black	
	Arial Narrow	
	Century Gothic	
Sans-serif fonts	Franklin Gothic	
	Impact	
	Tahoma	
	Trebuchet	
	Verdana	
Monospace fonts	Courier New	
	Lucida Console	
Cursive fonts	Comic Sans MS	

FIGURE 3.6 These fonts are usually preinstalled on Mac and Windows.

To see more samples of fonts common to Windows and Mac, check out: http://www.kathymarks.com/archives/2006/11/best_fonts_for_the_web_1.html and http://www.ampsoft.net/webdesign-l/WindowsMacFonts.html.

Because Trebuchet MS is more than one word, it has to be in quotes. If you do this in an inline style that's already inside double quotes, use single quotes on the name, like this <p style="font-family:'trebuchet ms', helvetica, arial, sans-serif;">

As much as you might want your Web pages' headlines to be displayed in Univers 87 Oblique, the odds of a user having that particular font are, to quote Elvis (Costello), "less than zero." Even Helvetica, perhaps the most popular sans-serif font of all time, is not included with Windows, although Windows has its own almost identical font, Microsoft Sans Serif. You can be certain, however, that every computer has, at minimum, Times New Roman, Arial, Verdana, and Courier, and any reasonably current computer almost certainly has the fonts listed in **Figure 3.6**.

"What about automatically downloading fonts as needed from my server to the user?" you ask. (You did ask, right?) Good question. Although CSS3 specifies a way a browser can request a font from your server in which to display the document, no browsers currently support this capability. But it is nice to think about, and one day it may be a reality. (Even then, the browser will never install the font on the user's computer but merely use it to display the page.)

Until the happy day when fonts are available on demand, in order to use specific fonts with CSS, you need to list the fonts, in order of preference, in which you would like the document to be displayed. This list must only be by family name—by that I mean you must use Helvetica or Times, not Helvetica Condensed or Times Expanded.

It is accepted practice to write a CSS declaration specifying a number of either serif or sans-serif fonts starting with the one you prefer first and ending with a generic font name such as serif or sans-serif. Here's an example with sans-serif fonts

```
body {font-family:"trebuchet ms", helvetica, arial, sans-serif;}
```

In the previous example using the font-family property, I am saying to the browser, "Display this document in Trebuchet MS, and if you don't have it, use Helvetica. If you don't have either of those, use Arial, and if all else fails, use whatever generic sans-serif font you do have." *It is very important to make the last item of a font-family declaration a generic declaration of either serif or sans-serif as a final fallback*. This ensures that, at a minimum, your document at least displays in the right *type* (no pun intended) of font.

And here's an example with serif fonts

```
font-family: {"hoefler text", times, serif;}
```

In the second example using the font-family property, I first declare Hoefler Text. However, because Windows users don't usually have Hoefler Text, they see the document displayed in the second choice, Times. If you put Times before Hoefler Text, everyone would see Times, because both the Mac and Windows platforms have that font.

Also, Vista, the Microsoft operating system, comes with a new collection of what I call the "VistaC" fonts, for obvious reasons, which are based on Microsoft's ClearFont technology: Calibri, Cambria, Candara, Consolas, Constantia, and Corbel—you can see what they look like at: http://www.modernlifeisrubbish.co.uk/article/new-vista-fonts-and-the-web. By adding these fonts first, Vista users will see them, and other operating systems will fall back to the second- and third-string fonts you specify.

Setting Up To Style a Document

The best way to learn about all the different aspects of fonts is to style a document. So set up your XHTML editor (such as Adobe Dreamweaver) and your browser to style the sample document (sample_XHTML_markup_ch1.htm) in the Chapter 1 folder on the *Stylin'* Web site (www.stylinwithcss.com). Here's how to proceed:

1. Download the sample documents folder from the *Stylin'* Web site and save it on your hard drive.

2. Navigate to the Chapter 1 folder and open the sample_XHTML_markup_ch1.htm file from the File menu of your XHTML editor.

3. Also open the same file in a Web browser.

   It's fine to open the file in two applications at once, because you are only writing to the file from the editor and are simply reading it in the browser.

4. Each time you make a change to the XHTML document and save, flip to your Web browser (Alt-Tab on Windows or Command-Tab on the Mac) and refresh the page in the browser using the F5 function key (or Command-R in Safari).

Now you will see the updated document displayed.

Using Embedded Styles (for Now)

To keep things simple, I'm going to start out by showing you how to write your CSS styles in a style element in the head of the document. Doing this means that you won't have to manage a separate style sheet, but the styles that you write will only be available to this one document. That's ideal for developing the layout of a single page, such as the examples we are going to be working on; later, you'll create a separate style sheet that can supply styles to multiple pages. Review the start of Chapter 2 if this doesn't make complete sense.

Let's use the XHTML document you created in Chapter 1 and modify it to include the style element in the document head, as illustrated by the highlighted code

```
<head>
<title>A Sample XHTML Document</title>
<meta http-equiv="Content-type" content="text/html;
charset=iso-8859-1" />
<meta http-equiv="Content-Language" content="en-us" />
<style type="text/css">


</style>
</head>
```

Add CSS for specifying a font family in this blank line

The blank line between the opening and closing tag of the `style` element is where you will add your CSS. When the browser encounters the opening tag of the `style` element, it stops interpreting the code as XHTML and starts interpreting it as CSS. When it encounters the closing tag of the `style` element, the browser reverts to treating the code as XHTML again. So anything you write within the `style` element must be in CSS syntax, the same syntax you use if the CSS is in a separate style sheet. This means any code within the `style` element is formatted as CSS like this

```
selector {property1:value; property2:value;}
```

You need to be aware of whether you are writing CSS or XHTML at any given moment during the development of your projects and make sure that you format your code accordingly.

Setting the Font Family for the Entire Page

To set the font family for the entire page, set it for the body of the document

```
<style type="text/css">
body {font-family: verdana, arial, sans-serif;}
</style>
```

Save your changes, flip to the browser, and refresh the page. What you see should look like **Figure 3.7**.

Because font-family is an inherited property, its value is passed to all its descendants, which, since body is the top-level element, are all the other elements in the markup. So with one line, you've made it so that everything displays in the desired font. Bathe for a moment in that glow of CSS magic. OK, moving right along...

FIGURE 3.7 Because font attributes are inherited, specifying the font for the body tag renders the entire document in the specified font.

All browsers, except Safari, add a blue border by default to any image that is enclosed in an a tag to indicate that it is clickable. I prefer to use a tooltip for this purpose and remove the default border, as I will illustrate later.

Sizing Fonts

You can use three types of values to size fonts. They are *absolute* (for example, pixels or inches), *relative* (for example, percentages or ems), and what I call the *sweatshirt keywords* (for example, x-small, small, large, and xx-large, among others). All three methods have advantages and disadvantages. Jeffrey Zeldman and other CCS mavens advocate keywords as the least problematic of the three (see A List Apart at www.alistapart.com/articles/sizematters/), but the keyword method requires some sophisticated CSS to make fonts display at consistent sizes in all browsers and only offers a limited number of font sizes. For this reason, and others I will cover as we go forward, I style font sizes in ems.

The Pros and Cons of Using Proportional Sizing

When you start to develop a style sheet, one key decision is the kind of units you will use to size type: absolute (points, inches, etc.) or relative (percentages, ems, etc.). The old way was to use pixels, but Internet Explorer, and other less-compliant browsers cannot scale type set in absolute units when the user selects a different size from a choice such as Type Size (exact wording varies between browsers) in the View menu. So now the trend is towards using relative sizes. Here are the pros and cons of doing that:

Pros:

- All type scales proportionally if the user uses the Text Size menu choice (it may be named differently in some browsers) to set the text larger or smaller. This is very user friendly and is an important step in making your site accessible to the visually impaired or to someone who has a super high-resolution monitor with pixels the size of grains of sand.

- As you fine-tune your design, you can proportionally change the size of all text by simply adjusting the body font-size; this changes the baseline size and all the other elements increase their size proportionally to that baseline.

Cons:

- If you are not careful, nested elements can display very small text (using keyword sizing prevents this) because font sizing is inherited

- It is possible for users to "break" a CSS page layout that hasn't been designed for text sizing. For example, if the user sets type to large sizes from the View menu, a "floating-columns" layout can display weirdness like the right column being forced down below the content area because it is too large to remain in place. In Chapter 6, where we create advanced CCS-based page layouts, we'll review this problem, and ways to prevent it, in detail.

Most browsers have a default size for 1 em (16 pixels high), and if you set text to 1 em, it takes on that default size. If you want text to be three-quarters of that size, set it to .75 ems. If you want it to be half, set it to .5 ems.

There is an excellent blog item and discussion on the thorny subject of sizing fonts by Richard Rutter at http://clagnut.com/blog/348/, so I'll not waste more space here except to say that if you care about people being able to size the type on your site, you need to read this. For an in-depth resource on font sizing, check out the CSS-Discuss site at http://css-discuss.incutio.com/?page=FontSize.

First, modify the body selector to look like this

```
<style type="text/css">

body {font-family: verdana, arial, sans-serif;
font-size:1em;}

</style>
```

Although this doesn't produce a visible effect, you now have a tweakable baseline size.

You might notice that the default sizes for common markup elements such as `<h1>` through `<h6>`, `<p>`, `<ul>`, and `<li>` are rather (read "very") large, and if you need to get any amount of content on the page, using these default sizes means the user must do lots of scrolling. Long hours of usability testing have taught me that scrolling is one of the least loved aspects of Web browsing. Also, I simply find that these large default sizes give the page a horsy, poorly designed look. But, when working in *proportional* ems, you can choose to make the overall font size a little smaller, because those users who want larger text sizes can get them easily by selecting View > Text Size from the browser menu and choosing Larger (or similar, depending on the browser).

Let's say you decide that the new baseline size is going to be 12 pixels (from a visual standpoint, that is; you will use percents and ems to actually specify the sizes). You set the body font size to .75 em, and text in a paragraph then displays at 75 percent of the browser's 16 pixel default size for paragraphs, or 12 pixels.

Remember, when you style the descendant elements, they inherit the new baseline size and the proportional effect is compounded—so, a font size of 1 em equals 12 pixels, .75 em equals 9 pixels, and so on.

The takeaway here is that if you are using a proportional value method (for example, ems) to size the fonts for the individual selectors, you are then able to provide the majority of viewers with smaller font sizes that are more aesthetically pleasing, that result in less scrolling, and that still give visually impaired users the option to override your font size decisions and increase the size of all type proportionally.

In the following examples, you work with the browser default size of 1em, and later, when you start building sites, you can adjust this baseline value to suit the needs of each design.

From the 1 em font-size baseline, let's set font sizes on each of the elements, starting with the line under the logo that reads "a New Riders book...." (**Figure 3.8**).

This line is an h3 element, so you're going to set it to .8 em. (I chose this number because I've done this before, and I know that's a nice size for it.) Here's what you write

```
<style type="text/css">

body {font-family: verdana, arial, sans-serif;
font-size:1em;}

h3 {font-size:.8em}

</style>
```

Figure 3.8 shows how this change looks.

FIGURE 3.8 The h3 headline is styled to be smaller.

You can see that the headline is now much smaller than its original default size. (You may be interested to know that by experimentation, I discovered its default size was equal to 1.2 ems, or 16 × 1.2 = 19.2 pixels.)

Let's now go on and set the font sizes for other elements in your markup, as follows

```
<style type="text/css">

body {font-family: verdana, arial, sans-serif;
font-size:100%;}

h3 {font-size:.8em}

p {font-size:.8em}

ol {font-size:.75em}

ul {font-size:.75em}

</style>
```

This results in **Figure 3.9**.

FIGURE 3.9 Tag selectors now let us specify sizes for all the tags in the document. Some tags are directly styled, while others inherit their sizes from their styled parent elements.

A couple of points about these styles: first, you didn't set a style for the list item (li) elements of the two lists, but you did for the ordered list (ol) and unordered list (ul) elements that respectively contain them. If you styled the li element, both lists would display in the same size, but because you styled the ol and ul elements instead, the li elements inherit their values, and you can later make the lists' items different sizes if you want.

Inherited Styles in Nested Tags

Secondly, although you are already making a nice improvement to the unstyled layout with which you started, the font size for the bulleted unordered list (ul) is very small, even though it's set to the same size as the ordered list (ol).

Inheritance of relative font sizes is buggy in IE6—see http://css-discuss.incutio.com/ ?page=InternetExplorerWinBugs.

This problem is caused by the fact that the ul element is set to .75 ems and the a elements nested down inside are set to .7 ems. The net result is that text in those a elements ends up displaying at .525 ems (.7 × .75). Inheritance of font sizes can work for you, and, as here, against you. Fortunately, the fix is easy—you simply set a contextual selector for this specific situation, like this

```
<style type="text/css">

body {font-family: verdana, arial, sans-serif; font-size:1em;}

h1 {font-size:1em}

h3 {font-size:.8em}

p {font-size:.8em}

ol {font-size:.75em}

ul {font-size:.75em}

ul a {font-size:inherit}

a {font-size:.7em}

</style>
```

Note we don't style the a element, but simply let it inherit its font size from its containing element, which is p in some cases and ol in others. In the case of the ol links, the a inherits from the li which inherits from the ol.

So you can see from these two comments that it makes sense to set the size of text at the highest level possible and then make adjustments by working your way down the document hierarchy, setting sizes at the highest level possible as you go. In other words, don't start with those highly nested links, but style text sizes top-down from the body tag. This minimizes the number of font-size rules you have to write, and maximizes the advantages of the Cascade.

You can now test the scalability of your ems-based layout:

1. Select Page > Text Size > Largest (in the IE7 menu) or View > Text Size > Increase a few times (in Firefox). Other browsers have similar choices. Note that everything scales up nicely for viewers who are visually impaired.

2. Vary the value of the font-size property of the body selector— try 80 percent and 120 percent, for example. Save and reload the page. Again, all the elements size proportionally. Those of

you who have spent hours changing the size attribute of hundreds of FONT tags in dozens of pages after it's decided that the type sizes are all too big or too small will appreciate the power and convenience of this capability. Next time the client makes some comment like, "The problem with you designers is you always make the type so bloody small," you can quadruple the font size of the body tag and thereby the entire site in about five seconds, and then politely say "Is *that* big enough for you?"

Let's move on to some other font-related CSS.

Font Properties

The relationship of font sizes is key to indicating the visual hierarchy of the content in your document. This is achieved through an understanding of the various font properties, and as we saw previously, an understanding of how font properties can be inherited through the structural hierarchy of your document. So let's now take a look at the font properties.

Font-Style Property

Example: h2 {font-style:italic;}

Other values: normal, oblique

Font style determines whether a font is italicized or not. It's that simple. If you want a piece of text to be italicized, you write this

p {font-style:italic;}

You can also write oblique instead of italic, but the result is the same.

There are only two useful settings for the font-style property: italic to make regular text italicized, and normal to make a section within italicized type regular "upright" text. In this example,

p {font-style:italic;}

span {font-style:normal;}

```
<p>This is italicized type with <span>a piece of non-italic
text</span> in the middle.</p>
```

The code produces the result in **Figure 3.10**.

FIGURE 3.10 The normal value for the font-style property causes a specified section of text to appear normal within a bit of italicized text.

Note on the Value Normal

normal causes any of the possible effects of a property not to be applied. Why might you want to do this? As I showed you in the font-style example in the main text, setting font-style:normal leaves the text in its regular state, rather than italicized. The reason this option is available is so you can selectively override a default or a global property you have set. Headlines h1 through h6 are bold by default, so if you want to unbold the h3 element, for example, you need to write h3 {font-weight:normal;}. If your style sheet states a {font-variant:small-caps;} so that all links are in small caps and you want one special set of links to be in regular upper- and lowercase type, you might write a declaration such as a.speciallink {font-variant:normal;}.

Font-Weight Property

Example: a {font-weight:bold;}

Possible values: 100, 200, and so on to 900, or lighter, normal, bold, and bolder.

The W3C recommendations for implementing this property simply state that each successive higher value (whether numerical or "weight" values) must produce boldness equal to or heavier than the previous lower value.

bold and bolder give two weights of boldness. lighter allows you to go one step in the other direction if you want a section within bold type to be, well, lighter. At least, that's the idea.

Figures 3.11A–D show a little test I ran on some different browsers.

Can you see more than two weights for any given browser among these results? Nor can I. I even tried different fonts, but to no avail. There really are only two results for all the font-weight values—bold or normal. Boldness variations would be a nice way to show a hierarchy in all kinds of data, especially when you could easily generate the different numerical values mathematically from middleware code (for example, ASP or PHP) to automatically highlight results that cross certain thresholds. However, the reality is that the browser makers have not chosen to take advantage of the concept of many different weights of text, which is a shame. There's room for improvement here, as the results show.

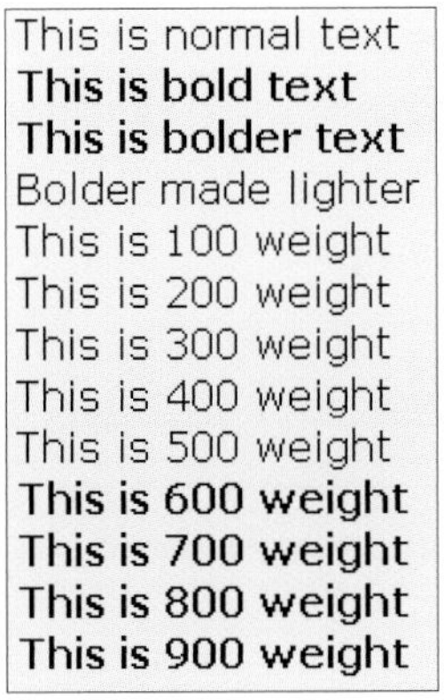

FIGURE 3.11A
Firefox Windows

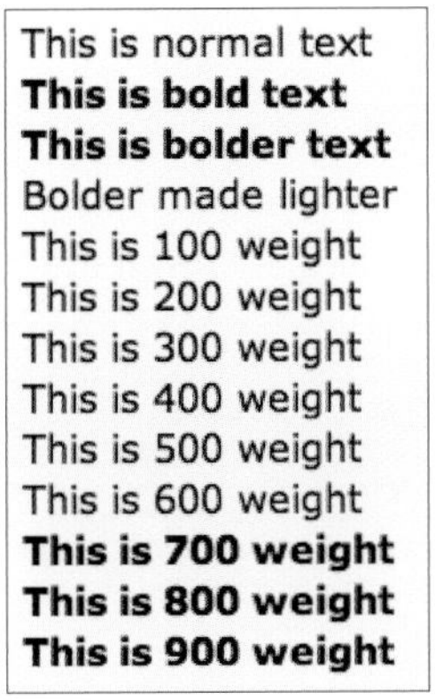

FIGURE 3.11B
Safari Mac

FIGURE 3.11C
IE6 Windows

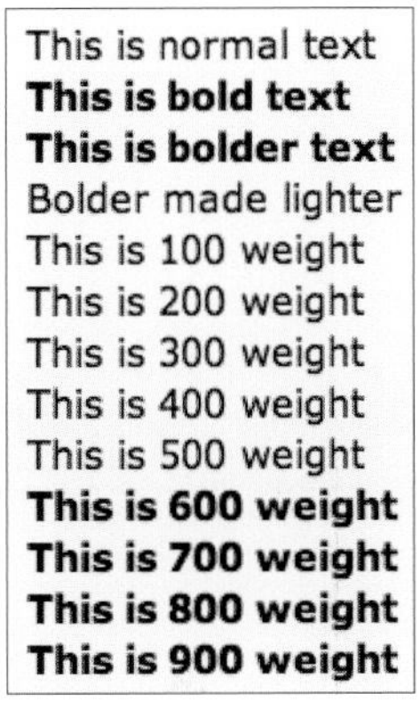

FIGURE 3.11D
Firefox Mac

Font-Variant Property

Example: `blockquote {font-variant:small-caps;}`

Values: `small-caps`, `normal`

This property accepts just one value (besides `normal`), and that is `small-caps`. This causes all lowercase letters to be set in small caps, like this

```
h3 {font-variant:small-caps;}
```

The code above produces the result in **Figure 3.12**.

FIGURE 3.12 Two paragraphs, one styled in small caps.

I often use `small-caps` with the `:first-line` pseudo-class (even IE6 supports it), which allows you to specify a style for the first line of an element. Typically, you would use it on a paragraph (see Chapter 2). Again, use this styling sparingly because text in all uppercase is harder to read because it lacks the visual cues provided by the ascenders and descenders of lowercase type.

The Font Property Shorthand

Example: `p {font: bold italic small-caps .75em verdana, arial, sans-serif;}`

```
<p>Here's a piece of text loaded up with every possible font
property.</p>
```

The code above produces the result in **Figure 3.13**.

FIGURE 3.13 Bolded, italicized, small-capped, sized, and font-family specified—all in a single CSS rule.

The `font` property is a nifty shortcut that lets you apply all of the font properties in a single declaration, which helps reduce the amount of CSS you have to write to achieve your desired font styling. You have to sequence the values in the correct order, however, so that the browser can interpret them correctly.

Two simple rules apply:

Rule 1: Values for `font-size` and `font-family` must always be declared.

Rule 2: The sequence for the values is as follows:

1. `font-weight`, `font-style`, `font-variant`, in any order, then

2. `font-size`, then

3. `font-family`

Jumping ahead somewhat, you can write the `font-size` property to also include the `line-height` property (which is a text property rather than a font property) by writing the size as 12px/150% or similar, which in print parlance results in 12 pixel text with 18 pixel leading. Line height is to CSS what leading is to typesetting in the world of print. You'll learn more about the `line-height` property in the "Text Properties" section next.

Text Properties

So now that you've looked at how to get the font you want, it's time to look at how to style text. If you want to indent a paragraph, create a superscript such as the 6 in 10^6, create more space between each letter of a headline, and many other type formatting tasks, you need to use the CSS text properties.

There are eight text-related CSS properties:

- `text-indent`
- `letter-spacing`
- `word-spacing`
- `text-decoration`

- `text-align`
- `line-height`
- `text-transform`
- `vertical-align`

Meet the Text Snake

A very important concept about how CSS manages text is that CSS puts a box around the text inside an element. For example, if you put a block of text in a paragraph p element, CSS sees the actual text as a long skinny line of text in a box, even if it gets broken across multiple lines in order to fit in the container. To make this clear, in **Figure 3.14**, the border of the containing element (the paragraph) is in red, and the border of the text box is in green.

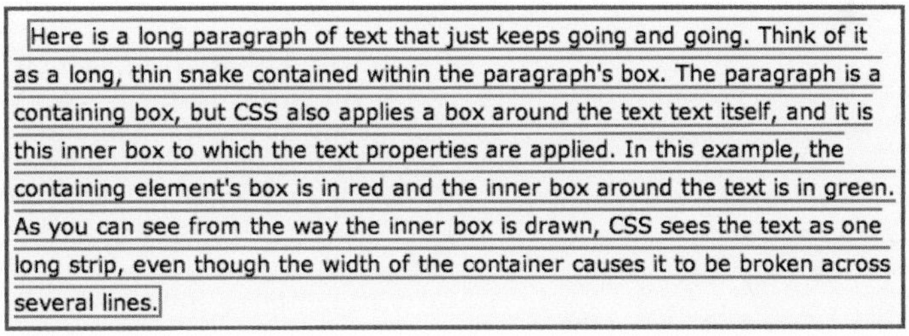

FIGURE 3.14 Text is contained within a long, skinny box that is often broken across multiple lines.

> Here is a long paragraph of text that just keeps going and going. Think of it as a long, thin snake contained within the paragraph's box. The paragraph is a containing box, but CSS also applies a box around the text text itself, and it is this inner box to which the text properties are applied. In this example, the containing element's box is in red and the inner box around the text is in green. As you can see from the way the inner box is drawn, CSS sees the text as one long strip, even though the width of the container causes it to be broken across several lines.

In this example, I marked up the text like this

```
<p><span>This is a long paragraph…(etc.)</span></p>
```

and applied the following styles

```
p {border:2px solid red;}
```

```
span {border:2px solid green;}
```

Note that the text box is broken across the lines and is only closed at the beginning of the first line and the end of the last line.

Knowing this can help you get things looking the way you want faster. For example, if you want to indent the first line of a paragraph, you can use the text property `text-indent`, as I did in Figure 3.14, and then you are moving the start position of the text box. Subsequent lines are not indented because to CSS, it's just one long piece of text.

If you want the whole paragraph indented, then you need to set the `margin-left` property of the paragraph; in other words, you have to push the whole container to the right. All you need to remember from all this is that text properties are applied to the long, thin, snake-like inner text box, not the box of the containing element.

Text-Indent Property

Example: p {text-indent:3em;}

Values: any length value (positive or negative)

Because I have already touched on it, let's start with the text-indent property. This property sets the start position of the text box in relation to the containing element. Normally, the left edge of the text box (the start of the first line, in the case of a multiple-line block) and the left edge of the container are the same.

If you set a positive value to the text-indent, then the text moves to the right, creating an indented paragraph (**Figure 3.15**).

FIGURE 3.15 Set a positive value for the text-indent property to create an indented paragraph.

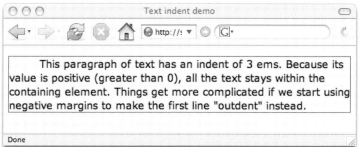

In these examples, the paragraph border is displayed in red for clarity—normally, it would not be shown.

However, if you set a negative value for text-indent, the first line hangs out to the left of the containing element. Be careful when you use negative margins to create a negative indent—in such a case, the first line of text actually hangs outside of its container, so make sure that there is a place for the hanging text to go. If the containing element abuts another element to its left, then the hanging text overlaps the latter element, or if it's close to the edge of the browser window, it is clipped (**Figure 3.16**).

FIGURE 3.16 This paragraph has a negative text indent for the first line but no corresponding left margin value, which causes the hanging text to be clipped.

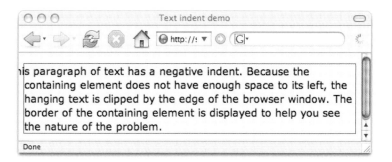

The way to avoid this problem is always to specify a positive left margin value greater than the specified negative indent. In **Figure 3.16**, the negative indent is –1.5 ems, but in **Figure 3.17**, there is also a left margin value of 2 ems.

FIGURE 3.17 This paragraph has a negative text indent and a corresponding left margin value that creates enough space for the hanging text in the first line.

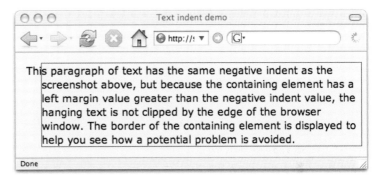

The code for the paragraph in **Figure 3.17** is as follows

```
p {text-indent:-1.5em; margin-left:2em; border:1px solid red;}
```

Hanging paragraphs can help give text that professionally styled look and give the reader clear visual entry points into the text blocks.

It's good practice to set indents and related margins in ems so that the indent remains proportional to the line length if the user (or you) changes the text size. In the case of a hanging indent, proportional sizing ensures that enough space for the hanging text is created, regardless of how large the user might scale the font.

If space is tight and you don't want spaces between paragraphs, you can set the margin top and margin bottom values of the paragraphs to 0 and use indents or negative indents instead of vertical space to provide a clear indication of where each paragraph starts.

Inherited Values are Computed Values

One more important note here: text-indent is inherited by child elements. For example, if you set a text-indent on a
div, all the paragraphs inside the div will have that text-indent value. However, as with all inherited CSS values, it's not
the defined value that's passed down but the computed value. Here's an example that explains the implications of this fact.

Let's say you have a div containing text that's 400 pixels wide with a 5 percent text indent. If this is the case, the indent for that text is 20 pixels (5 percent of 400). Within the div is a paragraph that's 200 pixels wide. As a child element, the paragraph inherits any text-indent value, so it is indented too, but the value it inherits is the result of the calculation made on the parent, that is, 20 pixels, not the defined 5 percent. As a result, it too has a 20 pixel indent even though it's half the width of the parent element. This ensures that all the paragraphs have nice matching indents, regardless of their widths. Of course, you can override this behavior by explicitly setting a different text-indent for child elements.

Letter-Spacing Property

Example: p {letter-spacing:.2em;}

Values: any length values (positive or negative)

This property produces what print designers call *tracking,* an overall spacing between letters. Positive values increase letter-spacing, while negative values decrease it. I highly recommend you use relative values, such as ems or percentages, rather than absolute values, such as pixels, so that the spacing remains proportional even if the user changes the font size. **Figure 3.18** gets you started.

FIGURE 3.18 In this example, you can see how changing the letter-spacing value changes the look of your text.

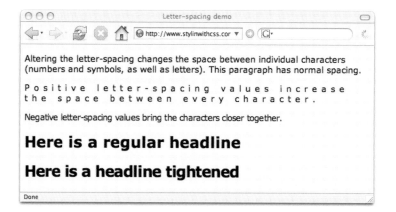

The default letter spacing appears more and more loose as the text gets larger. As you can see, you can give headlines that professional touch by tightening them up a bit.

Generally, body text doesn't need changes to the letter spacing, although it's a personal preference, and you can give your pages a unique look if the type is a little tighter or looser than is typical. Just go easy, as too much either way makes the type hard to read. Note the text and headline I tightened in Figure 3.18 only have .05 em (a twentieth of an em) of letter spacing removed from between each character; much more and the letters would start to merge into each other.

Word-Spacing Property

Example: p {word-spacing:.2em;}

Values: any length values (positive or negative)

Word spacing is very similar to letter spacing except, as you might imagine, the space changes between each word rather than between each letter. The first observation you should make here is that CSS treats any character or group of characters with white space around them as a word. Second, even more than letter spacing, word spacing can easily be overdone and result in some very hard-to-read text (**Figure 3.19**).

If you do use wide letter spacing, then the gaps between the words aren't as easy to differentiate, so that's a good time to add in a little word spacing, too.

FIGURE 3.19 Word spacing is one of those styles that is easy to overdo.

Text-Decoration Property

Example: .retailprice {text-decoration:line-through;}

Values: underline, overline, line-through, blink

You can see the result in **Figure 3.20** below. No, decorated text doesn't have holly and little bells on it; you can underline, overline, strike-through, and blink (but don't do it, please, because it is s-o-o-o-o annoying) text using this property.

FIGURE 3.20 These illustrations show what the various values can do, but the most useful application of text decoration is the control of underlining on links.

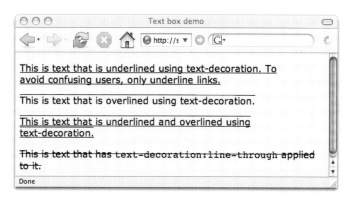

The primary application of text decoration is controlling the underlining of links. For example, it is usually obvious by their location and organization that sidebar navigation links are indeed links. They are much easier to read, and look nicer, without their default underlining, although you might add the underlining back onto a link when the user mouses over it to confirm that it's clickable. Conversely, you really want links within body copy to be underlined. It's a nice touch, and improves readability, if you remove the underlining of a link when the user mouses over it. Think long and hard before you add underlining to text that is not a link. Perhaps if you have a column of numbers, you might underline the last one before the total, or something like that, but Web users are so used to underlining as the visual cue for a link that you are setting them up for frustration and a lot of useless clicking if you underline text that is not actually a link.

Text-Align Property

Example: p {text-align:right;}

Values: left, right, center, justify

There are only four values for this property: left, center, right, and justify. The text aligns horizontally with respect to the containing element, and you must set the property on the containing element; in other words, if you want an h1 headline centered within a div, set the text-align of the div, not the h1. **Figure 3.21** shows the four possible text-align values in action.

FIGURE 3.21 The four text-align values as shown in Firefox for Mac.

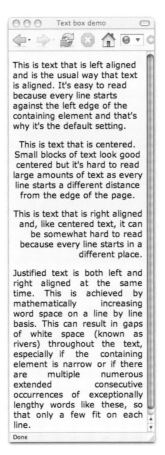

Line-Height Property

Example: p {line-height:1.5;}

Values: any numerical value (no value type is needed)

line-height is the CSS equivalent of *leading* (pronounced like the metal) in the world of print. Leading creates space between the lines of a block of text. Leading is defined not as the height of the space between the lines, but as the distance between the baseline of one line and the next. For the sake of readability, leading is greater than the height of the type so that there is space between the lines. By default, browsers set leading proportionately to the font size—typically at 118 percent of the font size, according to my tests—so there is always consistent space between the lines no matter what the font size.

In case you're wondering where the term "leading" came from, in the early days of printing, a strip of lead was used to space the lines of type.

FIGURE 3.22 A variation of the standard line height is a simple way to give a distinctive look to your site.

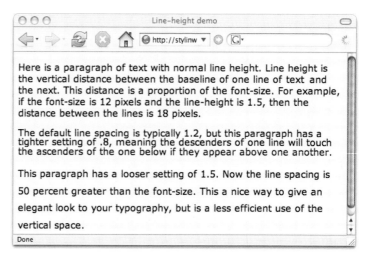

As shown in **Figure 3.22** above, the simplest way to change this default leading is to use the font: shorthand property and write a compound value for both font size and line height in one. For example:

div#intro {font:1.2em/1.4;}

In this case, the leading is 1.4 times the font size of 1.2 ems. Note that you don't need any units, such as ems or pixels, specified for the line-height part of the value, just a number. In this case, CSS simply takes the calculated size of whatever number of on-screen pixels 1.2 ems works out to be and multiplies it by 1.4 to arrive at the line height. If you later increase the font size to 1.5 ems, the line height (leading) is still 1.4 times the calculated amount of 1.5 ems. If the line height had been specified in a fixed unit, such as pixels, and you increased the font size, then the lines of text would start to overlap one another.

It's worth noting that any line height greater than the text height is shared both above and below the text. Let's take a simple example in pixels to illustrate this point, although for the reasons I gave earlier, using pixels is not the ideal way to set line height. However, it's easier to understand the math if I use pixels here. If you have a font size of 12 pixels and you set the line height to 20 pixels, the browser adds 4 pixels of space above the line of type and 4 below: 12 + 4 + 4 = 20. In the normal course of events, you don't notice this because the overall look in a multiline paragraph of text is that there are 8 pixels of space between each line. However, this might have a bearing for you on the first and last lines of text, which, in fact, only have 4 pixels of space above and below them respectively.

Vertical Centering of Single Lines of Text

It is natural to try using the `vertical-align` property to center elements vertically within a containing element, but it doesn't work. However, if you just want to center a single line of type within a containing element, that's doable. In CSS, you can achieve vertical centering, for a single line of text at least, by setting its line height equal to the height of the containing element. Because the line height is split between the top and bottom of the text, the text ends up centered vertically.

Vertically centering a block of text, such as a p element, within a containing element is almost impossible, although with some extra divs, it is doable. Rather than get into a lengthy explanation here, I refer you to "Vertical Centering in CSS" (www.jakpsatweb.cz/css/css-vertical-center-solution.html). You can do this, but it ain't pretty. Sometimes, you just have to wonder why such a basic necessity wasn't addressed in the CSS spec.

Text-Transform Property

Example: `p {text-transform: capitalize;}`

Values: `uppercase, lowercase, capitalize, none`

`text-transform` changes the capitalization of text within an element. You can force a line of text to have initial letters capitalized, all text uppercase, or all text lowercase. **Figure 3.23** shows the various options.

FIGURE 3.23 Text-transform lets you add newspaper-style headline formatting to text.

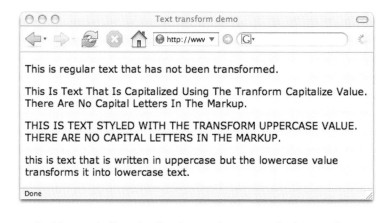

capitalize capitalizes the first letter of every word. This emulates the style of many headlines in ads, newspapers, and magazines, except that a human applying such styling tends to leave the capitalization off minor words such as "of," "as," and "and," as in "Tom and Jerry Go to Vegas." CSS capitalization simply produces "Tom And Jerry Go To Vegas." However, it's a nice effect for headlines, and if your content is coming from a database or another source such as XML, you can achieve this effect without touching the markup.

Use font-variant if you want large and small caps. Think also about tightening up the visual appearance with a small negative letter-spacing value (see "Letter-Spacing Property" earlier in this chapter).

Vertical-Align Property

Example: vertical-align:60%

Values: any length value, sub, sup, top, middle, bottom

vertical-align moves text up or down with respect to the baseline. As this example demonstrates, one of the most common uses is for superscript and subscript numbers in formulas and mathematical expressions, such as x^4-y^{-5} or N_3O. It's also the correct way to style asterisks and other markers within text to indicate footnotes. I don't like the way most browser style sub- and superscripts by default—the font size is too large and too high (or low, for subscript) for my liking. As illustrated here in **Figure 3.24**, a little styling can produce a much more professional look.

FIGURE 3.24 Superscripting and subscripting text lets you vary the vertical position of that text from the standard baseline. I have some styles in my standard text style sheet that improve the look of the default styling of these tags, as this example illustrates.

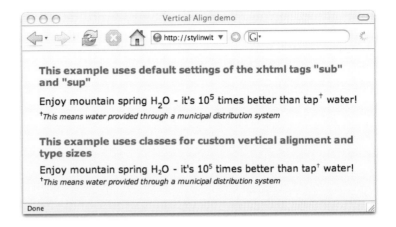

IE7 appears to have a hard time with sub- and superscripting, leaving large spaces around those characters.

So while the XHTML tags sup and sub create superscript or subscript text automatically, it's worth using vertical-align and text-size in combination to produce a more pleasing result.

Here's the code for this example

```
<style type="text/css">

body {font-family:verdana, arial, sans-serif; font-
size:100%;}

h4 {margin: 1.4em 20px .5em; color:#069;}

p {margin: 0 20px;}

p.custom sub {vertical-align:-.25em; font-size:65%;}

p.custom sup {vertical-align:.6em; font-size:65%;}

p.customsmall {font-size:.8em; vertical-align:1em}

</style>

</head>

<body>

<h4>This example uses default settings of the xhtml tags
"sub" and "sup"</h4>

<p>Enjoy mountain spring H<sub>2</sub>O - it's 10<sup>5</sup>
times better than tap<sup>&dagger;</sup> water!</p>

<p><sup>&dagger;</sup><em>This means water provided through a
municipal distribution system</em></p>

<h4>This example uses classes for custom vertical alignment
and type sizes</h4>
```

```
<p class="custom">Enjoy mountain spring H<sub>2</sub>O - it's
10<sup>5</sup> times better than tap<sup>&dagger;</sup>
water!</p>

<p class="customsmall"><sup>&dagger;</sup><em>This means
water provided through a municipal distribution system</em>
</p>

</body>
```

This covers the font and text properties of CSS. Let's end this chapter with a brief practical example of what we've learned.

Using Font and Text Styles

Using the markup we developed in Chapter 1, let's look at how we can transform a very ordinary-looking page into a more professional-looking piece. **Figure 3.25** shows the unstyled markup.

FIGURE 3.25 Here's the unstyled markup of the page we saw in Chapter 1.

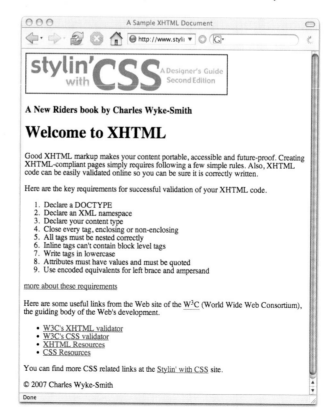

By applying only styles we learned in this chapter plus the `margin` and `background-color` properties, the page suddenly looks like someone actually designed it (**Figure 3.26**).

FIGURE 3.26 The styled page looks much spiffier.

Here are the styles:

1. `* {margin:0; padding:0;}`

    We start by "neutralizing" all the default margins and padding on the elements. These eat up a lot of vertical space in the unstyled version. By removing all the default margins and padding, only the elements we explicitly style have them.

2. `body {font-family:verdana, arial, sans-serif; font-size:100%; margin:1em; background-color:#DFE;}`

    These are baseline styles for the font and page margins. The `font-family` and `font-size` are inherited by all elements, and the all-round 1 em margin moves all the elements in from the edges of the page. We don't want our layout touching the edge of the browser window.

3. `img {border:0;}`

If you enclose an image in a link so that it is clickable, all browsers except Safari will put an ugly blue border around it to indicate this fact. I prefer to remove the border and use the `title` attribute to pop up text, such as "Go to Home Page," when the mouse moves over the image.

4. `h1 {font-size:1.1em; text-transform:uppercase; text-align:center; letter-spacing:.2em; margin:.5em 0;}`

The header is now centered with increased letter spacing and in all capitals.

5. `h3 {font-size:.7em; word-spacing:1em; letter-spacing:-.05em; border-bottom:1px solid #069; padding:0 0.5em 1em;}`

Here we've set tight letter spacing and wide word spacing.

6. `p {font-size:.75em; line-height:1.4em; text-indent:-1.75em; margin: 0.5em 2em;}`

Here we've reduced the type size and increased the line height. When we set the negative indent for the first line, we also set a corresponding margin so the text can't get clipped to the left.

7. `ul, ol {font-size:.75em; margin-left:6em; line-height:1.25; color:#444;}`

The large left margin indents the lists. We've also italicized them and increased line spacing for any lines that may wrap.

8. `#contentarea a {margin-left:6em;}`

The "More about…" link looks better moved right to align it under the list.

9. `a {color:#036; font-style:italic;}`

All the links are dark blue and italicized.

10. `a:hover {color:#069; text-decoration:none;}`

When hovered, the links get lighter, and the underlining is removed.

11. `acronym {border-bottom:1px dotted; cursor:default;}`

To show that the acronym has a tooltip when rolled, we use a dashed underline (a solid underline would indicate a link). Additionally, we change the cursor to the pointer to encourage users to linger long enough to let the tooltip pop up.

12. `#homepagefooter {border-top:1px solid #069;}`

    Adds a blue horizontal rule above the footer.

13. `#homepagefooter p {font-size:.7em; text-align:center; text-indent:0em; border-top:1px solid #069; padding-top:.5em;}`

    Finally, we size and center the footer text and add a border to the top, padded away from its text, to separate the footer from the content. Note that we remove the `text-indent` that we would otherwise inherit from the less specific p declaration earlier in the styles.

While this might seem like a lot of work for a single page, remember that once styles like these are in a style sheet, they are applied to all the pages that are linked to it, so you can get a whole Web site's-worth of mileage out of the work you put into styling a page like this.

Now that you understand the basics of CSS and how to style text, let's move on to creating multicolumn page layouts.

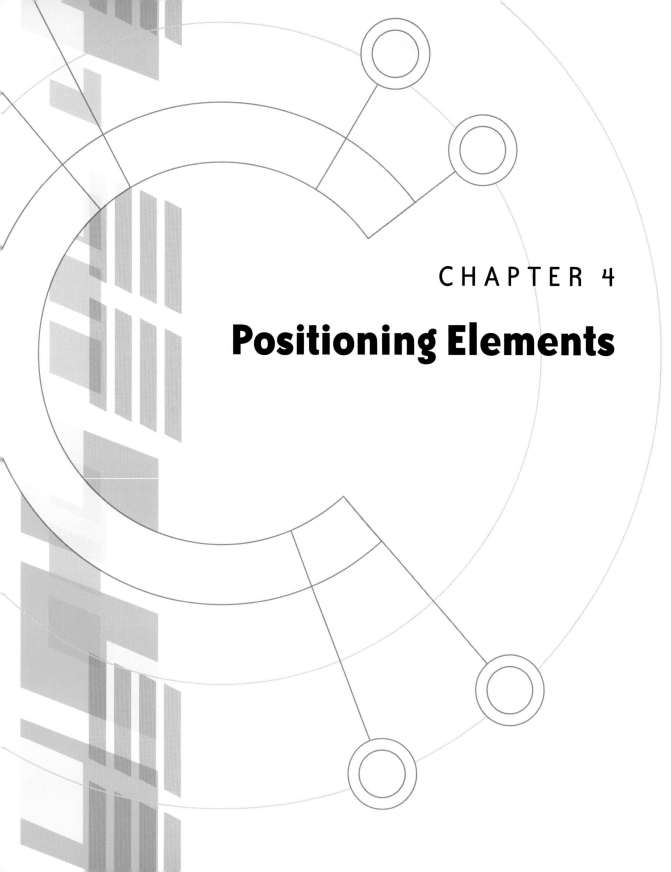

CHAPTER 4

Positioning Elements

ONE OF THE KEY STEPS in the adoption of Web standards has been the abandonment of tables as a means of laying out pages. Tables were never meant to be used in this way—they were intended to be used for laying out grids of data, in a similar manner to an Excel spreadsheet. However, before the development of CSS, tables were used to create a page grid into which elements could be organized into columns. This meant adding nasty presentational hacks—such as spacer GIFs, line breaks, and non-breaking spaces—into the markup to achieve the desired layout. With CSS, you can position XHTML elements with great accuracy without adding presentational elements into your markup.

With the application of CSS properties, such as margins, padding, and borders, and CSS techniques, such as floating and clearing, you can achieve the same—and even better—results than in the past. You can do this while keeping your markup lean and clean, and while sharing the styles you write between like elements of your layout. This results in lightweight and easy-to-read code.

How well you succeed with these techniques depends on how well you understand the *box model*, the `position` *property*, and the *display property*. The box model describes the positioning controls that exist for every element in your markup. The `position` property defines the positional relationship between these elements on the page. The `display` property determines whether elements stack or sit side-by-side, or even display on the page at all. Let's look at each in turn.

Understanding the Box Model

To learn more about the box model see http://www.w3.org/TR/REC-CSS2/box.html.

Every element you create in your markup produces a box on the page, so an XHTML page is actually an arrangement of boxes.

By default, the border of each element box isn't visible and the background of the box is transparent, so I understand if you're wondering where all the boxes are. With CSS, it's easy to turn on the borders and color the backgrounds of the boxes. You can then start to see your page structure in a whole new light.

For example, here is part of the page we styled at the end of the last chapter, only this time with the borders turned on (**Figure 4.1**).

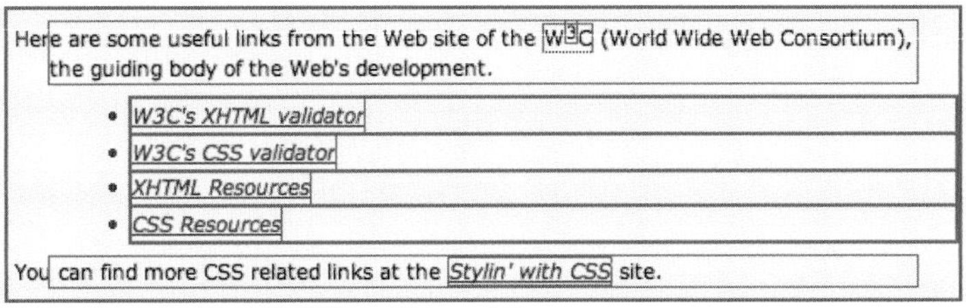

FIGURE 4.1 With borders on, you can see that the inline link elements "shrink-wrap" their text, but the block-level list items that enclose them stretch right across the page to fill their containing element (except where their margins prevent them from doing so). Note also the negative margins on the paragraphs make them extend to the left out of their element boxes.

Here are some useful links from the Web site of the W3C (World Wide Web Consortium), the guiding body of the Web's development.

- W3C's XHTML validator
- W3C's CSS validator
- XHTML Resources
- CSS Resources

You can find more CSS related links at the Stylin' with CSS site.

In this example, we let the browser simply arrange the block and inline elements down the page. To create layouts that are more interesting than this default XHTML layout presented by the browser, you need to understand how to control the appearance and placement of element boxes. Step one is to understand the box model (**Figure 4.2**), which defines the properties that make up each box.

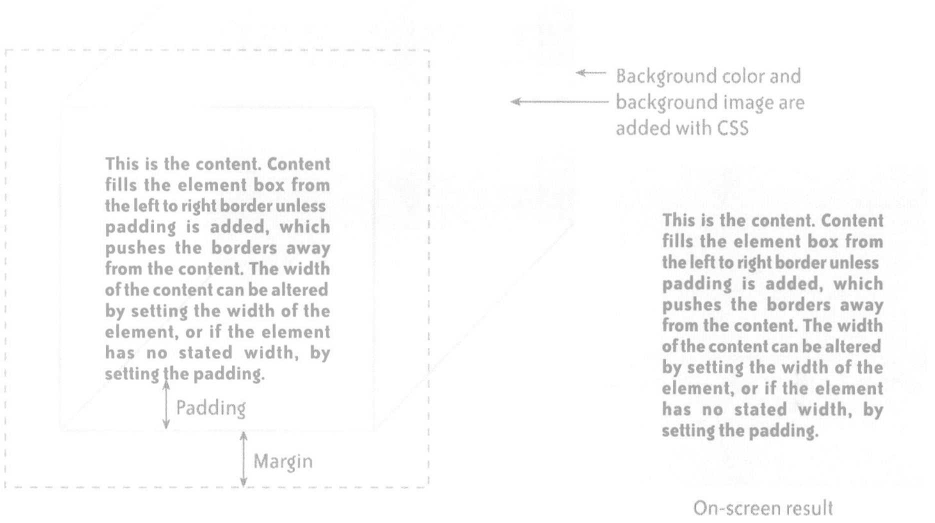

This is the content. Content fills the element box from the left to right border unless padding is added, which pushes the borders away from the content. The width of the content can be altered by setting the width of the element, or if the element has no stated width, by setting the padding.

Padding

Margin

Background color and background image are added with CSS

This is the content. Content fills the element box from the left to right border unless padding is added, which pushes the borders away from the content. The width of the content can be altered by setting the width of the element, or if the element has no stated width, by setting the padding.

On-screen result

FIGURE 4.2 This box model diagram shows the relationship between margins, border, and padding of an XHTML element. In the box model, the foreground, which is typically text or an image, is defined in the XHTML markup, but a background color or background image can only be added with CSS.

Note that the exact widths of `thin`, `medium`, and `thick` lines are not actually defined in the CSS specifications, so these widths may vary between browsers. The line styles, with the exception of `solid`, which is a simple unbroken line, also are not explicitly defined in the CSS specifications; a dashed line may have different dash and space lengths from browser to browser.

You can adjust three aspects of the box with CSS:

- **Border.** You can set the thickness, style, and color of the border.

- **Margin.** You can set the distance between this box and adjacent elements.

- **Padding.** You can set the distance of a box's content from its border.

A simple way to think about these properties is that margins push outward from the border and padding pushes inward from the border. Because a box has four sides, properties associated with margin, border, and padding each have four settings: top, right, bottom, and left.

The Box Border

Border has three associated properties:

- **Width.** This includes `thin`, `medium`, `thick`, or any unit (ems, px, %, and so on).

- **Style.** This includes `none`, `hidden`, `dotted`, `dashed`, `solid`, `double`, `groove`, `ridge`, `inset`, and `outset`.

- **Color.** This includes any color value (for example, RGB, hex, or keyword).

A common way to style a box is to make all four sides the same color, style, and thickness. You might write something like this, specifying each of these three properties individually:

```
p.warning {border-width:4px}
```

```
p.warning {border-style:solid}
```

```
p.warning {border-color:#F33;}
```

But when you want to style all four sides with the same width, style, and color, as we do here, you can write a shorthand version, using the border property like this:

Here I also add a couple of pixels of padding all round to prevent the text touching the border.

```
p.warning {border:4px solid #F33; padding:2px}
```

Whichever way you choose to do it, any paragraph with the "warning" class would have an attention-grabbing, four-pixel-wide solid red line around it, as shown in **Figure 4.3**.

The shorthand border property causes the same value be applied to all four sides, but if you want to specify some difference between the sides, you can do that easily. Say we want the border to be solid and red on all four sides, but want the right and bottom sides thinner for visual interest. We have to use two rules to achieve the desired result: The first rule uses border to specify the styling common to all four sides, and the second rule uses border-width to specify the border width differences.

```
p.warning {border:solid #F33; padding:2px;}
```

```
p.warning {border-width:4px 2px 2px 4px;}
```

which results in **Figure 4.4**.

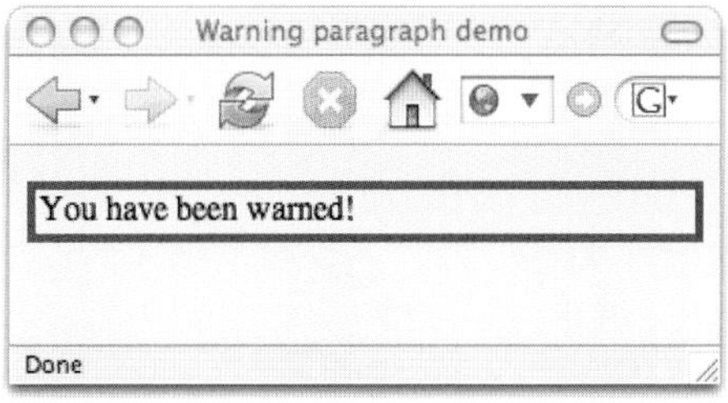

FIGURE 4.3 Here, because I want all four sides to be the same, I can style the border with the shorthand bor-der property. Some padding prevents the text from touching the border.

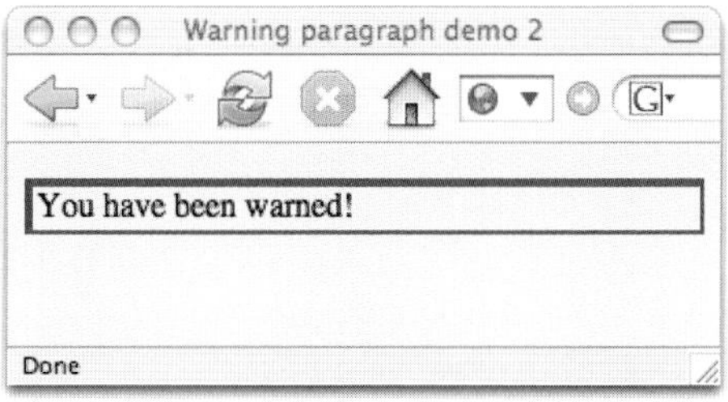

FIGURE 4.4 By splitting out the box's styles over two rules, the box's sides can have both common (color and padding) and different (line width) styles.

It is very helpful to temporarily display the border of a box during development so that you can more clearly see the effects of styles such as `margin` and `padding`. By default, the styles for element boxes are: border width set to `medium`, border style set to `none`, and border color set to `black`. Because the border style is set to `none`, the box doesn't display. So, all you need to do to quickly display a paragraph's box, for example, is write this

```
p {border:solid;}
```

This sets the border style to a solid line and the box displays; the color and width are already set by default. Note, however, that adding borders can alter the layout because borders add dimension to the element, which may or not matter, depending on where that element is in your layout. An alternate way to display a box is to add

Shorthand Styling

It gets tedious to write a separate style for each of the four sides of an element, whether you are specifying margins, padding, or borders. CSS offers some shorthand ways to specify these, one after another within a single declaration. In such a declaration, the order of the sides of the box is always top, right, bottom, left. You can remember this as TRouBLe, which you will be in if you forget, or you can visualize the order as the hands on a clock going around from 12. So, if you want to specify the margins on an element, instead of writing

```
{margin-top:5px; margin-right:10px; margin-bottom:12px; margin-left:8px;}
```

you can simply write

```
{margin:5px 10px 12px 8px;}
```

Note that there is just a space between each of the four values; you don't need a delimiter such as a comma. You don't have to specify all four values—if you don't provide one, the opposite side's value is used as the missing value.

```
{margin:12px 10px 6px;}
```

In this example, because the last value, left, is missing, the right value is used and the left margin is set to 10px.

In this next example

```
{margin:12px 10px;}
```

only the first two values, top and right, are set, so the missing values for bottom and left are set to 12px and 10px, respectively.

Finally, if only one value is supplied

```
{margin:12px;}
```

then all four sides are set to this value.

Using this shorthand, you can't just specify bottom and left without providing some values to top and right, even if those values are both zero. In such a case, you can write 0 without supplying a value type like this

```
{border:0 0 2px 4px;}
```

a background color so that the box's area is visible, but the box does not change size.

The Box Padding

Padding adds space between the box's content and the border of the box. As part of the inside of the box, it takes on the color of the box's background. **Figure 4.5** shows two paragraphs, one with and one without padding.

FIGURE 4.5 If you display an element's border, you will almost always add padding to prevent the content from touching it.

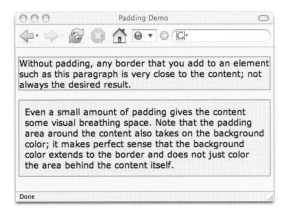

Where designers once used table cell padding and spacer GIFs, which added lots of extra presentational markup, you can now achieve the same effect economically by adding CSS padding styles.

The Box Margins

Margins are slightly more complex than borders and padding. First, most block level elements (paragraphs, headings, lists, and so on) have default margins, as we saw earlier in the chapter.

In **Figure 4.6**, you can see a heading and two paragraphs displayed three times. The first example shows the heading and two paragraphs as they appear by default. The second example shows the same arrangement of a heading and two paragraphs, but this time with their borders and background turned on so you can see how margins create space between them. The third example shows what happens when the margins are set to zero: The elements then touch one another.

It's good practice to place the following declaration at the top of a style sheet

```
* {margin:0; padding:0;}
```

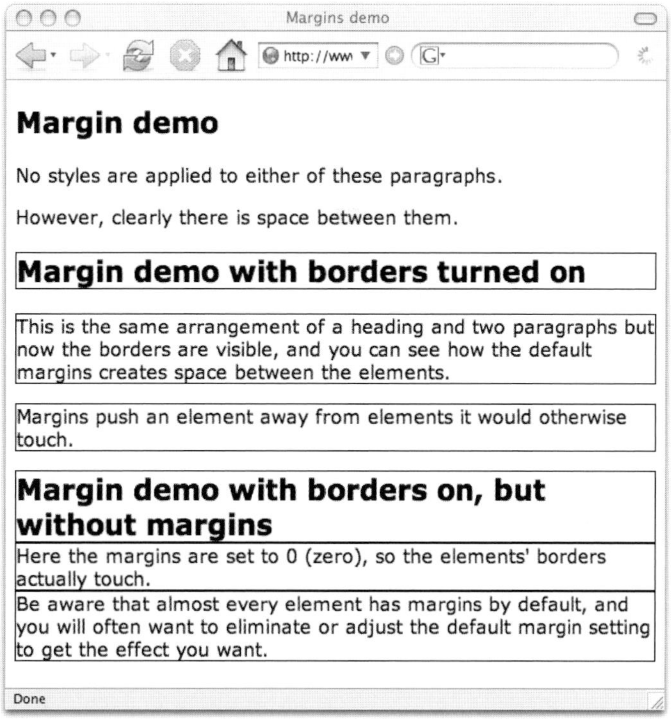

FIGURE 4.6 Learning to control margins around the elements is a key skill—it's important to realize that almost every element has margins by default.

FIGURE 4.6 Learning to control margins around the elements is a key skill—it's important to realize that almost every element has margins by default.

This sets the default margins and padding of *all* elements to zero so that you don't get confused by which margins and padding the browser sets and which you set. Once you put this in your style sheet, all the default margins and padding will disappear. Now you can add them back to just the elements that you want to have margins as you style the page. As you will see later, different browsers apply default padding and margins differently to element sets, such as forms and lists, and "neutralizing" the default settings in this way, and then adding your own, results in a more consistent cross-browser experience.

Often, you will want to mix units when you set margins for text elements, such as paragraphs. For example, the left and right margins of a paragraph might be set in pixels so that the text remains a fixed distance from a navigation sidebar, but you might set the top and bottom margins in ems so that the vertical spacing between paragraphs is relative to the size of the paragraphs' text, like this

```
p {font-size:1em; margin:.75em 30px;}
```

In this example, the space between the paragraphs is always three-quarters of the height of the text; if you increase the overall type size in the body tag, not only does the paragraphs' text get bigger, but the space between the paragraphs also increases proportionately. The left and right margins, set in pixels, remain unchanged. We'll look at this concept further when we start constructing page layouts in Chapter 5.

Collapsing Margins

Say the following aloud: "Vertical margins collapse." You need to remember this important fact. Let me explain what this means and why it's important. Imagine that you have three paragraphs, one after the other, and each is styled with this rule

```
p {width:400px; height:50px; border:1px solid #000;

margin-top:50px; margin-bottom:30px; background-color:#CCC;}
```

Although vertical margins collapse, horizontal margins do not. Instead, horizontal margins act as you would expect—margin settings are added together to create space between horizontally adjacent elements.

Because the bottom margin of the first paragraph is adjacent to the top margin of the second, you might reasonably assume that there are 80 pixels (50 + 30) between the two paragraphs, but you'd be wrong. The distance between them is actually 50 pixels. *When top and bottom margins meet, they overlap until one of the margins touches the border of the other element.* In this case, the larger top margin of the lower paragraph touches first, so it determines how far apart the elements are set—50 pixels (**Figure 4.7**). This effect is known as *collapsing*.

FIGURE 4.7 Vertical margins collapse. They overlap until one element touches the border of the other.

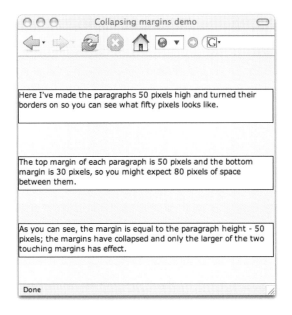

This collapsing margin effect ensures that when an element is first or last in a group of headings, paragraphs, or lists, for example, the element can be kept away from the top or bottom of the page or the containing element. When the same elements appear between other elements, both margins are not needed, so they simply collapse into each other, and the larger one sets the distance.

How Big Is a Box?

The way the box model works is at the heart of some of the most frustrating aspects of CSS for beginner and expert alike. Note in the discussion that follows that we are talking about block level elements, such as headings, paragraphs, and lists; inline elements behave differently.

Let's go step by step and review the box model in a little more depth. We'll discuss setting the width of a box here, since managing element width is critical to creating multicolumn layouts, but you can also apply the same (il)logic to the height.

You can set the width of an element box (hereafter simply called a box) using the `width` property

```
p {width:400px;}
```

Then you can turn the background color on so that you can see the box without affecting its width in any way

```
p {width:400px; background-color:#EEE;}
```

Figure 4.8 shows a 400-pixel-wide element with background color on.

FIGURE 4.8 By setting the width property, the element does not default to the width of the containing element. In this case, the containing element is the body element, which by default is the width of the browser window.

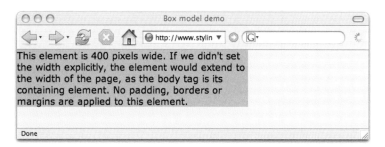

Without any padding, the content is this width also, and it touches the sides of the box. That makes perfect sense, but this logic goes

out the window when you start adding padding and borders. Let's add a padding of 20 pixels to each side of the content, like this

```
p {width:400px; background-color:#EEE; padding:0 20px;}
```

You might expect that if you pad a 400-pixel-wide box by 40 pixels, the content gets squeezed down to 360 pixels, but you would be wrong. Instead, in the wonderful, wacky world of CSS, the box gets bigger by 40 pixels (**Figure 4.9**).

FIGURE 4.9 Adding padding causes the box to get wider.

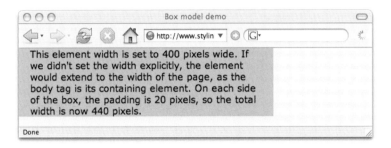

If you then add a 6-pixel border to the right and left sides of the box

```
p {width:400px; margin: 0; padding:0 20px; border:#000 solid;
border-width: 0 6px 0 6px; background-color:#CCC;}
```

the box grows wider by 12 pixels (**Figure 4.10**). Now the original 400-pixel-wide box is a total of 452 pixels wide (6 + 20 + 400 + 20 + 6 = 452).

FIGURE 4.10 Adding borders causes the box to grow even wider.

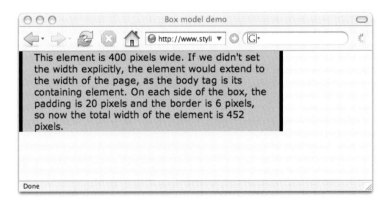

Let's now add right and left margins to create space around the sides of the element (**Figure 4.11**)

```
p {width:400px; margin: 0 30px; padding:0 20px; border:#000
solid; border-width: 0 6px 0 6px; background-color:#CCC;}
```

FIGURE 4.11 Margins create space around an element.

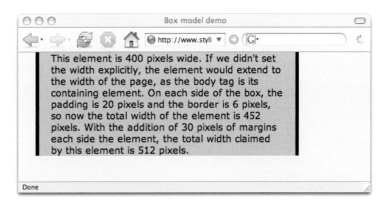

This element is 400 pixels wide. If we didn't set the width explicitly, the element would extend to the width of the page, as the body tag is its containing element. On each side of the box, the padding is 20 pixels and the border is 6 pixels, so now the total width of the element is 452 pixels. With the addition of 30 pixels of margins each side the element, the total width claimed by this element is 512 pixels.

Box Model Observation 1#: Dimensioned boxes (width is specified) expand to occupy more horizontal space as padding, borders, and margins are added. Effectively, the width property sets the width of the box's content, not the box itself, when the box's width is stated.

Adding margins, 30 pixels to each side, in this case, increases the overall space occupied by the element since the margins are outside of the box. However, although you might expect the border of the box and the padding within *not* to increase the box's width, they do.

This behavior can have important implications if you build a layout with multiple columns where the columns must maintain their widths for the layout to work. "Floated layouts," which you will learn about in the next chapter, can display incorrectly if a column width gets inadvertently altered by changes to the padding, margins, or borders. Typically, you create a column in your layout using a dimensioned (defined width) div and then nest all the column's content elements (headings, paragraphs, navigation lists, and so on) inside it.

CREATING A SINGLE COLUMN WITH CONTAINED ELEMENTS

To illustrate the basics of this technique, here's an example where I have a div sized at 170 pixels with a heading and a paragraph inside it.

```
<div id="column">

    <h4>An h4 heading</h4>

    <p>The heading and this paragraph...</p>

</div>
```

and CSS for the div

```
div#column {width:170px;}
```

I've added a ruler graphic along the top of the page so you can see the width change as the CSS changes (**Figure 4.12**).

Box Model Observation #2: Undimensioned elements (no width set) will always expand to fill the width of their containing element. Because of this, adding horizontal margins, borders, and padding to an undimensioned element does *cause the content to change width.*

I've colored the backgrounds of the heading and the paragraph so you can see that they completely fill the column horizontally. Block level elements have a default size of auto, which effectively means "as large as possible." Which leads us to the next observation.

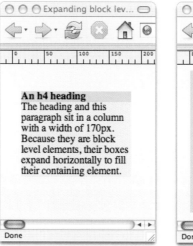

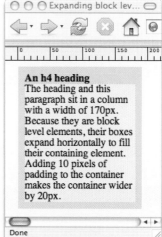

FIGURE 4.12 Without any padding applied to the container, the block level heading and paragraph fill the width of the column.

FIGURE 4.13 Adding padding to the containing element also adds width to it. Note that the container is now 190 pixels wide. For clarity, I've colored the background of the div in the pink color.

Faced with the text jammed against the sides of the column like this, one's first instinct is to add some padding to the div to create some breathing space around the type (**Figure 4.13**).

```
div#column {width:170px; padding:10px;}
```

As you can see from the ruler in the screenshot, the 10 pixels of padding added to each side of the column has increased its width to 190 pixels. While this neatly pads all elements inside the div away from the edges with a single style, in order to keep the overall width at 170 pixels, we would now have to subtract the corresponding amount (10+10=20 pixels) from the current box width value and set it to 150 pixels. It gets tiresome to keep changing the column width every time you alter the column padding, especially with a multi-column layout.

An alternative is to apply identical margins to every element inside the column, but again, that can mean a lot of elements to keep track of and change if we decide to adjust the distance between the column's sides and its content.

The simple solution is to add another div immediately inside the column div

```
<div id="column">

  <div id="column_inner">

    <h4>An h4 heading</h4>

    <p>The heading and this paragraph...</p>

  </div>

</div>
```

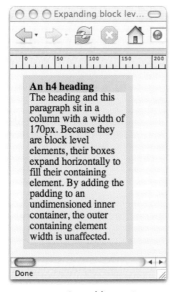

FIGURE 4.14 By padding an inner div, the width of the column, as defined by the outer div, remains unchanged.

and apply the padding to this inner div instead, like this

```
div#column {width:170px; padding:10px;}

div#inner_column {padding:10px;}
```

This allows you to have a single style to control the column padding, without having issues with the column changing width (**Figure 4.14**).

The inner div is undimensioned, so Box Model Observation #2 applies, and the content gets squeezed down. Now I can adjust the one margin setting and move all the elements inside the column away from its edge and the column's width remains unchanged. I will use this technique of placing an inner div in a column in many of the page layouts in the next chapter, so make sure you understand the concept illustrated by these last three screenshots before moving on.

The takeaway from this box model discussion is that, with all modern, standards-compliant browsers, when you set the width of an element, you are really setting the width of the content within it, and any padding, borders, and margins you set increase the overall space the element occupies over and above the specified width value.

Now let's look at the other key technique you need to understand when it comes to creating CCS-based layouts—floating and clearing.

After all I've said about avoiding presentational markup, you might be wondering why I am adding markup just to achieve a presentational effect. My answer would be divs, unlike tables for example, do not visually affect the layout unless we style them, so I think it is a worthwhile trade-off, especially for those learning CSS, who have enough to think about without pulling out a calculator every time they change the borders or padding on an element.

Floating and Clearing

Another powerful technique you can use to organize your layout on the page involves combining floating and clearing, using the float and clear properties. Floating an element is a way of moving it out of the normal flow of the document. Elements that follow a floated element will move up to sit next to the floated element if there is room. The clear property enables you to stop elements moving up next to a floated element. If, for example, you have two paragraphs and only want the first to sit next to the floated element, even though both would fit, you can "clear" the second one so it is positioned under the floated element. Let's look at both these properties in more detail.

The Float Property

The float property is primarily used to flow text around images, but it is also the basis for one of the ways to create multi-column layouts.

Let's start with an example of how to flow text around an image.

```
img {float:left; margin:0 4px 4px 0;}
```

This markup floats the image to the left, so that the text wraps around it to its right. (**Figure 4.15**).

FIGURE 4.15 A floated image is removed from the document flow. If a text element follows it in the markup, that element's text will wrap around it.

For the float to work, the markup should look like this with the image first

```
<img ....../>
```

```
<p>...the paragraph text...</p>
```

In short, when you float an image or any element, you are asking it to be pushed as far as possible to the left (or right, in the case of float:right) of the parent element; in this case, body. The paragraph (with a red border in the screenshot above) doesn't see the floated element as preceding it in the document flow, so it also takes the top left corner position of the parent; however, its content, the text, wraps itself around the floated image.

From here, it's a simple step to use float to form columns (**Figure 4.16**).

```
p {float:left; width:200px; margin:0;}
```

```
img {float:left; margin:0 4px 4px 0;}
```

FIGURE 4.16 When the fixed width paragraph is floated next to the floated image, it forms a column and no longer wraps the image.

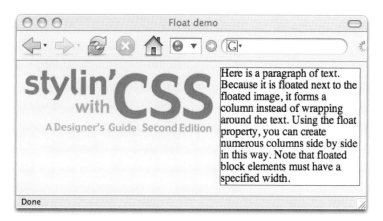

There are many more rules that govern floats, and you can read about them in Eric Meyer's book Cascading Style Sheets 2.0 Programmer's Reference (2001, McGraw-Hill Osborne Media). In short, as Eric writes, "When an element is floated, … these (float) rules say 'place the element as high, and as far to one side, as possible'"

Even though it was published years ago, this book is an essential reference for any serious CSS programmer as it contains a level of detail about the inner workings of CSS that is almost impossible to find elsewhere.

When you float both the image and the "widthed" paragraph like this, the text-wrapping effect stops, and the text forms a column next to the image. This is the principle of creating multi-column layouts using floats. As long as each element has width and is floated, and there is room for them to do so, they line up like columns. (Images implicitly have width and don't need CSS dimensions when floated to behave this way.) If you do this with three floated, fixed-width divs, you get three containers into which you can put other elements (and they too can be floated if you want). You'll see all of this in action in Chapter 5.

The Clear Property

The other property that is frequently used with float is clear. Any element that has room to do so will move up next to a floated element, but sometimes, you don't want this to happen; you want it to clear—that is, to sit below (not beside) the floated element. To demonstrate this point, **Figure 4.17** shows a layout where each item comprises an image with text next to it, achieved by floating the images. It's like the example shown in **Figure 4.16**, but repeated three times.

FIGURE 4.17 Because there is room, the third image and its text can float up next to the second image—not the desired effect.

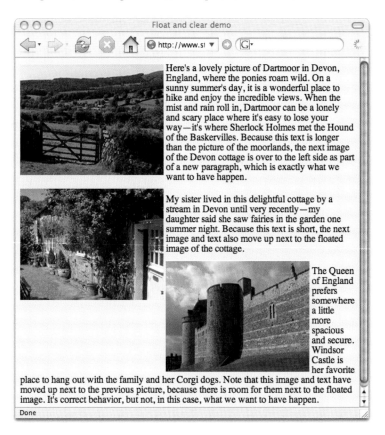

Here's the XHTML (with the content edited to save space)

```
<img src="../images/dartmoor-view.jpg" />

<p> Here's a lovely picture of Dartmoor... </p>

<img src="../images/english-cottage.jpg" />
```

```
<p> My sister lived in this delightful cottage ... </p>

<img src="../images/winsor-castle_walls.jpg" />

<p> The Queen of England...</p>
```

to which we apply this CSS

```
p {margin:0 0 10px 0;}

img {float:left; margin:0 4px 4px 0;}
```

Each image should float next to its associated text down the page. However, when there is not enough text to clear the bottom of a floated image, as in paragraph two in **Figure 4.17**, the next image/paragraph pair moves up next to the float also.

In this example, the layout displays correctly in the browser; the third item has room to sit next to the previous floated element, so it does. Of course, this is *not* what we want visually. The fix here is to add a non-floated element into the markup that has a clear property applied to it to force the third item to start below the second. Here's the markup with an extra div element and an associated style added

```
<img src="../images/dartmoor-view.jpg" />

<p> Here's a lovely picture of Dartmoor... </p>

<img src="../images/english-cottage.jpg" />

<p> My sister lived in this delightful cottage ... </p>

<div class="clearthefloats"></div>

<img src="../images/winsor-castle_walls.jpg" />

<p> The Queen of England...</p>
```

and then we just need to add a clearing class to the CSS

```
p {margin:0 0 10px 0;}

img {float:left; margin:0 4px 4px 0;}

.clearthefloats {clear:both;}
```

With the additional markup and the clearing class in the CSS (which can clear elements floated both left and right), the page now displays correctly (**Figure 4.18**).

FIGURE 4.18 With the clearing element added, the layout displays correctly.

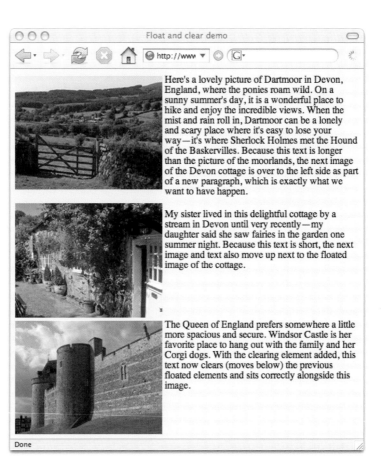

Here's a lovely picture of Dartmoor in Devon, England, where the ponies roam wild. On a sunny summer's day, it is a wonderful place to hike and enjoy the incredible views. When the mist and rain roll in, Dartmoor can be a lonely and scary place where it's easy to lose your way—it's where Sherlock Holmes met the Hound of the Baskervilles. Because this text is longer than the picture of the moorlands, the next image of the Devon cottage is over to the left side as part of a new paragraph, which is exactly what we want to have happen.

My sister lived in this delightful cottage by a stream in Devon until very recently—my daughter said she saw fairies in the garden one summer night. Because this text is short, the next image and text also move up next to the floated image of the cottage.

The Queen of England prefers somewhere a little more spacious and secure. Windsor Castle is her favorite place to hang out with the family and her Corgi dogs. With the clearing element added, this text now clears (moves below) the previous floated elements and sits correctly alongside this image.

The value of both *on the* clear *property means that the* div *clears (sits below) elements floated both left and right. You could have used the value* left *in this case, but by using* both, *if you switch the float on the images to* right *later, the* clear *still works.*

This new "cleared" element added between the second and third paragraphs is now positioned (invisibly, because it has no content associated with it) beneath the second image. Because the third image and paragraph follow this cleared element in the markup, they are positioned below it, and the desired layout is achieved.

Clearing floats is an important technique to master when you are creating CSS layouts. The sidebar "The Aslett Clearing Method" discusses a useful technique that allows you to clear floats using only CSS and a single class in your markup. We will study floats and clearing further, but this is enough information to get you started using floats as the basis of many CSS page layouts. Now let's move on to the position property.

The Aslett Clearing Method

Named after its creator, Tony Aslett (www.csscreator.com), the Aslett Clearing Method forces a container such as a div to enclose floated content nested within it, which it would not normally do. This technique uses the CSS :after pseudo-class to insert a hidden bit of non-floated content (a period with no height) after all the other content inside that container. The code also applies clearing to this non-floated content, and the container is thereby forced to enclose it. Here's the code:

```
.clearfix:after {
  content: ".";
  display: block;
  height: 0;
  clear: both;
  visibility: hidden;
}
.clearfix {display: inline-table;}
/* backslash hack hides from IE mac \*/
* html .clearfix {height: 1%;}
.clearfix {display: block;}
/* end backslash hack */
```

You can add this code at the end of a style sheet so it's available to your pages. (I've added it to the end of the text_n_colors.css file in the downloads for you.) Then any time you need a container to enclose floated content, simply add the class clearfix to the container, like this:

```
<div class="clearfix">
```

and the container will instantly enclose any floated content within it. A couple of good uses of this technique are

1. To force a footer to sit below floated columns (see Chapter 5 for examples of layouts with floated columns). Add the clearfix class to a wrapper div around the columns, and this container will then always expand vertically to enclose the columns, no matter how long they get. An element such as footer div that follows the closing tag of the wrapper div in the markup will then always sit below the longest column.

2. To add a border around a number of floated elements. Enclose the floated elements in a wrapper div and add the clearfix class to this wrapper so it encloses the floated elements. Then style the border of this containing element.

This is one of those techniques where you don't know why you would need it until you need it; one day, though, you will. It sure beats adding lots of clearing divs into your markup and is very simple to use.

Note that IE6 incorrectly causes a div that contains floated elements to enclose those elements, so this is just one more reason to develop in a standards-compliant browser and test with IE afterwards.

To learn more about the Aslett Clearing Method, check out Position Is Everything (www.positioniseverything.net/easyclearing.html).

The Position Property

At the heart of CSS-based layouts is the position property. The position property determines the reference point for the positioning of each element box.

Let's look at what this means.

There are four values for the position property: static, absolute, fixed, and relative. static is the default. These terms didn't seem to map to what they actually do when I first encountered them. To help you avoid puzzling over what each does, let's take a quick look at each using a simple example with four paragraphs. In each case, I will leave paragraphs one, two, and four in the default static positioning and alter the property value of paragraph three. I have added the class specialpara for the third paragraph in the markup (not shown), so I can change its position property without affecting the other paragraphs.

Static Positioning

First, let's see our four paragraphs all with the default position of static (**Figure 4.19**).

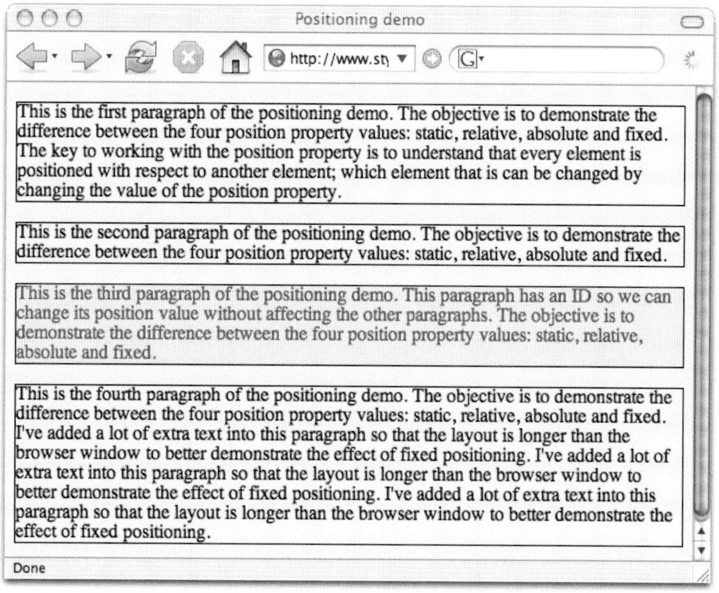

FIGURE 4.19 With the four paragraphs each displayed with the default position property value, static, they stack one above the other, as normal document flow dictates.

With static positioning, each element is simply laid out one after the other, so the paragraphs appear under each other, with their default margin settings creating the space between them.

To break away from this sequential layout of elements provided by the default static positioning, you must change a box's position property to one of the three other possible values.

Relative Positioning

Let's set the third paragraph to the relative position. You can then move this paragraph with respect to its default position using the properties top, left, bottom, and right. Normally, providing values for just top and left produces the result you want. In this example

```
p#specialpara {position:relative; top:30px; left:20px;}
```

produces the result shown in **Figure 4.20**.

FIGURE 4.20 Relative positioning allows you to use the left and right properties to move the element with respect to its normal position in the document flow.

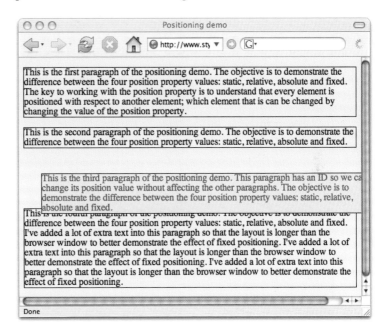

Now the top of your paragraph is moved down by 30 pixels and right by 20 pixels. However, as you have noticed, although the element moves relative to its original position, nothing else changes. The space occupied by the original static element is retained, as is the positioning of the other elements.

The lesson here is that if you move an element in this way, you must allow space for it. In the example shown in **Figure 4.19**, you might take the next step of adding a `margin-top` value of 30 pixels or greater to the fourth paragraph to move it down, thus preventing it from being overlapped by the repositioned third paragraph.

Absolute Positioning

Absolute positioning is a whole different animal from `static` and `relative`, since this type of positioning takes an element entirely out of the flow of the document. Let's modify the code you used for relative positioning by changing `relative` to `absolute`

```
p#specialpara {position:absolute; top:30px; left:20px;}
```

Figure 4.21 shows the results.

FIGURE 4.21 Absolute positioning enables you to remove an element from the document flow and position it with respect to another element—here, the default positioning context, body.

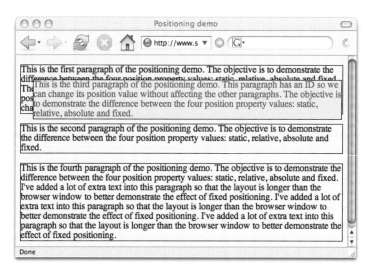

In **Figure 4.21**, you can see that the space previously occupied by the element is gone. The absolutely-positioned element has become entirely independent of the surrounding elements in the markup, and it is now positioned with respect to the top-level element, body. And this brings us neatly to the important concept of *positioning context*, which is the recurring subject of the rest of this chapter.

Let's start thinking about this concept by saying that *the **default** positioning context of an absolutely-positioned element is the body element*. As **Figure 4.21** shows, the offset provided by the top and left values moves the element with respect to the body element— the top ancestor container in our markup hierarchy—not with respect to the element's default position in the document flow, as is the case with `relative`.

Because the absolutely positioned element's positioning context is `body`, the element moves when the page is scrolled to retain its relationship to the body element, which also moves when the page scrolls.

Before we see how we can use a different element than `body` as the positioning context for an absolutely positioned element, let's cover the last of the four positioning properties—fixed positioning.

Fixed Positioning

Fixed positioning is similar to absolute positioning, except that the element's positioning context is the viewport (the browser window or the screen of a handheld device, for example), so the element does not move when the page is scrolled. **Figures 4.22** and **4.23** show the effects of fixed positioning.

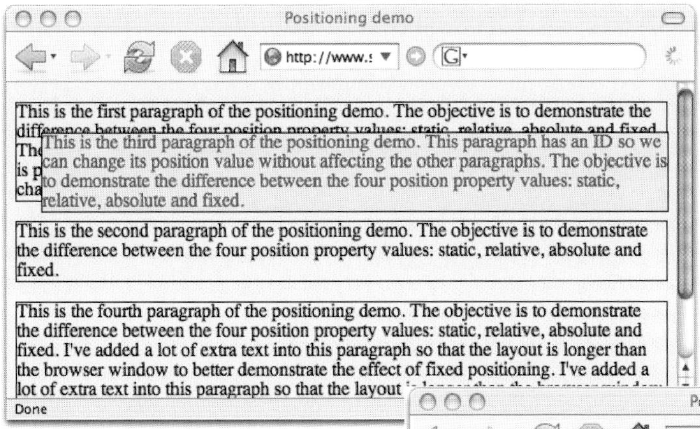

FIGURE 4.22 Fixed positioning looks a lot like absolute positioning...

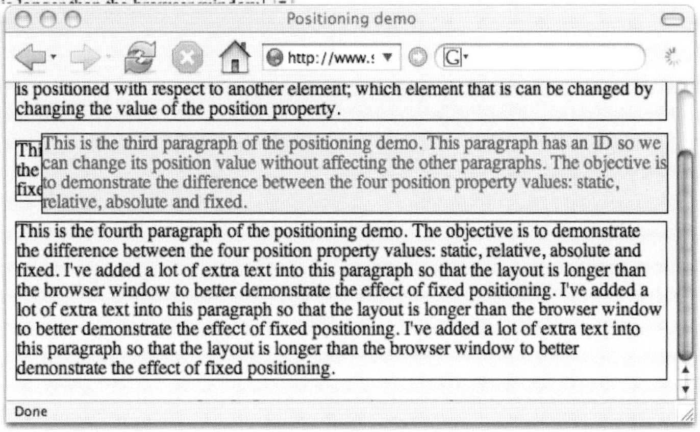

FIGURE 4.23 ...until you scroll the page—the fixed element does not move.

This "nailed-to-the-browser-window" effect enables you to simulate the effect of now-deprecated frames. For example, you can create a navigation element that stays put when the page scrolls without all the headaches of managing multiple documents in a frameset. However, IDWIMIE; `position:fixed` does not work in Internet Explorer 6, although it does work in Internet Explorer 7. You can find a neat workaround to make fixed positioning work in Internet Explorer 6 at TagSoup.com (http://devnull.tagsoup.com/fixed).

Positioning Context

Because positioning context is such an important concept to grasp if you want to escape from table-based layouts, some more explanation is useful. Put simply, *contextual positioning* means that when you move an element using the properties `top`, `left`, `right`, or `bottom`, you are moving that element with respect to another element. That other element is known as its *positioning context.* As you saw in "Absolute Positioning" earlier, the positioning context of an absolutely positioned element is `body`—that is, unless you change it. For example, `body` is the containing element of all other elements in your markup, but you can use any ancestor element as a positioning context of another element by changing the ancestor's `position` value to `relative`.

Let's look at this markup

```
<body>

<div id="outer">The outer div

<div id="inner">This is some text...</div>

</div>

</body>
```

and this CSS

```
div#outer_div {width:250px; margin:50px 40px; border-top:3px
solid red;}

div#inner_div {top:10px; left:20px; background:#AAA;}
```

FIGURE 4.24 Here are two nested paragraphs. I've added a red border to the top of the outer div and colored the inner div gray. Because the inner div is static (default) positioning, top and left properties are ignored.

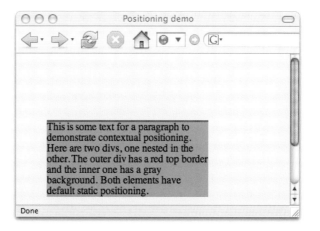

The text should properly be wrapped in a paragraph to define it semantically, but for clarity in this demo, I have just put the text directly into the inner div.

Any close study of this code begs the question: Why isn't the inner div 10 pixels down from the top of the outer one and 20 pixels to the left, as specified? Instead the two elements both share the same origin (top-left) point. The answer is that the inner (and irrelevantly, the outer) div has the default positioning of static. This means it is in the regular document flow, and because the outer div has no content, the inner div starts in the same place. Only when you set an element to one of the other three positioning options—relative, absolute, or fixed—do the top, left, right, and bottom properties actually do anything. Let's see this in action by setting the inner div's position property to absolute.

```
div#outer_div {width:250px; margin:50px 40px; border-top:3px
solid red;}
```

```
div#inner_div {position:absolute; top:10px; left:20px;
background:#AAA;}
```

But absolutely positioned with respect to what? Because there is no other relatively positioned element for it to reference, it positions itself by default with respect to the body element.

The top border of the outer div is set to red so you can see where it is. Its margins push it 50 pixels down and 40 pixels left of the top corner of the browser window. Because the inner div's position property is set to absolute, it is positioned relative to body, because *body is the default positioning context*. It entirely ignores its parent (outer div) element, and its top and left properties offset it with respect to body, as shown in **Figure 4.25**.

FIGURE 4.25 Although the inner div (gray background) is inside the outer div (indicated by its red top border) in the markup, its absolute display positioning dictates that, without any other relative positioned element to use as a context, it positions itself relative to the body element.

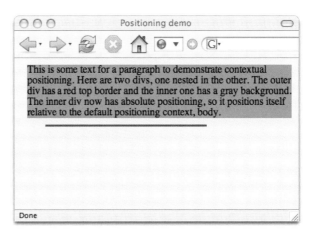

If you use margins and padding carefully, in most cases, all that you need to organize your page layouts is static positioning. Many beginning CSS designers mistakenly set the position property of almost every element only to find it hard to control all these freed-up elements. Don't change the position *property of an element from the default* static *unless you really need to.*

FIGURE 4.26 Once the outer div has a relative positioning, absolutely positioned descendants position themselves relative to it, as defined by their top and left attributes.

If you then set the `position` property of the outer div to `relative`, the positioning context of the absolutely positioned inner div is now the outer div, as shown in **Figure 4.26**. Setting the `top` and `left` properties of the inner div now positions it with respect to the outer div. If you now set the `left` and `top` position properties of the outer div to anything other than zero, the inner div would move to maintain its positioning relationship to the outer div—its positioning context. Get it?

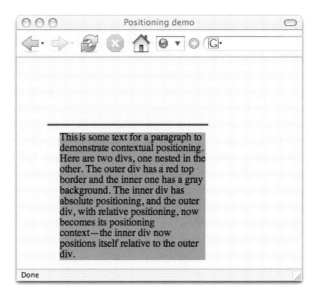

We'll look at a practical example of the uses of the `position` property, right after we look at the `display` property.

The Display Property

Just as every element has a `position` property, every element also has a `display` property. Although there are quite a number of `display` property values, the most commonly used elements have a default `display` property value of either `block` or `inline`. In case you slept through class during the previous chapters, the difference between `block` and `inline` elements is

- `Block` elements, such as paragraphs, headings, and lists, sit one above another when displayed in the browser.

- `Inline` elements, such as `a`, `span`, and `img`, sit side-by-side when they are displayed in the browser and only appear on a new line if there is insufficient room on the previous one.

The ability to change `block` elements to `inline` elements, and vice versa, like this

block by default

```
p {display:inline;}
```

inline by default

```
a {display:block}
```

is a powerful capability that allows you, for example, to force an inline element to fill its containing element. We will do this with links later when we create CSS drop-down menus.

One other value for `display` worth mentioning here is `none`. When an element's `display` property is set to `none`, that element, and any elements nested inside it, are not displayed on the page. Any space that was occupied by the element is removed; it's as if the related markup did not exist. (This contrasts with the `visibility` property, which simply has the values `visible` or `hidden`. If an element's `visibility` is set to `hidden`, the element is hidden, but the space it occupied remains.) Next, you'll learn how to toggle the `display` property of elements between `none` and `block` as the mouse moves over them to enable functionality such as drop-down menus. JavaScript can also toggle this property to cause elements to appear or disappear when defined user actions occur. Let's look at an example that combines what we have just learned about `position` and the `display` properties.

Positioning/Display Example

During the summer of 2007, I coded the CSS for *icyou.com*, a video-sharing site about healthcare created by the company for whom I work, Benefitfocus.com. Almost every page of this site offers an index of small thumbnail pictures that you can click to play related videos. To save screen real estate, we decided to have the description of each video only appear when the user moused over the thumbnail, as shown here in **Figure 4.27**.

FIGURE 4.27 A thumbnail on the icyou.com site displays an informational pop-up when the user mouses over it.

Here's how we did that. First, this is the markup of one thumbnail

```
<div class="video_selection">

  <a href="#"><img src="../images/23_diabetes_testimonial-
  1.jpg" alt="Blood pressure video" /></a>
```

```
<p> Bobby is a #2 Diabetic who weighed 274 pounds. After a
change in diet he is no longer on medication. Runtime: 46
sec.</p>

<h2><a href="#">Living with Diabetes; Bobby's story</a></h2>

</div>
```

which, unstyled, looks like this (**Figure 4.28**).

FIGURE 4.28 Here are all the elements we need to create the thumbnail area and its associated pop-up.

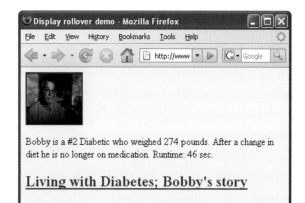

Let's do some basic styling on this markup (**Figure 4.29**).

```
div {width:92px; border:2px solid #069; padding:5px;}

h2, p {font-size:.7em; font-family:Arial, sans-serif;
margin:0;}

p {width:80px; border:1px solid gray; padding:.3em;
background-color:#FFD;}
```

FIGURE 4.29 The first step is to style the appearance and widths of the elements.

This series of screenshots were made on my Windows computer, where I have TechSmith's Snag-It, an excellent screenshot tool that can capture the cursor—key to illustrating this demo.

We've added a border to the containing div and some padding to keep the contents away from the edge (increasing its stated width, of course!). Now the div is 106 pixels wide (92 + 2 + 2 + 5 + 5 = 106). We've also set the font for h2 and paragraph and removed the default margins from both.

We have created a similar box with padding around the paragraph. This is going to be our pop-up—it's just not positioned or popping yet.

Now the fun begins. We are going to take the paragraph out of the document flow by changing its display setting to absolute. At the same time, we will set the div's display property to relative so that it becomes the positioning context for the absolutely-positioned paragraph. Remember, this relatively-positioned context element must be an ancestor of the absolutely-positioned element. In this case, the div is the parent of the paragraph, so we're fine (**Figure 4.30**).

```
div {position:relative; width:92px; border:2px solid #069;
padding:5px;}

h2, p {font-size:.7em; font-family:Arial, sans-serif;}

p {position:absolute; left:96px; top:15px; width:80px;
border:1px solid gray; padding:.3em; background-color:#FFD;}
```

FIGURE 4.30 The absolutely positioned pop-up element is now positioned where we want it to appear relative to the containing div.

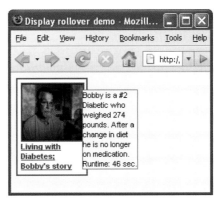

The left and top settings on the absolutely-positioned paragraph push it across and down so it sits nicely to the right of the image.

The final step is to hide the pop-up until the user moves the mouse inside the div. To do this, we will use the :hover pseudo class (**Figures 4.31A and B**).

```
div {position:relative; width:92px; border:2px solid #069;
padding:5px;}
```

```
h2, p {font-size:.7em; font-family:Arial, sans-serif;
margin:0;}
```

```
p {position:absolute; display:none; width:80px; left:96px;
top:15px; border:1px solid gray; padding:.3em; background-
color:#FFD;}
```

```
div:hover p, p:hover {display:block;}
```

FIGURES 4.31A AND 4.31B The display property used in combination with the :hover pseudo-class enables us to have the pop-up appear when the user moves the pointer into the div.

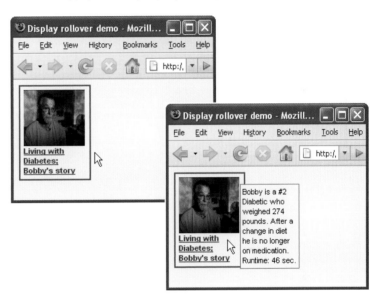

The paragraph is now normally hidden; its display property is set to none. However, the last highlighted line of code says: If the mouse hovers over the div, display the paragraph, or, if the mouse is over the paragraph (which happens if the user moves off the div and on to the paragraph once it is displayed), keep on displaying it. As soon as the user moves off either the div or the displayed paragraph, the rule no longer applies, and the paragraph is hidden again.

And there we have a simple pop-up effect with only CSS. Actually, there is a small IDWIMIE catch—IE6 only supports the :hover pseudo-class on a (links), so we need to add a JavaScript file, as an IE behavior, called csshover.htc, to enable IE to respond to hovers on any element like all the grown-up browsers can. (See the sidebar "The Hover Behavior for Internet Explorer 6.")

```
body {behavior:url(csshover.htc);}
```

Note that this code assumes that the `csshover.htc` file is in the same folder as the XHTML; normally, you would have the code in a JavaScript folder with any other JavaScript that relates to your site and link to it with a relative path.

The Hover Behavior for Internet Explorer 6

Before CSS2, only links could provide a response to being hovered over. Using the `:hover` pseudo-class on a selector enables you to define a response when any element is hovered over; for example, here's the CSS for a div with a blue background that turns red when the div is hovered over.

```
div#respond {background-color:blue;}
```

```
div#respond:hover {background-color:red;}
```

This is a very useful feature, and the key to creating CSS-based menus, but Internet Explorer 6 doesn't produce a hover effect for any selector except a, a link. Fortunately, a very smart programmer, Peter Nederlof, came up with an Internet Explorer behavior that solves this problem. The file is called `csshover.htc` and you can download it from www.xs4all.nl/~peterned/hovercraft.html. Here's how you add it to the CSS.

```
body {font:1em verdana, arial, sans-serif; behavior:url(css/
csshover.htc);}
```

In this example, as the URL for this file indicates, I created a new folder called `css` in the same folder as the files for this example and put the `csshover.htc` file in that folder. If you decide to put the file in a different location, you will need to modify the URL.

The ccsshover.htc file is included in the Stylin' download folder for this chapter, and also in the JavaScript folder in the Stylib CSS library folder.

With the `csshover.htc` file associated with your file in this way, Internet Explorer can respond to hovers. Now, across all of our target browsers, the background of the list item turns white when it is hovered over.

Take time to review and understand the three important examples shown in this chapter:

- Creating a column with an inner div and nested elements

- Clearing floated elements

- Controlling the positioning and display of elements using the `position` and `display` properties

These techniques are integral to creating page layouts with CSS, which is the subject of our next chapter.

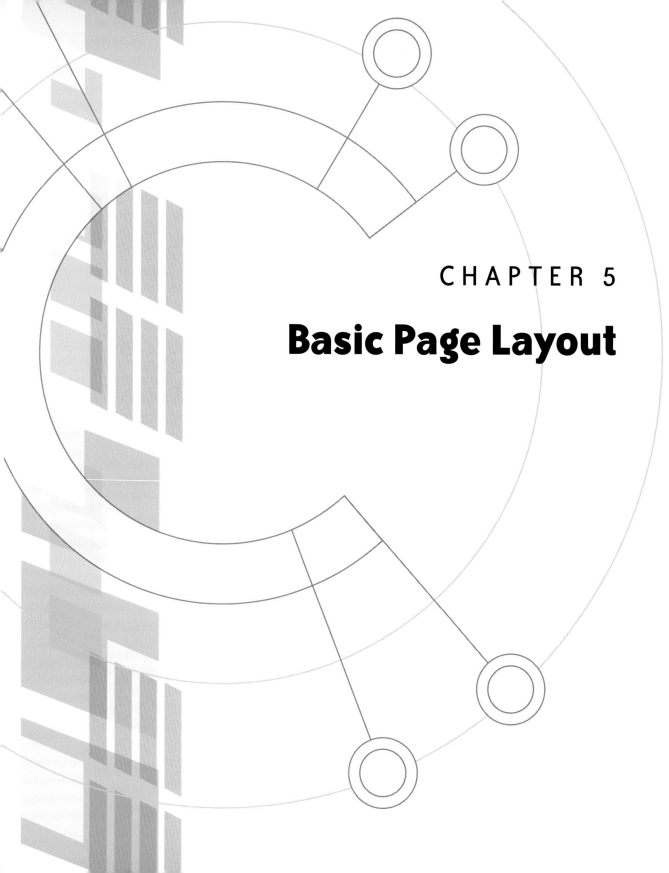

CHAPTER 5

Basic Page Layout

AT THE END OF CHAPTER 3, we styled a page of text in a single, long column. While you may lay out a simple one-column page like this once in while, usually you want to have more than one column in order to make the most of the horizontal space and offer users plenty to look at and interact with before they have to scroll.

If you dig down under the hood of most site designs, they are based on two- or three-column layouts, even though that fact is sometimes visually well disguised. In this chapter, I am going to introduce you to ways in which these layouts are created using XHTML and CSS. You can think of any page layout I show in this chapter as being like the chassis of a car—it's not visible to the user, but it's the underlying framework on which the shiny bodywork of a great site design is built. In subsequent chapters, we will see how to add the visual design into a layout's framework, but first we are going to look at the workings of these underlying page layouts.

Some of the layouts we will look at are simple arrangements of fixed width columns, while others offer sophisticated features, such as "constrained liquidness" (my term), where the layout can automatically expand its width to best fit any browser window, but only over a specified range. You don't need to understand exactly how these layouts work to use them. Just start your design with an XHTML template and its associated CSS from the *Stylib* library, and you can immediately begin to add the visual design of your page and its content, without the often tedious work of creating an underlying "chassis" that works reliably across many different browsers. Let's start by looking at some existing multi-column Web sites and their key features.

Stylib files can be found at: http:// www.stylinwithcss.com/stylib.

Some Multi-Column Layouts

A basic use of columns is to organize a list of navigation links down the left or right side of the page next to a main content area. Let's take a look at an example of this. Jing is a new screen recording technology in development from TechSmith, creators of the industry-standard SnagIt screen capture software, and the Jing blog at http://blog.jingproject.com/ is an excellent example of a liquid two-column layout (**Figure 5.1**).

Visit this site and then adjust the width of your browser to see what is meant by *liquid*; the main content changes its width as the browser changes size, with the text automatically rewrapping to the new line length as the width changes. Note, however, that the layout reaches a minimum width where it will become no smaller—then the right edge of the browser window simply covers it up. We will discover how to implement both of these features—liquid layout and minimum width—later in this chapter.

Perhaps the most common layout is three columns, typically with left navigation, content in the middle, and the right column for what I generically call promos—the advertisements, links to other sites, news headlines, and calls to action that frequently need a place somewhere on the page. Here's a three-column product page on Amazon.com, which puts the navigation in the header so it can use two columns to tell you about the product and the third to help you buy it (**Figure 5.2**).

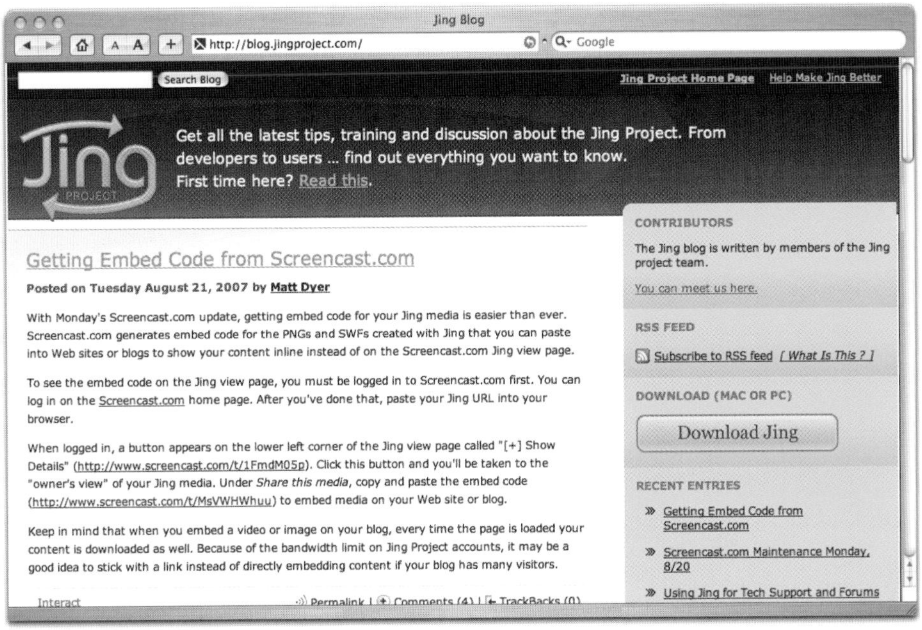

FIGURE 5.1 The Jing blog uses a two-column liquid layout.

FIGURE 5.2 Amazon's three-column product page layout has a liquid center.

Four-column layouts can easily look cluttered and are more difficult to design successfully, but in the masterful hands of Jeffrey Zeldman and team the understated four-column home page of A List Apart (http://www.alistapart.com) looks clean and elegant (**Figure 5.3**).

FIGURE 5.3 A List Apart's four-column home page.

As illustrated in the examples above, virtually every layout, regardless of the number of columns, has at the top a horizontal area, commonly known as the header, that spans the width of the page. The header's primary purpose is to present the brand identity of the site so users know which site they are on, but it's also frequently used for navigation elements, as the Amazon and A List Apart screenshots show. Also, most pages have a corresponding footer element that can provide navigation links once the user gets to the bottom of the page, and often holds copyright and legal disclaimers that need to be present on every page. The rest of this chapter is dedicated to showing you how to work with style sheets to create layouts with headers, multiple columns, and footers.

Introducing *Stylib*—the *Stylin'* Library

In the course of creating Web sites, I have found myself writing the same pieces of code over and over again. Multi-column layouts, navigation links, and forms are just some of the things I have coded with XHTML and CSS many, many times. While the underlying similarities of the components of these sites are often not apparent because of the differences in colors, fonts, and other visual attributes, their underlying XHTML markup and the "mechanics" of the CSS that organize that markup on the screen change very little. Recently, to reduce the frequent sense of dèjá-vu, I started to develop a library that I now call *Stylib*. This library, a collection of XHTML, CSS, and JavaScript files, not only contains all the elements I commonly use in my design work, but also has two important characteristics. First, the components are designed to work together rather like Lego® bricks, and secondly, the parts that I might want to change from one site to the next—the type sizes and colors, for example—are broken out from the code for the underlying layout. This means I can make visual changes, such as color and type size, without worrying about affecting the workings of the menu or whatever it is I am styling.

The Stylib library is at an early stage, and I welcome your feedback and any contributions you want to make to the library. The only requirement is that you supply a valid XHTML page with the related CSS embedded in the head of the document, and that it only requires a single class on the containing div to invoke the CSS. Everyone who contributes a component that is included will get a credit in the code.

As part of this book, you can download the *Stylib* CSS library from the stylinwithcss.com site—I am going to use it throughout the upcoming chapters, and you can see (and download) the finished examples and the *Stylib* library as a basis for your own site designs. Rather than explain all the details of how it works right now, we'll just start using it, and see the features as we go along.

Width Matters

Remember as you read this chapter that all these layouts increase their vertical height automatically, according to the content within them. If you add more content, the layout increases its height to accommodate it, and that is exactly what you want to have happen. However, controlling the *horizontal* width of these layouts is key to the way they function. Users detest horizontal scrolling, so it's important to ensure they do not have to do that. Also, most of these layouts are based on using elements that are floated using CSS to create columns, and these kinds of layouts can display incorrectly if they do not maintain key width dimensions. All this will be explained in detail as we look at the examples, but remember: You want to create layouts that expand vertically to accommodate any amount of content, without changing their width. Setting and controlling the layout width is the primary skill I am trying to teach.

Floated Versus Absolutely-Positioned Layouts

There are two basic approaches to creating columns in your page layouts. You can float them side-by-side in the manner we saw in the last chapter when we created a column of text next to an image, or you can use absolute positioning and fix the width and location of the columns across the page.

Floated columns are quick and easy to implement, but require that you be very careful to ensure that you don't accidentally cause the total width of the columns to exceed the width of the layout (for example, by increasing the width of columns by adding a large image into it). This kind of problem will cause the right column to be forced down and under the left one—not a pretty sight. However, the use of the overflow property combined with the "inner div" approach that I showed earlier (and that we will use in the following examples) can prevent this problem. With one exception, all the layouts I am about to show you use this floating-column technique.

Absolutely-positioned columns do have a couple of notable advantages. First, you can sequence the markup to put the content first, or certainly earlier, which some claim can improve search engine visibility. (Personally, I think referring links, good title tags, and judicious use of keywords in headings and copy are the keys to being found by search engines, but let's have that conversation another day.) Second, the columns stay in their specified location under all circumstances, and the layout cannot "break" like a floated layout can. However, because the columns are absolutely positioned, they are removed from the document flow and therefore have no sense of their relationship to one another. Not only does this mean that it's difficult to create fluid layouts with absolute positioning, but also a footer below the columns doesn't get pushed down as content is added to the page, because the columns are entirely independent and don't interact with one another. While there are some ways to rectify this problem with JavaScript (such as the Nifty Corners code discussed later in this chapter), I tend to stick with the floated-column layouts. I'll show you one absolutely-positioned layout at the

This is the most simple layout I am going to show, but it's probably going to take the longest to explain. Many of the techniques in this layout appear in the others, so I am going to explain them one time here, and then not repeat myself in subsequent examples.

end of the chapter, so you can compare how the two methods stack up against one another.

A Simple Two-Column Fixed-Width Layout

In the first example, I introduce a very common layout. It contains a narrow left column for navigation and a wider right column that holds the page's content. In this example, both the navigation and content column are fixed widths, and the layout centers itself in the browser window if the browser window is made wider than the width of the layout (**Figure 5.4**).

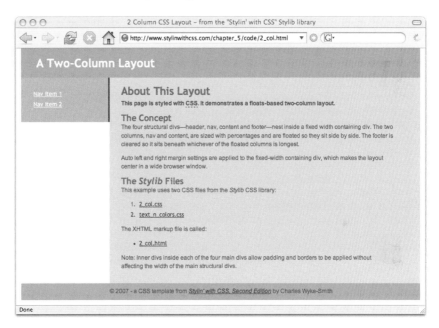

FIGURE 5.4 A two-column layout from the *Stylib* library. The left column is only as long as its content. We'll see how to visually extend this column later in the chapter.

```
<!DOCTYPE html PUBLIC "-//W3C//DTD XHTML 1.0 Strict//EN"
"http://www.w3.org/TR/xhtml1/DTD/xhtml1-strict.dtd">

<html xmlns="http://www.w3.org/1999/xhtml">

<head>

<meta http-equiv="Content-Type" content="text/html;
charset=iso-8859-1" />

<title>2 column layout</title>

<link href="../../lib/css_styles/layouts/2_col.css"
media="all" rel="stylesheet" />

<link href="../../lib/css_styles/text/text_n_colors.css"
media="all" rel="stylesheet" />
```

the layout and text stylesheets

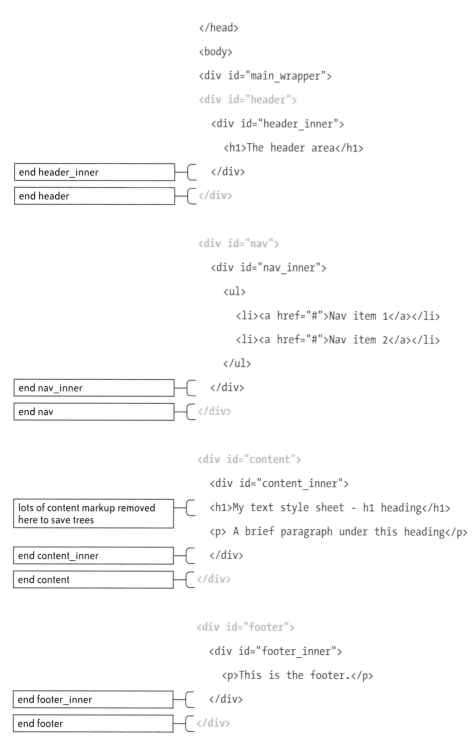

```
</head>
<body>
<div id="main_wrapper">
<div id="header">
    <div id="header_inner">
        <h1>The header area</h1>
```

end header_inner — `</div>`
end header — `</div>`

```
<div id="nav">
    <div id="nav_inner">
        <ul>
            <li><a href="#">Nav item 1</a></li>
            <li><a href="#">Nav item 2</a></li>
        </ul>
```

end nav_inner — `</div>`
end nav — `</div>`

```
<div id="content">
    <div id="content_inner">
```

lots of content markup removed here to save trees —

```
        <h1>My text style sheet - h1 heading</h1>
        <p> A brief paragraph under this heading</p>
```

end content_inner — `</div>`
end content — `</div>`

```
<div id="footer">
    <div id="footer_inner">
        <p>This is the footer.</p>
```

end footer_inner — `</div>`
end footer — `</div>`

```
end main wrapper        </div>

                        </body>

                        </html>
```

This may look like a lot of code, but if we break it down, you will see there are only a few key pieces to it.

First, find where the head tag closes `</head>` about a third of the way down. Above it is the code the browser needs to display the page, and below, following the body tag, is the content that will be displayed.

Starting from the very top, after the required DOCTYPE and XHTML tag comes the head of the document, which contains the title tag and two link tags. The link tags connect two style sheets in the *Stylib* library to this page, which provide the page with the CSS for the page layout and the text stylings, respectively. We will examine these style sheets in detail in a moment.

In the body of the document are four divs—header, nav(igation), content, and footer—with their respective inner divs. Let's see what it takes to lay these divs out so that nav and content divs sit side-by-side, with the full-width header and footer above and below them, respectively. Here's the CSS that makes this happen, which is in the linked style sheet `2_col.css`. (The link to this style sheet is high-lighted at the top of the code above.)

There is a second style sheet linked to this page called text_n_colors.css, which you can find in the Stylib library. This style sheet is used in every example in this chapter. It sets colors of the backgrounds of the columns and styles all the text ele-ments on the page. By adding a class such as "olive" or "lime" to the body tag, you can invoke one of the several different page color schemes included in this style sheet—in the examples where the markup doesn't have a class on the body tag (such as the example above), then this style sheet's default color scheme is used. I am not showing this style sheet here because it's not the focus of this chapter, and with all the various color schemes, it is almost 400 lines of CSS. Anyway, the focus here is the way in which CSS can be used to organize the page layout. Just realize that the page colors and styles of the text come from the text_n_colors style sheet, which we will look at in Chapter 7, and are not part of the page layout CSS that follows.

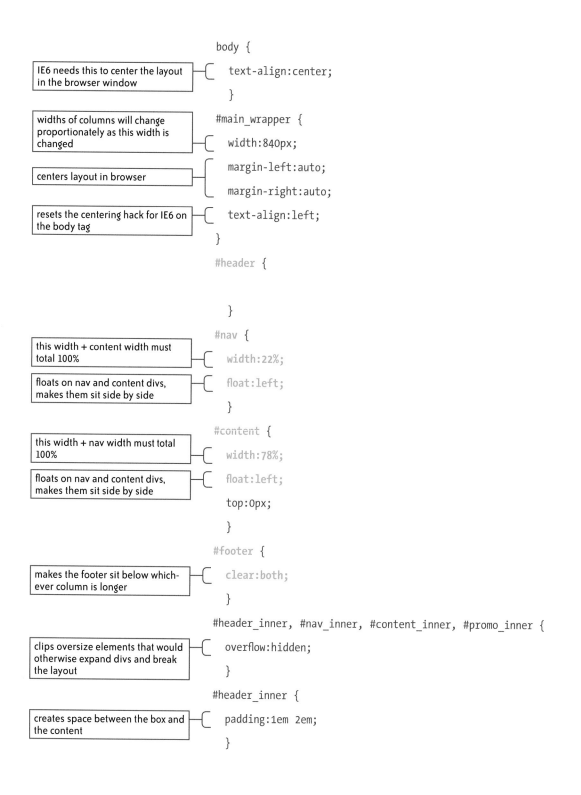

```
body {

    text-align:center;

}

#main_wrapper {

    width:840px;

    margin-left:auto;

    margin-right:auto;

    text-align:left;

}

#header {



}

#nav {

    width:22%;

    float:left;

}

#content {

    width:78%;

    float:left;

    top:0px;

}

#footer {

    clear:both;

}

#header_inner, #nav_inner, #content_inner, #promo_inner {

    overflow:hidden;

}

#header_inner {

    padding:1em 2em;

}
```

IE6 needs this to center the layout in the browser window

widths of columns will change proportionately as this width is changed

centers layout in browser

resets the centering hack for IE6 on the body tag

this width + content width must total 100%

floats on nav and content divs, makes them sit side by side

this width + nav width must total 100%

floats on nav and content divs, makes them sit side by side

makes the footer sit below whichever column is longer

clips oversize elements that would otherwise expand divs and break the layout

creates space between the box and the content

```
#nav_inner {

    padding:1em .8em;

    border-right:3px solid #B33;

}

#content_inner {

    padding:0 1em 1em 1.5em;

}

#footer_inner {

    padding:.5em 1em;

    text-align:center;

}
```

creates space between the box and the content

creates space between the box and the content

creates space between the box and the content

You can alter the proportional widths of the two columns by changing their width percentages; just be sure to make the two column widths total 100%.

Without this CSS, the four main divs (highlighted in the XHTML) would be stacked one above the other across the width of the browser by default. The CSS that converts that default arrangement into the two-column layout is simply the five lines highlighted in the CSS above. The nav and content divs are floated, which will make them sit side-by-side, and each has a percentage width applied to it that together totals 100% so they are the same width as the header and footer.

The footer has a `clear:both` rule to ensure that it sits below whichever of the two columns is longest as determined by their content. Document flow does all the rest of the work for us—the header and footer are by default the full width of the `main_wrapper` containing element.

As its name suggests, the `main_wrapper` div encloses the entire layout, and I have given it an arbitrary width of 840 pixels. This div sets the overall width of the layout because it's the parent of the four divs, and therefore its width determines the width of the footer, the header, and the combined width of the columns. The beauty of this arrangement is two-fold. First, by simply adjusting the width of the `main_wrapper` div, we can modify the overall layout width (the elements inside change size proportionately, and their code doesn't have to change). Second, just by adding `auto` left and right margins to the `main_wrapper` div (see the code above), the layout centers itself nicely in the browser window if the user makes the browser window wider than the `main_wrapper` div; currently, 840 pixels.

IDWIMIE 6—IE6 needs us to add a little work-around in the form of the addition of a special JavaScript to get the auto-centering of the layout to work; `min-width` *and* `max-width` *simply don't work in IE6. In the Stylib JavaScript folder, you will find a file called minmax.js. Just link it to the page by adding* `<script type="JavaScript" src="../../lib/js_tools/ minmax.js"></script>` *somewhere in the head of the page, usually right after the links to the CSS files. You may need to adjust the file path to link to this file, depending on where you put the Stylib library on your server.*

Occasionally, you may need to remove the overflow setting on a div, such as when it contains a menu with a drop-down element that appears when the user points at it. If overflow is set to hidden, the drop-down won't display outside of the div area—and it's fine to remove the overflow setting for this kind of need. The overflow settings are only insurance against problems caused by adding oversize content and are not integral to the working of the layout.

Know Your Inner Div

The other things I'll note before we get into the content for this page are the inner divs. In the style sheet, the CSS for these inner divs is at the end, after the main CSS for the page layout. I demonstrated the usefulness of inner divs in Chapter 4. Although they add a little extra markup, I believe they greatly simplify styling and modifying your layout, as they solve all the commonly encountered box model problems of columns getting larger as you apply margins, borders, and padding.

I like to use inner divs on the elements that have critical widths associated with them. If I don't, every time I add a one-pixel border around that div, I have to remember to subtract two pixels off the stated width (left + right) in order to keep the div's width constant. It gets tedious fast, and you end up with stated widths in the CSS that don't reflect the actual width of the divs. However, some designers don't like the idea of the extra markup in their XHTML. If that's you, with all these examples, you can if you want, remove the inner divs (don't forget to remove their closing tag, too!) and move their associated styles onto the main div—from `inner_nav` to `nav`, for example. If you do this, remember that you need to subtract the total width of any left and right borders and padding from the stated width of the div. Let's look at the CSS that relates to these inner divs.

Prevent Unwanted Overflow

I've written a single rule for all the inner divs, using a group selector, which hides the overflow of oversized content within them.

The CSS `overflow` property controls how elements deal with content within them. The default setting, `visible,` causes the element to expand to enclose the content within it. For example, if you add a large image into the narrow `nav` column, that column would normally expand vertically and horizontally to display the entire image. Unexpected changes in column width like this are the curse of floated layouts, as the rightmost column will move down under the left column if the columns get pushed over to the right, and it suddenly doesn't have room to sit where it belongs. With the `overflow: hidden` rule applied, instead of getting larger, the column will retain its defined width and simply display the part of the image that *does* fit—it does not change size. Of course, it's good practice not to add oversized elements in the first place, but sometimes you won't have control over the content in the future.

If I had added the three-pixel red border to the nav div itself, the layout would then be 100% (which the browser calculates from the parent element, so it equals 840 pixels) + 3 more pixels. This makes the layout too wide to fit the wrapper, so the floating content column then moves under the nav. Try temporarily moving this border style from nav_inner *to* nav *to see what I mean.*

Freely Style Your Inner Divs

You can merrily apply borders, margins, and padding to the inner divs. Because they do not have an explicit width, they always fill their respective column divs. I was able to add the red line down the side of the navigation by adding it to the inner div. I could do this without affecting the width of the critical "outer" div width and thereby breaking the layout. Just remember: Don't apply visual styles directly to those main column divs; style their related "inner" divs instead.

Styling the Text

The *Stylib* library contains a style sheet for text elements that is also linked to this page called `text_n_colors.css`. Any well-marked-up text should display nicely using this style sheet. Everyone's personal text styling preferences are different, and this reflects some of mine; for example, I like headings to sit nice and tight on top of the text that follows them. The default browser settings leave a sizable margin underneath headings, so this style sheet sets headings to have a `margin-bottom` value of 0.

A Simple Two-Column Liquid Layout

A layout designed to fit a small monitor can look like a postage stamp on a large one, so creating a liquid layout that can change width to more closely fit the width of any monitor is a user-friendly thing to do. To make our two-column layout liquid, we need to remove the fixed-width setting on the `main_wrapper` div, so the layout's width can change with the browser window's width.

On the `main_wrapper` div, make the following incredibly simple change:

```
width:840px;
```

Creating a liquid layout from the fixed-width layout is easy. Simply deleting the `width:840px;` setting from the `main_wrapper`, the layout instantly changes width as the browser window width changes. The now undimensioned `main_wrapper` springs to the full width of its parent, `body`, which is by default the full width of the browser. As both columns are sized in percentages, they now both change size proportionately with any changes in the browser window width, and "liquidness" is attained. Note the auto margins do nothing now, as the layout always fills the available horizontal space in the browser (**Figures 5.5–5.6**).

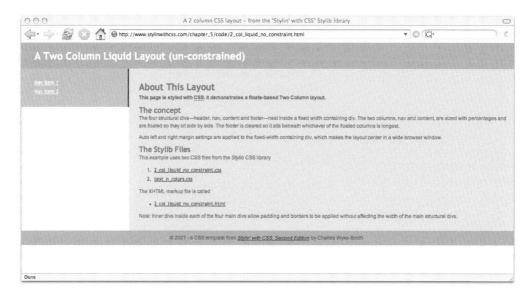

FIGURE 5.5 Here's our first step in converting the fixed width layout to a liquid layout. As the browser width changes, the width of the columns changes proportionately. Note, however, that when the browser window is wide, the line length can get too long for easy readability.

FIGURE 5.6 When this same two-column liquid layout is displayed in a narrow browser window, the content gets crushed down—the line lengths are absurdly short, and the navigation links are almost entirely obscured.

There is a major user experience problem with the layout as it stands at this point, and it's one that goes unfixed on many liquid layouts: The browser window dictates the width of the layout,

As in the first layout (and all of them), you will need to use a script tag in the header to link the min-max.js file from the Stylib library to have auto-centering work in IE6.

however absurd the visual result may be, as illustrated in **Figures 5.5 and 5.6**. The liquid page can get crushed down to a point where the line length of the content is just a few words, or almost worse, the page can be so wide on a large monitor that when you read to the end of one incredibly long line, your eye can't find its way back to the start of the next. Also, you usually want only the content column to change width, not the navigation column. Let's look at how we can improve our new liquid layout to fix these issues.

Use a Little Constraint

The CSS properties `max-width` and `min-width` do as their names suggest and allow you to set how large or small respectively an element can become. By adding these properties to the `main_wrapper`, we can constrain our page to only be liquid between a certain range of values, like this

```
width:840px;
```

sets maximum layout width ──┤ `max-width:960px;`

sets minimum layout width ──┤ `min-width:720px;`

We are stating here that the layout can expand or contract 120 pixels from our previous 840-pixel fixed width, but no more.

I like to have to have a minimum of six and a maximum of 15 words to a line; you can play with the min/max settings to get just the right range for your pages. Note that if you set the min and max widths in ems, then the number of words per line is always the same, even if the user scales the overall font size.

Now, when the layout reaches either the stated minimum or maximum width, it's as if the page has a fixed width applied to it. After reaching minimum width, the right edge of the browser window moves over the now-fixed-width layout. Going the other way, after the browser window goes beyond the layout's maximum size, the layout gets no wider. Then our auto margins kick in again, and the "max'd out" layout centers itself in the browser window as it did with the fixed width version we looked at previously. Much nicer.

A couple more quick changes will ensure that only the content column changes width.

```
#nav {
    width:22%;
    width:140px;
    float:left;
}
```

the content margin must match this value ──┤

```
#content {

    float:left;

    width:78%;

    margin-left:140px;

}
```

margin must equal width of nav column

Because we have fixed the width of the navigation column, then the only useable value for the content column, if it is to remain liquid, is auto, which means as wide as the containing element—in this case main_wrapper. (Because auto is the default width, we don't need to state it in our CSS.) Of course, if the content column is this full width, it would leave no space for the navigation column, so we add a 140-pixel margin to the content column to create a visual space for it.

To Float or Not To Float?

This causes the floated content column to sit down the page below the navigation column. That's as high as it is able to float up, because it is now full width and the earlier-in-the-markup nav gets dibs on the corner.

By unfloating the content column, it returns to the document flow and sits up in the top-left corner of the page. The navigation column then floats up, also into the top-left corner, over the content div's empty left margin area.

All this might be a little difficult to grasp, but what we have done is position both elements with their top-left corners in the top-left corner of the containing element, body. The floated nav is not in the document flow, so it sits up as high and as far to the left as it can within the containing element. The content div is now first in the document flow, so it also moves into the top-left position. It's only the left margin on the content area that pushes it away from this position and prevents it from being under the navigation column. Temporarily remove the left margin on the content area to see what I mean.

With these changes made, we now have a user-friendly "liquid-but-constrained" layout that we can use as the basis of a page design (**Figures 5.7–5.8**).

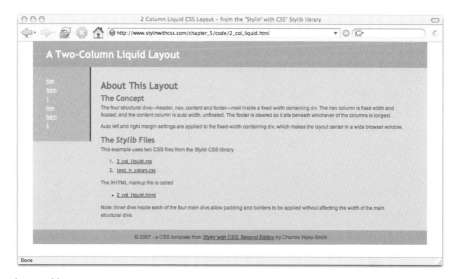

FIGURE 5.7 With the min/max width applied, the layout reaches a maximum width and then centers itself in the browser window.

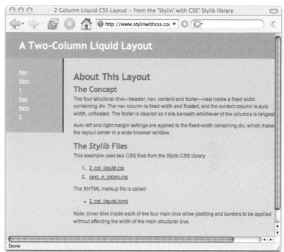

FIGURE 5.8. Going the other way with the min/max width applied, the layout reaches a minimum width and then gets no smaller; the browser window now starts to cover it up.

A Three-Column Fixed-Width Layout

A fixed-width three-column layout works in the same way as the two-column version. The only additional work is to add another column div into the markup, float it like the other columns, and then share the 100% width among the three columns to our liking. Here's the new markup. The only thing that is different from the two-column markup is the new promo div (highlighted) that follows the content div (**Figure 5.9**).

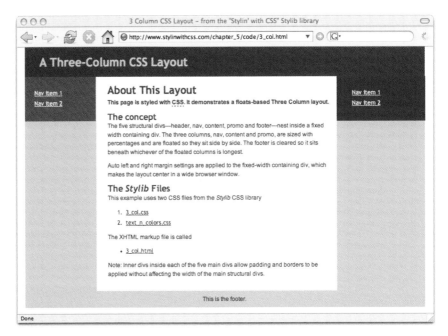

FIGURE 5.9 A three-column fixed-width layout.

Here's the associated XHTML:

```
<body>

<div id="main_wrapper" class="clearfix">

<div id="header">

  <div id="header_inner">

    <h1>The header area</h1>
```

end header_inner ─┤ `    </div>`

end header ─┤ `</div>`

```
<div id="nav">

  <div id="nav_inner">

    <ul>

      <li><a href="#">Nav item 1</a></li>

      <li><a href="#">Nav item 2</a></li>

    </ul>
```

end nav_inner ─┤ `    </div>`

end nav ─┤ `</div>`

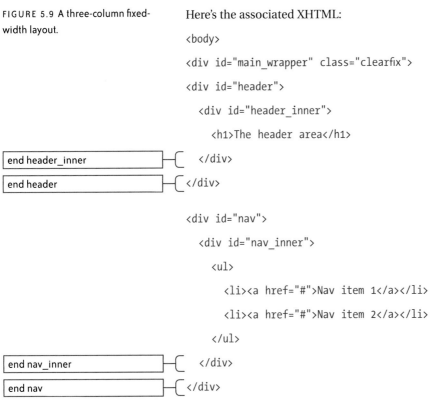

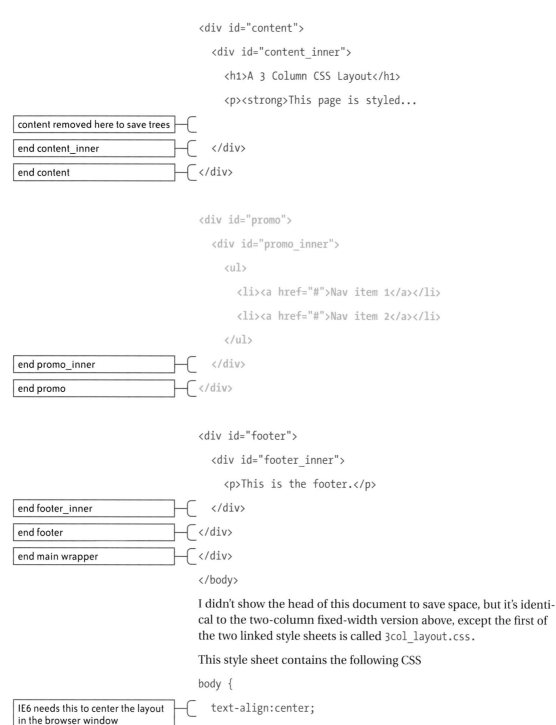

```
<div id="content">

  <div id="content_inner">

    <h1>A 3 Column CSS Layout</h1>

    <p><strong>This page is styled...
```

content removed here to save trees

```
  </div>
```
end content_inner

```
</div>
```
end content

```
<div id="promo">

  <div id="promo_inner">

    <ul>

      <li><a href="#">Nav item 1</a></li>

      <li><a href="#">Nav item 2</a></li>

    </ul>
```
end promo_inner
```
    </div>
```
end promo
```
  </div>
```

```
<div id="footer">

  <div id="footer_inner">

    <p>This is the footer.</p>
```
end footer_inner
```
    </div>
```
end footer
```
  </div>
```
end main wrapper
```
</div>
```
```
</body>
```

I didn't show the head of this document to save space, but it's identical to the two-column fixed-width version above, except the first of the two linked style sheets is called 3col_layout.css.

This style sheet contains the following CSS

```
body {
```
IE6 needs this to center the layout in the browser window
```
  text-align:center;

}
```

widths of columns will scale proportionately if this width is changed

centers max'd layout in browser

centers max'd layout in browser

prevents page inheriting IE6 centering hack on body

no header styles yet

inner divs code removed below here to save space—same code as in two-col version above

```css
#main_wrapper {

    width:840px;

    margin-left:auto;

    margin-right:auto;

    text_align:left:

}

#header {

}

#nav {

    width:18%;

    float:left;

}

#content {

    width:60%;

    float:left;

}

#promo {

    width:22%;

    float:left;

}

#footer {

    clear:both;

}
```

The highlighted code in the XHTML and CSS above are the only changes you need to make to the two-column layout. If you understood the two-column version, there isn't much more to say about the three-column version.

Now we will start to look at some more advanced CSS. You saw how easy it was to convert a two-column fixed layout into a liquid layout, but in order to create a three-column liquid layout, we have to get very creative.

A Three-Column Liquid Layout

See the challenge at Mezzoblue blog at http://www.mezzoblue.com/ archives/2004/01/23/friday_chall/

Things get more complex if we want to add a liquid center to our three-column layout, where the content area changes width as the browser window is resized, but the side columns remain a fixed size. As we have seen, it's simple to make a liquid content area with just a left column because that left column never moves relative to its reference point—the top-left of its container. When there is a right column too, it's a very different story, as the right column must constantly reposition itself as the center column changes width, and this turns out to be a complex thing to do with CSS. In fact, in 2004 Dave Shea, of Zen Garden fame, issued a challenge to see if anyone could solve this problem—one that had even him stumped.

CSS maven Ryan Brill quickly worked out the answer—use negative margins—and his solution has become a CSS classic now used in numerous liquid layout sites. With a tip o' the hat to Ryan, here's how it's done (**Figures 5.10** and **5.11**).

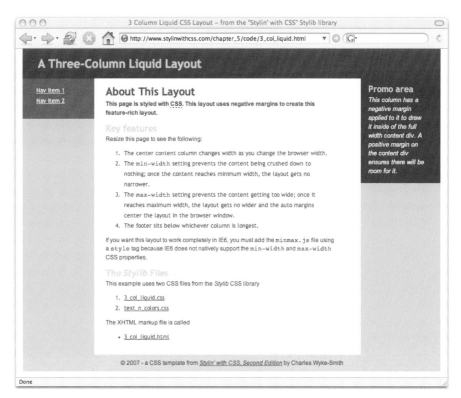

FIGURE 5.10 A three-column liquid layout at the point where it hits maximum width and starts to center itself in the browser window.

FIGURE 5.11 A three-column liquid layout at the point where it hits minimum width and the right edge of the browser starts to cover the layout.

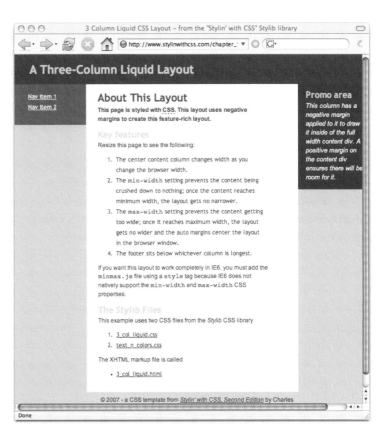

First, we add a couple more divs. The first one encloses the three columns, and the second goes inside it and only encloses the left and center columns.

```
<body>

<div id="main_wrapper">

  <div id="header">

    <div id="header_inner">

      <h2>The header</h2>

    </div>

  </div>

  <div id="threecolwrap">

    <div id="twocolwrap">

      <div id="nav">
```

encloses the three columns —

encloses the left and center columns —

the left column —

```
                                    <div id="nav_inner">

                                       <h3>Left nav</h3>

                                       <ul>
```
links removed to save space ─┤
```
                                          <li><a href="#">Link 1</a></li>

                                       </ul>

                                    </div>
```
end nav div ─┤
```
                                 </div>
```
the center column ─┤
```
                                 <div id="content">
```
start of page content ─┤
```
                                    <div id="content_inner">

                                       <h1>A Three Column Liquid layout</h1>

```
tree-saving removal of content ─┤
end content inner ─┤
```
                                    </div>
```
end of content div ─┤
```
                                 </div>
```
end of twocolwrap div ─┤
```
                              </div>

                              <div id="promo">

                                 <div id="promo_inner">

                                    <h3>Promo area</h3>
```
content removed here ─┤
```
                                    <p>

                                    </p>
```
end of inner promo div ─┤
```
                                 </div>
```
end of promo div ─┤
```
                              </div>
```
end of threecolwrap div ─┤
```
                           </div>

                           <div id="footer">

                              <div id="footer_inner">

                                 <p>&copy; 2007 - a CSS template from <a href="http://
                                 www.stylinwithcss.com">Stylin' with CSS, Second
                                 Edition</a> by Charles Wyke-Smith</p>
```
end of footer inner div ─┤
```
                              </div>
```
end footer div ─┤
```
                           </div>
```
end main_wrapper div ─┤
```
                        </div>

                     </body>
```

This is the same markup as we have used in earlier examples, with the addition of the two highlighted wrapper divs. The associated CSS looks like this

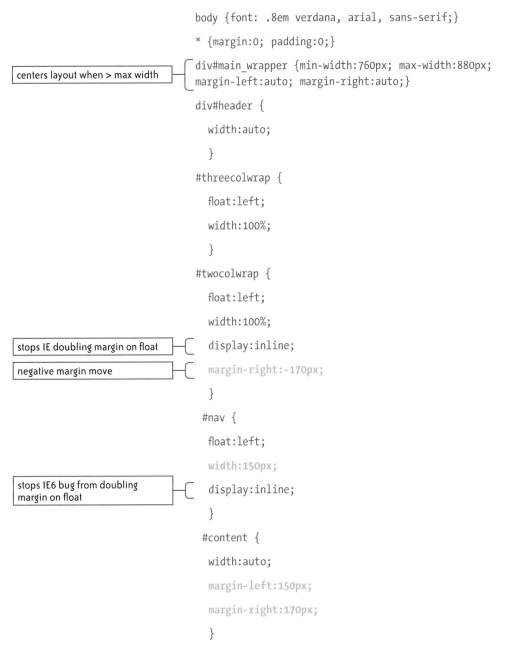

```
body {font: .8em verdana, arial, sans-serif;}

* {margin:0; padding:0;}

div#main_wrapper {min-width:760px; max-width:880px;
margin-left:auto; margin-right:auto;}
```

centers layout when > max width

```
div#header {

    width:auto;

    }

#threecolwrap {

    float:left;

    width:100%;

    }

#twocolwrap {

    float:left;

    width:100%;
```

stops IE doubling margin on float

```
    display:inline;
```

negative margin move

```
    margin-right:-170px;

    }

#nav {

    float:left;

    width:150px;
```

stops IE6 bug from doubling margin on float

```
    display:inline;

    }

#content {

    width:auto;

    margin-left:150px;

    margin-right:170px;

    }
```

```
#promo {

  float:left;

  width:170px;

  }

 #footer {

  width:100%;

  clear:both;

  float:left;

  }
```

In this layout also, the center column does not have a specified width. It would not be able to change size if it did, so its natural tendency is to expand to the width of the layout. Of course, if it did that, there would be no room for the side columns, so we apply margins equal to the width of the side columns to push the content column in on each side. The problem is that, even after doing this, without some extra magic, the right column would sit with its left edge aligned to the right side of the container and therefore be in the wrong location or, if the browser window was narrow, be off-screen.

Ryan Brill's insight was to set a negative margin on the two-column wrapper, which would suck the right column back into the page and keep its right edge aligned with the right edge of the container. It's a thing of beauty. Every time I create this layout, I think I get a little closer to understanding how it actually works! What I do know is that this is probably the most useful page layout of them all—as they would say in England: "Absolutely brill!"

Making All the Columns the Same Length

Unlike table-based layouts, div-based layouts do not result in all the columns being the same length. Divs are simply as tall as the content they contain and expand vertically as more content is added. It can be more visually pleasing to have all columns go full height, especially on long pages where the side columns would otherwise move up off-screen as the user scrolls down, leaving empty space on each side of the content. You can fix a div's height, but this is not useful if the size or quantity of the content changes. You need to keep flexibility in the page length so the page is as tall as it needs to be to accommodate the content. So what we need is flexible height, while still having all the columns appear to be the same height— and the operative word here is *appear*. All we need to do is create the *illusion* that the columns are the same height. Here are the two best ways to do that:

- **Faux columns**—Add a graphic to the layout's background that is the same color and width of the columns, to create the illusion that the columns extend right down the page.

- **Programmatically extend the divs**—Add a JavaScript that finds the height of the longest column as the page loads and instantly sets the other columns to this height.

Let's look at the pros and cons of these two methods.

Faux Columns

The faux columns' method involves adding a background graphic to the wrapper div of the page that is the same width and color as the column we want to visually extend. Background images can be set to repeat down the page, so that as the page height increases, the graphic always repeats itself enough times to fill the available space.

TWO-COLUMN LIQUID LAYOUT WITH FAUX COLUMNS

Let's use the fixed-width two-column liquid example we looked at earlier in the chapter and visually extend the columns to full height. The navigation column is 140 pixels wide, with the red right border on the inner div part being of that width, so the artwork I make looks like this (**Figure 5.12**):

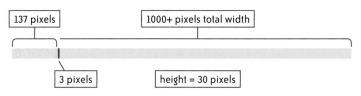

FIGURE 5.12 The faux art work will be added to the `mainwrapper` div that extends across the full width of the layout, so I made the artwork wider than the `max-width` value; only the part that fits within the div is visible. The CSS setting `repeat-y` will make it repeat vertically down the page.

Now I add the artwork to the background of the `main_wrapper` div like this:

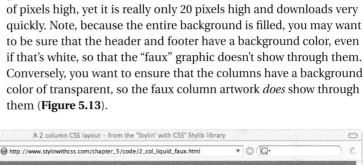

```
#main_wrapper {
    max-width:960px;
    min-width:720px;
    margin-left:auto;
    margin-right:auto;
    text-align:left;
    background:url(../../../chapter_5/code/images/2_col_faux_
    art.gif) repeat-y;
}
```

sets maximum layout width

sets minimum layout width

centers layout in browser

centers layout in browser

resets the centering hack for IE6 on the body tag

The ../ in the file path means "up one folder level." In my current file organization, the chapter_5 folder is three levels up from this CSS file. Your path from the CSS to the image may need to be different.

The repeat-y setting makes the graphic repeat ("tile") as many times as needed in order to fill the container. Because the main_wrapper div encloses the entire layout, the graphic tiles the entire background. In this way, it instantly fills an area that could be thousands of pixels high, yet it is really only 20 pixels high and downloads very quickly. Note, because the entire background is filled, you may want to be sure that the header and footer have a background color, even if that's white, so that the "faux" graphic doesn't show through them. Conversely, you want to ensure that the columns have a background color of transparent, so the faux column artwork *does* show through them (**Figure 5.13**).

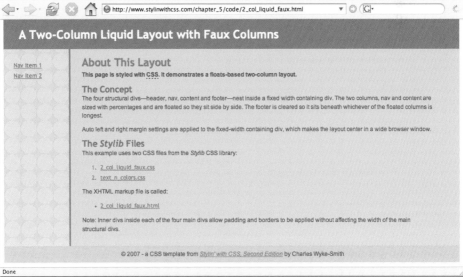

FIGURE 5.13 A two-column liquid layout with faux columns from the *Stylib* library.

Even though the navigation column is still the same short length as in the two-column liquid layout earlier in this chapter, the visual result is very different—the columns now appear to extend full-height each side of the content area. All it takes is a little care with the artwork to ensure that the horizontal dimensions of the elements in the piece of artwork match the widths of the columns.

THREE-COLUMN LIQUID LAYOUT WITH FAUX COLUMNS

If you need to add faux columns to the liquid three-column layout that we saw prior to this exercise, you will need to make separate graphics to visually extend the left and right columns, like this (**Figure 5.14**):

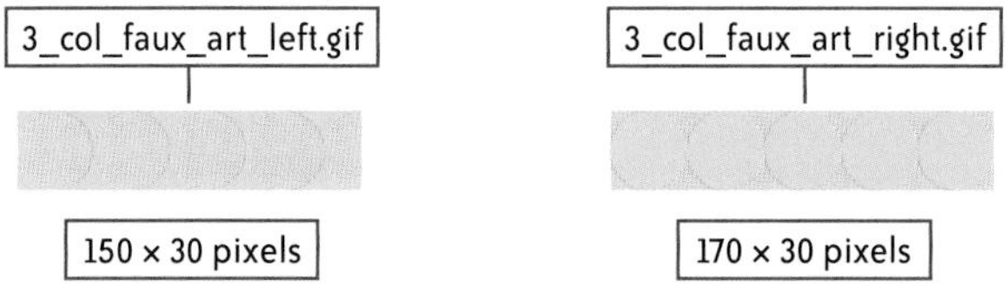

FIGURE 5.14 To create faux columns for the liquid three-column layout, these two pieces of artwork can be added to the twocolumnwrap and threecolumnwrap divs respectively.

3_col_faux_art_left.gif

3_col_faux_art_right.gif

150 × 30 pixels

170 × 30 pixels

The left graphic is the width of the left column, 150 pixels, and the right graphic is the width of the right column. We add the graphics into two different wrappers—the left one into the two-column wrapper, and the right one into the three-column wrapper.

```
#threecolwrap {

    float:left;

    width:100%;

    background:url(../../../chapter_5/code/images/3_col_faux_
    art_right.gif) repeat-y right;

    }

#twocolwrap {

    float:left;

    width:100%;

    display:inline;

    margin-right:-170px;

    background:url(../../../chapter_5/code/images/3_col_faux_
    art_left_blend.jpg) repeat-y left;

    }
```

stops IE doubling margin on float

neg margin move

The three-column wrapper extends the full width of the layout, so we can use it to add the faux graphic for the right column, but we must set the `right` setting to the `background` property to position the artwork in the top right rather than the default top left of the container.

Also, these backgrounds don't have to be flat color—any design that can repeat vertically can be used, as the examples here illustrate. Note that I set the `background-color` of the nav and promo columns themselves to `transparent` so we see the faux column graphic's full height (**Figure 5.15**).

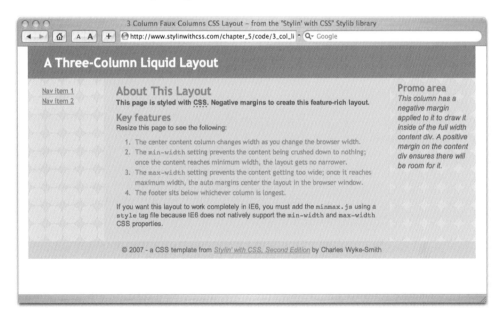

FIGURE 5.15 A three-column liquid layout with faux columns from the *Stylib* library.

Also, it's possible that the side columns might, if the page has very little content, be longer than the center column. Because the center column has no faux background, this would result in a space below the center column in the same way that there is space below the side columns in the earlier examples. To fix this, we remove the background color fill from the content column and move it to the background of the `main_wrapper` div, which is always the height of the layout. With the side columns full length now, the only place the main wrapper can be visible is in the content area—just what we need. (Alternatively, but not illustrated here, you could also add a background image to `main_wrapper`, and have a faux column effect on all three columns—totally stylin'!)

The code changes to do this are:

```
body {background:#BB9;}
```

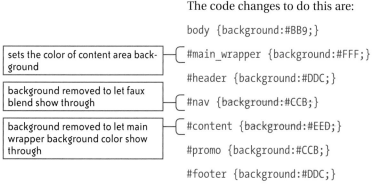

sets the color of content area background

```
#main_wrapper {background:#FFF;}

#header {background:#DDC;}
```

background removed to let faux blend show through

```
#nav {background:#CCB;}
```

background removed to let main wrapper background color show through

```
#content {background:#EED;}

#promo {background:#CCB;}

#footer {background:#DDC;}
```

Faux columns are a little time-consuming to execute, and if you change the column sizes, you have to go back and rework the graphics, but they let you create more interesting things than just solid backgrounds and solve the full-length column problem very nicely.

Programmatically Extend Columns (and Round Their Corners!)

Another way that you can have columns of equal length is to use JavaScript to determine which of the columns is the longest and have it match up to the length of the others. This type of application of JavaScript is known as *DOM scripting*. The Document Object Model is the browser's view of the hierarchy of all tags and all their attributes in your page. CSS uses the DOM to set tag attributes, but JavaScript is a powerful scripting language that can also get (as well as set) all the attributes of all elements in the DOM (such as the height of divs) and perform all kinds of processes on them. There are a number of JavaScript scripts out there that can enable you to match up the height of elements. They usually require you to identify the columns to be compared to the JavaScript, by adding the same class to each column div.

My favorite code to use for this purpose is NiftyCorners by Alessandro Fulciniti. Not only can this handy script instantly provide you with equal length columns, but it can also, as its name suggests, round the corners off any element. (The rounded-corner look quickly became the definitive design feature of the Web 2.0 sites.) Let's see how to use NiftyCorners to create equal length, rounded-corner columns for our three-column fixed-width layout that we saw earlier in the chapter.

Modification to the Nifty Cube File

Note that I have made a small mod to the niftycorners.js file so that it can be located somewhere other than in the same folder as the XHTML page, and can be referenced by multiple pages. All I did was modify one function in this file from this

```
function AddCss(){

niftyCss=true;

var l=CreateEl("link");

l.setAttribute("type","text/css");

l.setAttribute("rel","stylesheet");

l.setAttribute("href","niftyCorners.css");

l.setAttribute("media","screen");

document.getElementsByTagName("head")[0].appendChild(l);

}
```

to this

```
function AddCss(path){

niftyCss=true;

var l=CreateEl("link");

l.setAttribute("type","text/css");

l.setAttribute("rel","stylesheet");

l.setAttribute("href",path);

l.setAttribute("media","screen");

document.getElementsByTagName("head")[0].appendChild(l);

}
```

Now I can pass the relative path to the file from each XHTML page, as you can see from the three-column rounded-corners code. If you use the Nifty Corners version in the *Stylib* library, the above change is already made, but if you download a new version from the Nifty Cube site at http://www.html.it/articoli/niftycube/index.html, you will need to make these changes to make it work with the *Stylib* files.

For this example, I am using the three-column fixed-width layout we saw earlier, with the following changes (**Figure 5.16**).

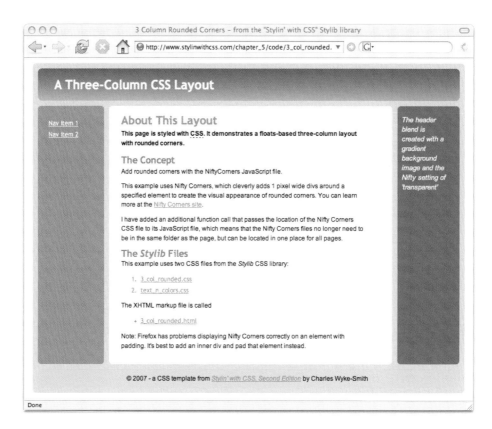

FIGURE 5.16 The NiftyCorners JavaScript can make several columns the same length and optionally round their corners.

The NiftyCorners JavaScript file needs to be linked from the head of the page like this

```
<script type="text/javascript" src="../../lib/nifty_corners/
javascript/niftycube.js"></script>
```

Then we add the code that associates the NiftyCorners code with the elements we want to extend.

```
<script type="text/javascript">

window.onload=function(){

Nifty("div#nav,div#content,div#promo","medium same-height");

Nifty("div#header,div#footer","medium");

AddCss ("../../lib/nifty_corners/css/niftyCorners.css");

}

</script>
```

the nav, content, and promo columns have medium radius rounding applied and are set to the same height

header and footer have medium radius rounding applied

provide relative path to the NiftyCorners.css file

With the appropriate settings applied to the columns, we now need to create space around them so the columns don't touch anymore. It would be very nice to simply apply the rounded corners to the inner divs, but the boxes don't display correctly if you do this—some of the rounded corners have strange-looking straight edges. So we are going to add margins around the main divs and then subtract the same amount off the width of the boxes so the layout retains its original width; it doesn't matter if the layout gets a little taller.

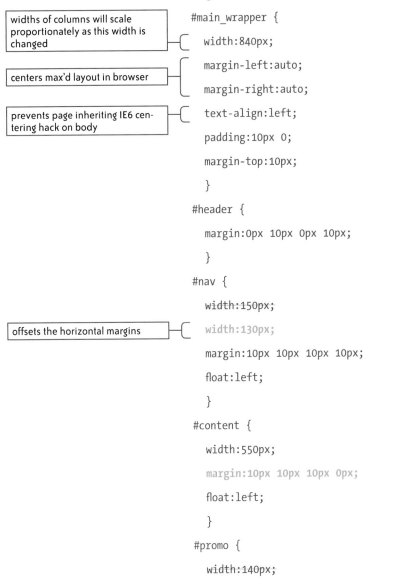

widths of columns will scale proportionately as this width is changed

centers max'd layout in browser

prevents page inheriting IE6 centering hack on body

offsets the horizontal margins

```
#main_wrapper {

    width:840px;

    margin-left:auto;

    margin-right:auto;

    text-align:left;

    padding:10px 0;

    margin-top:10px;

    }
#header {

    margin:0px 10px 0px 10px;

    }
#nav {

    width:150px;

    width:130px;

    margin:10px 10px 10px 10px;

    float:left;

    }
#content {

    width:550px;

    margin:10px 10px 10px 0px;

    float:left;

    }
#promo {

    width:140px;
```

offsets the horizontal margins applied to the content div

```
width:120px;

margin:10px 0 10px 0;

float:left;

}

#footer {

margin:0 10px;

clear:both;

}
```

Of course, the user must have JavaScript turned on in the browser, and about 95% of all users do (source: thecounter.com Oct 07 global stats). In this case, it's not a big deal if JavaScript is not on, as the only difference is that the boxes are not rounded but have regular square corners.

The total of horizontal margins added equals 40 pixels so I subtracted 20 pixels off both the left and right columns to maintain the 840 pixels width.

NiftyCorners ends the problem of creating adjustable-size rounded-corner boxes by adding as many as four background graphics to an element (XHTML elements can only have one background image), using techniques such as adding three extra span wrappers inside the div. The drawback of NiftyCorners is that you can't add curved borders; it has to be a block of solid color. The CSS3 spec includes curved corners, but only Firefox can currently render them.

An Absolutely-Positioned Layout

I said I would show one absolutely-positioned layout before the end of the chapter, so here is a three-column layout created using absolute positioning (**Figure 5.17**).

Let's start with the markup:

the olive class adds the 'olive' color scheme from text_n_colors.css

```
<body class="olive">

<div id="main_wrapper">

<div id="header">

  <div id="header_inner">

  <h2>Header</h2>

  </div>

</div>
```

```
<div id="content">

    <div id="content_inner">

    <h1>A Three-Column CSS Layout</h1>

        <p><strong>This page is styled with <abbr
        title="Cascading Style Sheets">CSS</abbr>...
```

content removed here to save space

```

        </p>

        </div>
```
end content inner_div

```
        <div id="footer">

        <div id="footer_inner"><p>The footer</p></div>

        </div>
```
end content div
```
    </div>


    <div id="nav">

        <div id="nav_inner">

            <ul>

            <li><a href="#">Link 1</a></li>

            <li><a href="#">Link 2</a></li>

            </ul>

        </div>

    </div>


    <div id="promo">

        <div id="promo_inner">

        <p>the promo area</p>

        </div>
```
end promo div
```
    </div>
```
end main wrapper
```
    </div>

    </body>
```

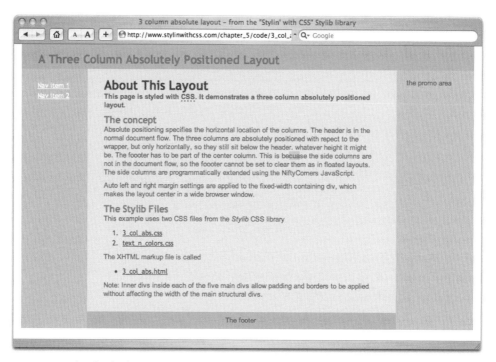

FIGURE 5.17 This absolutely-positioned layout includes the footer in the center column because the footer cannot clear the absolutely-positioned columns. If you can live with this limitation, this is an industrial-strength layout.

Most notable about this markup, in contrast to the floating layouts we have seen so far, is that the order of the divs in the markup does not reflect the order in which the elements appear on the page. The content area here directly follows the header, and the navigation and promo columns are at the very end. (You don't have to do this, but it is generally accepted that it helps search engine visibility to have the content as high in the markup as possible.) The footer is between the closing inner content div and the closing content div. Let's look at this markup step by step to more clearly understand what's going on here.

Because we are absolutely positioning the three columns, and positioning them on the page stating their left or right position (with respect to their positioning context, mainwrapper—see the CSS below), it doesn't matter what order we state them in the markup. It's as if we are pinning the columns next to each other to the page at the specified point, like postcards on a corkboard, so the order in which we do that doesn't matter.

Here's the CSS that creates the page layout, with the all-important positioning rules highlighted:

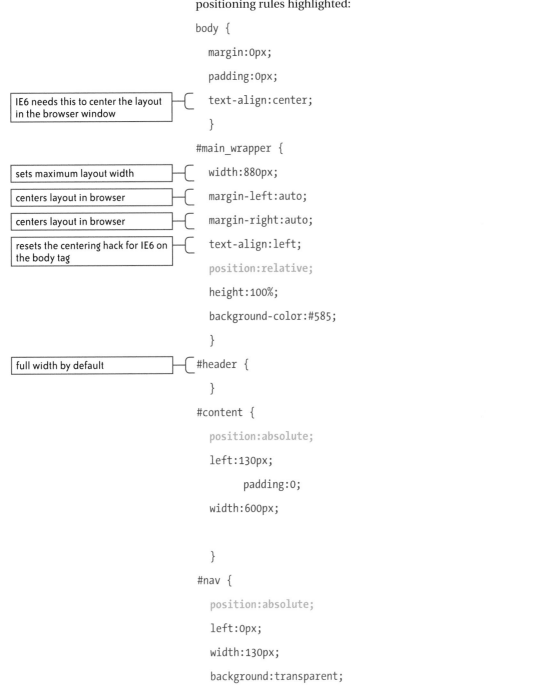

```
body {

    margin:0px;

    padding:0px;

    text-align:center;

}
```

IE6 needs this to center the layout in the browser window

```
#main_wrapper {

    width:880px;

    margin-left:auto;

    margin-right:auto;

    text-align:left;

    position:relative;

    height:100%;

    background-color:#585;

}
```

sets maximum layout width

centers layout in browser

centers layout in browser

resets the centering hack for IE6 on the body tag

```
#header {

}
```

full width by default

```
#content {

    position:absolute;

    left:130px;

        padding:0;

    width:600px;


}
#nav {

    position:absolute;

    left:0px;

    width:130px;

    background:transparent;
```

```
        margin-bottom:300px;

        }

    #promo {

        position:absolute;

        right:0px;

        width:150px;

        background:transparent;

        }
```

full width by default ──┤ `#footer {`

```
        }
```

prevents oversize elements from
breaking the layout ──┤ `#header_inner, #nav_inner, #content_inner, #promo_inner {`

```
        overflow:hidden;

        }

    #header_inner {

        padding:1em 2em;

        }

    #nav_inner {

        margin:1em 1.2em;

        }

    #content_inner {

        margin:2em 2.5em 0em 2em;

        padding:0;

        }

    #promo_inner {

        margin:1em 1.2em;

        }

    #footer_inner {

        text-align:center;

        }
```

As I mentioned at the top of the chapter, absolutely-positioned elements like these columns are out of the document flow, so they can't push a footer down like the columns in the floated layouts we've looked at. Unless we resort to using some JavaScript and adding several classes to the markup (see http://www.shauninman.com/archive/2004/05/14/clear_positioned_elements), there is a small compromise that we need to make with respect to the footer. If we want it to always be positioned at the bottom of the layout, it cannot be full width and can only be the width of the content column, as illustrated by **Figure 5.17**. I don't think that's a big deal, especially if we use NiftyCorners to match up the column lengths and give a nice, finished look to the layout. To move the footer into the content area, I placed the footer markup inside of the main content div but outside of the content inner div. This allows the footer to extend the full width of the content area and not be affected by the padding on the content's inner div.

The key piece of code in this CSS is the `position:relative` on the `mainwrapper` div. This provides the positioning context for the absolutely-positioned columns. Without this, the columns would always position themselves with respect to the body and attach themselves to the edge of the browser window. Positioned with respect to `mainwrapper`, which is itself a fixed width and centered in the browser window, the columns become part of a layout that can position itself in the middle of the page once the width of the browser window exceeds the stated width of the layout.

So this brings us to the end of this chapter on layouts. In Chapter 6, we will look at interface components, such as menus, tables, and forms, and then in the final chapter, we will see how to combine the templates from this chapter and the components from Chapter 6 to create complete Web page layouts.

Designing Interface Components

I USE *interface components* as my term for all the supporting elements of your page's content: lists, menus, forms, tables, and so on. In this chapter, we will look at how these components should be written in XHTML to be valid and accessible, and then see how to style them with CSS in a variety of ways to meet the design needs of your projects.

Let's start with tables.

Styling Tables

It's widely known that tables have been misused in the past to create page layouts full of presentational markup. However, that does not mean that we shouldn't embrace the use of tables for their designated purpose—laying out grids of data in rows and columns in the same manner as a spreadsheet is laid out in Microsoft Excel.

Here's a default table displayed in Firefox (**Figure 6.1**).

FIGURE 6.1 Default table display with borders turned on using the XHTML border attribute.

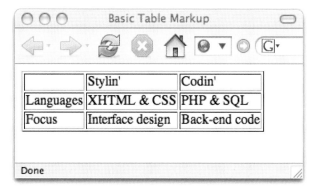

The markup looks like this:

```
<table border="1">

  <tr>

    <td> </td>

    <td>Stylin'</td>

    <td>Codin'</td>

  </tr>

  <tr>

    <td>Languages</td>

    <td>XHTML &amp; CSS</td>

    <td>PHP &amp; SQL</td>

  </tr>

  <tr>

    <td>Focus</td>

    <td>Interface design</td>
```

```
        <td>Back-end code</td>

    </tr>

</table>
```

The above screenshot is how we are used to seeing tables displayed. Observe how I've added the highlighted presentational border style on the table tag to turn on the grid; otherwise, the data would just float on the page, and it would be hard to see the relationships of the columns and rows. We'll remove it shortly.

Every designer should devour the work of Edward Tufte, starting with the dry-sounding but utterly fascinating book The Visual Display of Quantitative Information, 2nd Edition, *Cheshire, CT: Graphics Press. ISBN 0961392142. Essential reading.*

There is an awful lot of what Edward Tufte would call "chart-junk" in this default display. The boxes around the table and around every data point attract your eye more than the data itself.

The markup is also very minimal—a table element contains three table rows tr, each of which contains three table data td elements (cells).

Let's look at some ways we can improve the visual appearance of this table. We'll begin with some improvements to the markup that will give us both plenty of hooks for our CSS, and, most importantly, more clearly indicate the relationships between the data elements.

FIGURE 6.2 The improved markup makes the meaning of the table clearer to both sighted users and to low-vision users who rely on screen readers.

	Stylin'	Codin'
Languages	XHTML & CSS	PHP & SQL
Focus	Interface design	Back-end code

My Books (window title: Basic Table Markup)

Talking screen readers have a hard time with tables; without additional help, they read the heading row first and then the data row by row, which is not an ideal way for a person with low vision to hear the information. Just try reading the table information above aloud to someone so they understand it. You really need to state the names of the labels before you read each of the data points in the columns (or rows, depending on how you decide to read it), and good markup can help a screen reader do just that. Let's give our table markup a semantic tune-up (see **Figure 6.2**).

```
<table border="1" summary="Summary of my books">

  <caption>

    <strong>My Books</strong>

  </caption>

  <tr>

    <th scope="col"> </th>

    <th scope="col">Stylin'</th>

    <th scope="col">Codin'</th>

  </tr>

  <tr>

    <th scope="row">Languages</th>

    <td>XHTML &amp; CSS</td>

    <td>PHP &amp; SQL</td>

  </tr>

  <tr>

    <th scope="row">Focus</th>

    <td>Interface design</td>

    <td>Back-end code</td>

  </tr>

</table>
```

For a more in-depth discussion of the use of these table elements in creating accessible markup, read Zoe Gillianwater's article "Using Tables Appropriately" at http://www. communitymx.com/content/article. cfm?cid=0BEA6.

Much better. Note that our table markup now has a summary attribute, a caption tag, and most importantly, table headings (th) that differentiate the heading cells from the data cells, which by default display bold. Each of these headings has a scope attribute that indicates whether it relates to a column or a row.

Now that we have some better markup, we can remove the border="1" attribute from the table tag, and replace it with a class that we can use in our style sheet to target all the elements of our table.

```
<table class="basic_lines" border="1" summary="Summary of my books">
```

Now we just see the data (see **Figure 6.3**).

FIGURE 6.3 Without any cell borders, it's not so easy to see the relationships in the data.

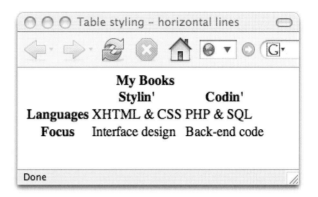

My objective when styling tables is to add the minimal amount of visual elements to enable the user to make sense of the data. For example, let's see if we can avoid using any vertical lines at all, like this (see **Figure 6.4**):

```
table.basic_lines {

    width:300px;

    border-top:3px solid #069;

}
```

sets the width on the layout

a top border for the table

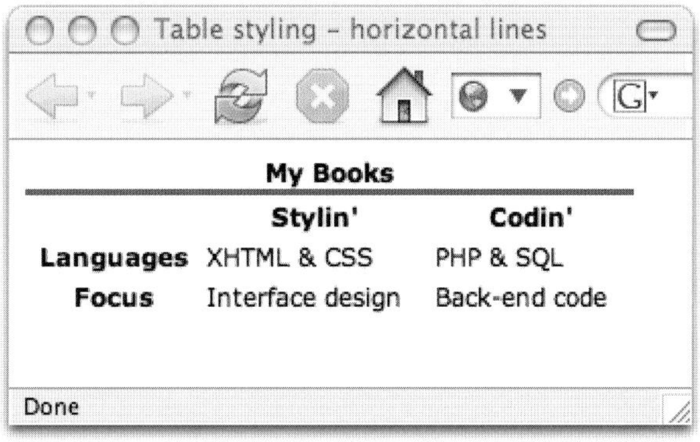

FIGURE 6.4 We start styling by putting a thick border across the top of the table. Note the caption by default displays outside the table, even though it is within its tags.

A sans-serif font family and a crisp blue line under the caption (which appears above the table even though it follows the table tag in the markup) make a good start. Now let's add some lines to the headings and data (see **Figure 6.5**).

```
body {

    font: .8em verdana, sans-serif;

    }

table.basic_lines {

    width:300px;

    border-top:3px solid #069;

    }

table.basic_lines th {

    border-bottom:2px solid #069;

    }

table.basic_lines td {

    border-bottom:1px solid #069;

    }
```

FIGURE 6.5 A mix of thick and thin lines helps further differentiate the data from the headings. But what's with those little gaps in the lines?

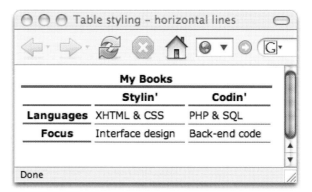

Quite nice. Now a little cleanup is all that's needed. Let's create some space around the text and close up those gaps in the lines (see **Figure 6.6**).

```
body {

    font: .8em verdana, sans-serif;

    }

table.basic_lines {

    width:300px;
```

removes the space between the cells ⎯⎤

```
    border-collapse:collapse;

    border-top:3px solid #069;

    }
table.basic_lines caption {
```

space between the table and the caption ⎯⎤

```
    margin-bottom:6px;

    }
table.basic_lines th {

    border-bottom:2px solid #069;

    }
table.basic_lines td {

    border-bottom:1px solid #069;

    }
table.basic_lines td, table.basic_lines th {
```

some space around the text in each cell ⎯⎤

```
    padding:5px 3px;

    }
```

FIGURE 6.6 The finished styling gives a clean, minimalist look to the table that aids understanding instead of distracting from the data.

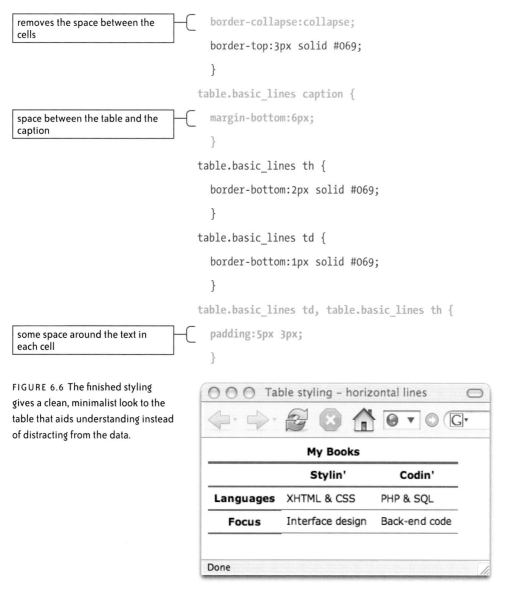

Table styling – horizontal lines

	My Books	
	Stylin'	**Codin'**
Languages	XHTML & CSS	PHP & SQL
Focus	Interface design	Back-end code

Done

Note the use of the border-collapse property on the table tag. Border collapsing reduces that double border we saw in the default style to a single border line between the two cells. We aren't showing the vertical lines on this table, but if we were, there would be one on the edge of each cell with a space between them, as we saw in the default style example earlier. Because we weren't displaying those vertical lines, we were just seeing the space, and by collapsing the borders, that space is closed up. I also added a little padding inside the cells to give the text some breathing space, and put a few pixels of space between the caption and the table. We end up with a simple, clean look, especially when compared with the 10-box default version with which we started.

Now that you understand the basics of table markup, let's take a look at the complete markup for a variation on the same markup, shown in **Figure 6.7**, which I call Bars-n-Stripes.

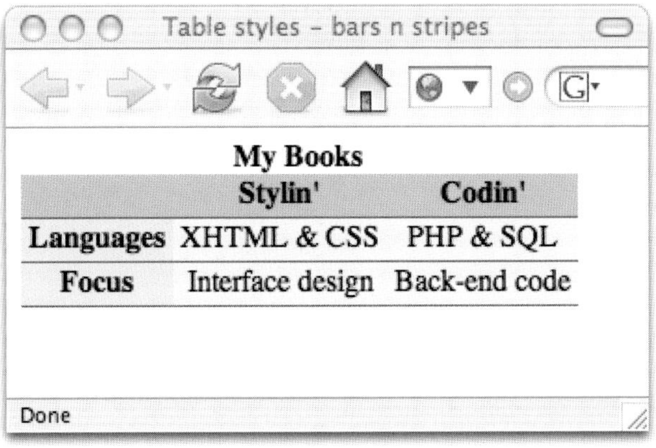

FIGURE 6.7 A different styling of the same markup, but this time with colored backgrounds.

```
table.bars_n_stripes {

    width:300px;

    border-collapse:collapse;

    }

table.bars_n_stripes td {
```

table data area ──┤ `    background-color:#FFFFCC;`

```
    }
```

labels column ──┤ `table.bars_n_stripes th {`

```
    background-color:#CCFFCC;

    }
```

headings row ──┤ `table.bars_n_stripes th[scope="col"] {`

colors top row of cells—IDWIMIE (previous rule applies to IE6) ──┤ `    background-color:#99CCCC;`

```
    }
```

some space between the text and the edge of each cell

a thin line under each row of the table

```
table.bars_n_stripes td, table.bars_n_stripes th  {

   padding:3px 3px;

   border-bottom:1px solid #069;

}
```

This table has a 300-pixel fixed width. If you remove that setting, the table will widen as you add more text.

After the previous example, this one is quite easy to understand, with one notable comment. You'll notice the use of a pseudo-class attribute selector—the rule only applies if the element has the attribute scope="col". This enables me to target rules at the top row of cells and get that deep green-blue color on just the top row. Of course, poor old IE6 doesn't understand pseudo-classes so the result in IE6 is that the top row is the same green as the Languages and Focus cells, but it's still an acceptable result. This is what's known as "graceful degradation," or "progressive enhancement" to the perennially positive amongst us; either way, what it means is that some people, depending on their viewing setup, get a better experience than others, but as I like to say, as long as everyone gets an *acceptable* experience, that's OK. This comment leads me right to my last table example, which only Safari and Firefox are capable of displaying exactly as I intend, but which all other browsers make an acceptable job of displaying.

> ### Most People Only Use One Browser at a Time
>
> Something that frequently happens to me is that one of the designers I am working with shows me something that looks OK in, say, IE6, and then says "But look how much better it looks in Firefox! What will people say?" My answer is "Nothing!" People who see the site in IE6 aren't looking at it in both IE6 and Firefox. Only geeks like us do that. As long as the site looks OK to IE6 users, with nothing obviously broken, they have no idea what they are missing. My point: Don't obsess about getting everything to look exactly the same in every browser—it can't be done, and only you know how "perfect" actually looks.

In this next table layout, which for obvious reasons I call *tic-tac-toe*, the outer edges of outer cells of the table do not have borders on them. It doesn't matter how many rows and columns the table has—the outer edge cells don't have outer borders, but all the inner cells have borders on all four sides. I've duplicated the table cells in the markup in both directions so you can see the effect better. The final styling is shown in **Figures 6.8 and 6.9.**

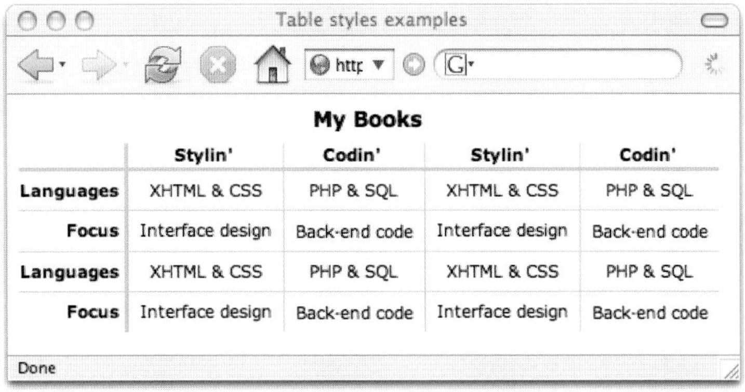

FIGURE 6.8 The open edges of the outer cells of this "tic-tac-toe"-style table are achieved with attribute selectors and pseudo-classes.

Achieving this effect required extensive use of pseudo-classes, which IE6 doesn't understand, but the design degrades quite gracefully in that browser.

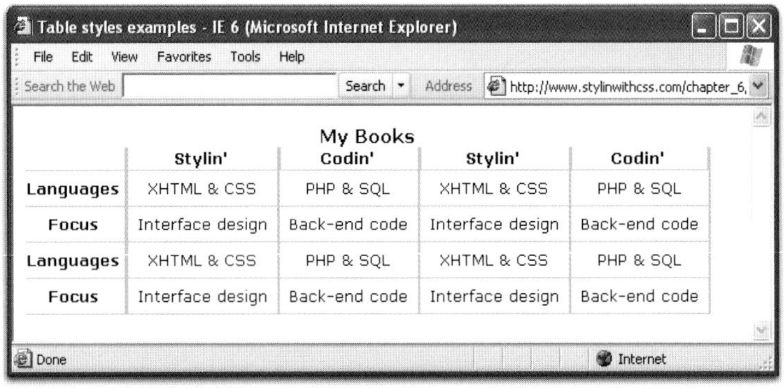

FIGURE 6.9 IE6 doesn't understand pseudo-classes, so it cannot render all the details of this design as specified in the pseudo-class rules. However, the presentation is still quite pleasing.

Let's start at the beginning to see how it was created.

```
table {
    border-collapse:collapse;
}
table.tic_tac_toe td {
    border-right: 1px solid #99CCCC;
    border-bottom: 1px solid #99CCCC;
}
```

creates the grid of table cells

labels column (and headings until we override below)

```
table.tic_tac_toe th {

    border-right:3px solid #99CCCC;

    border-bottom: 1px solid #99CCCC;

    padding-right:.3em;

}
```

I started by styling the borders of the td and th cells. The table cells share borders once I collapse them. Because I didn't want the top and left borders on the outer edges, I simply styled the bottom and right border of every cell, which resulted in **Figure 6.9**.

As noted, this is also the total extent to which IE, with its almost nonexistent pseudo-class support, can render this example. On to the more compliant browsers.

Let's deal with the top row next. You can see that I need to get a thicker line under the headings row and have every right border on the headings be thin, except for the first one. Let's add a couple of selectors to do that (see **Figure 6.10**).

headings row

```
table.tic_tac_toe th[scope="col"] {

    border-right:1px solid #99CCCC;

    border-bottom:3px solid #99CCCC;

}
```

first cell of headings row

```
table.tic_tac_toe th[scope="col"]:first-child {

    border-right:3px solid #99CCCC;

}
```

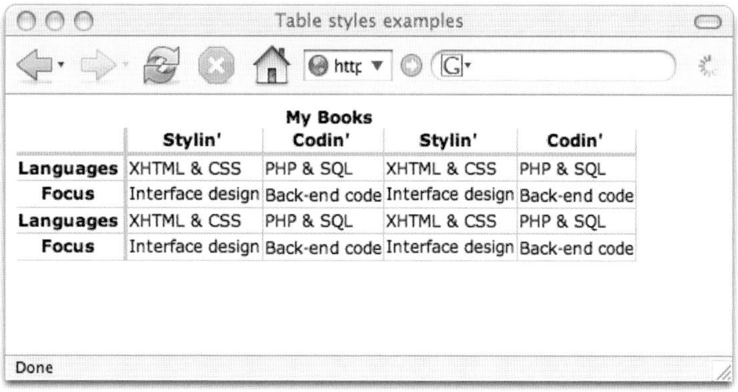

FIGURE 6.10 The borders on the heading rows are now styled.

	Stylin'	Codin'	Stylin'	Codin'
		My Books		
Languages	XHTML & CSS	PHP & SQL	XHTML & CSS	PHP & SQL
Focus	Interface design	Back-end code	Interface design	Back-end code
Languages	XHTML & CSS	PHP & SQL	XHTML & CSS	PHP & SQL
Focus	Interface design	Back-end code	Interface design	Back-end code

I use an attribute selector to target the top row—the th cells with col scope—to set all their right borders to 1 pixel and the left borders to 3 pixels. Then I need to get the right border of just the first cell of the first row to go back to being 3 pixels. To target just this cell, I combine an attribute selector with the first-child pseudo class, like this: th[scope="col"]:first-child, which means "the first th with the scope of col", and then I style its right border to be 3 pixels thick.

All that's now left to do is to take the bottom and right border off the bottom and right cells of the table, respectively. Their current styles are the right and bottom borders we added to the ths and tds in the first step. Let's start with the ths.

First, we need to target the right border of the last cell of the heading's row (the last th with the scope of row) and the bottom border of the heading's column (the last th with the scope of col).

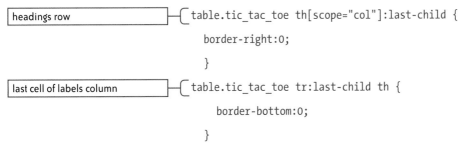

headings row

```
table.tic_tac_toe th[scope="col"]:last-child {

    border-right:0;

}
```

last cell of labels column

```
table.tic_tac_toe tr:last-child th {

    border-bottom:0;

}
```

Now let's remove the bottom borders of the last row of the table (actually of that row's cells—the tds) and the right borders of the last column of tds, as shown in **Figure 6.11**.

FIGURE 6.11 The bottom borders are removed from the bottom row of cells, and the right borders are removed from the right-most column of cells.

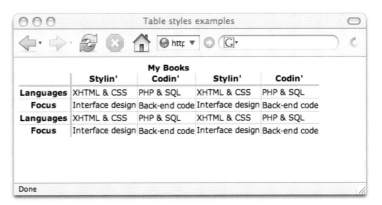

		My Books		
	Stylin'	**Codin'**	**Stylin'**	**Codin'**
Languages	XHTML & CSS	PHP & SQL	XHTML & CSS	PHP & SQL
Focus	Interface design	Back-end code	Interface design	Back-end code
Languages	XHTML & CSS	PHP & SQL	XHTML & CSS	PHP & SQL
Focus	Interface design	Back-end code	Interface design	Back-end code

```
table.tic_tac_toe tr:last-child td {

    border-bottom: 0;
```

```
    }

    table.tic_tac_toe td:last-child {

        border-right:0;

    }
```

The first selector targets the cells of the last row of the table. The second selector simply needs to say td:last-child because the last cell of each row is a last child; its parent is the table row. Here's the finished code. The selectors are in a slightly different order from the step-by-step, partly for clarity and partly because some of them need to be where they are to override preceding styles.

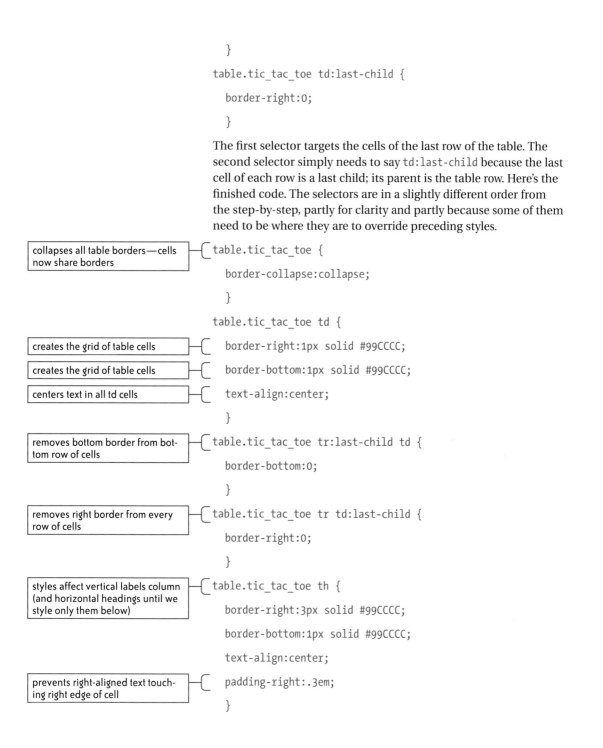

```
                          ┌─ table.tic_tac_toe {
collapses all table borders—cells ─┤
now share borders          └─
                               border-collapse:collapse;

                            }

                            table.tic_tac_toe td {

creates the grid of table cells ─┤─       border-right:1px solid #99CCCC;

creates the grid of table cells ─┤─       border-bottom:1px solid #99CCCC;

centers text in all td cells ─┤─       text-align:center;

                            }

removes bottom border from bot- ─┤─ table.tic_tac_toe tr:last-child td {
tom row of cells            └─
                               border-bottom:0;

                            }

removes right border from every ─┤─ table.tic_tac_toe tr td:last-child {
row of cells                └─
                               border-right:0;

                            }

styles affect vertical labels column ─┤─ table.tic_tac_toe th {
(and horizontal headings until we
style only them below)          border-right:3px solid #99CCCC;

                               border-bottom:1px solid #99CCCC;

                               text-align:center;

prevents right-aligned text touch- ─┤─       padding-right:.3em;
ing right edge of cell
                            }
```

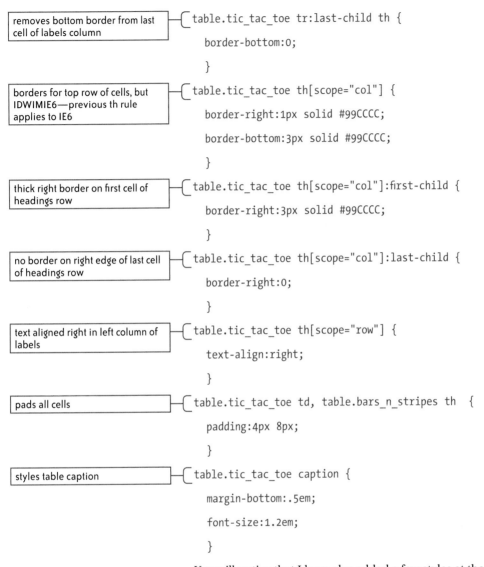

removes bottom border from last
cell of labels column
```
table.tic_tac_toe tr:last-child th {

    border-bottom:0;

}
```

borders for top row of cells, but
IDWIMIE6—previous th rule
applies to IE6
```
table.tic_tac_toe th[scope="col"] {

    border-right:1px solid #99CCCC;

    border-bottom:3px solid #99CCCC;

}
```

thick right border on first cell of
headings row
```
table.tic_tac_toe th[scope="col"]:first-child {

    border-right:3px solid #99CCCC;

}
```

no border on right edge of last cell
of headings row
```
table.tic_tac_toe th[scope="col"]:last-child {

    border-right:0;

}
```

text aligned right in left column of
labels
```
table.tic_tac_toe th[scope="row"] {

    text-align:right;

}
```

pads all cells
```
table.tic_tac_toe td, table.bars_n_stripes th {

    padding:4px 8px;

}
```

styles table caption
```
table.tic_tac_toe caption {

    margin-bottom:.5em;

    font-size:1.2em;

}
```

You will notice that I have also added a few styles at the end to align
the headings' column text to the right, and to provide some space
around the text, as you can see in **Figure 6.12**. Note I hide from IE
the text-align:right on the left column by using an attribute selector, which IE doesn't understand. If I did it any other way then *all*
headings would be right-aligned, which would look wrong along the
top row of headings; they really have to be centered. IE6 users simply see the left column of headings centered also, as shown in the
previous screenshot—graceful enough, I think.

FIGURE 6.12 The finished "tic-tac-toe" table.

My Books				
	Stylin'	**Codin'**	**Stylin'**	**Codin'**
Languages	XHTML & CSS	PHP & SQL	XHTML & CSS	PHP & SQL
Focus	Interface design	Back-end code	Interface design	Back-end code
Languages	XHTML & CSS	PHP & SQL	XHTML & CSS	PHP & SQL
Focus	Interface design	Back-end code	Interface design	Back-end code

This section of the chapter was intended to give you a sense of what's possible with styling tables to make them a visually appealing area of your page and to draw focus to the information in your data; they don't have to be a boring bunch of boxes that your viewer's eye skips over as fast as possible. I'll finish by saying there are other XHTML elements associated with tables that I haven't covered here. If you really want to become an XHTML table expert, take a look at an article (and the pages linked to the article) called "Bring on the Tables" on Roger Johansson's excellent 456 Berea Street site at http://www.456bereastreet.com/archive/200410/bring_on_the_tables/.

Styling Forms

Processing form data is outside of the scope of this book, but if you want to learn how forms send data to a server, check if that data is valid (for example , if e-mail addresses have an @ in them), present any errors back to user for correction and then write validated data into a file or a database, check out my book, Codin' for the Web, *also published by New Riders. It's written to be the next step in building your Web development skills after you have mastered the techniques shown here in* Stylin'.

Forms are vital to most Web sites because they are the means by which user-entered data can be sent from the browser across the Internet to the site's Web server. From simple log-ins and sign-ups, through to multi-page e-commerce checkouts, forms are everywhere, and understanding how to create them is a key skill for every Web developer. Because of their importance, I am going to start by showing you in some detail how forms work and how their XHTML is written before moving on to ways in which you can style them.

How Forms Work

The purpose of a form is to gather various pieces of data from the user. When the form is submitted, usually by clicking a button, the form data, structured as a set of name/value pairs, such as user_name=tracey, is passed to the server to be processed by a server-side script written in a language such as PHP, Java, or Perl. Even though you might not be the person writing that server-side code, you need to know how to create forms in XHTML so that they send the correctly structured data to the server for processing when the user hits the Submit button.

Form Markup

Here's a form, shown in **Figure 6.13**, that uses each of the different types of XHTML form elements.

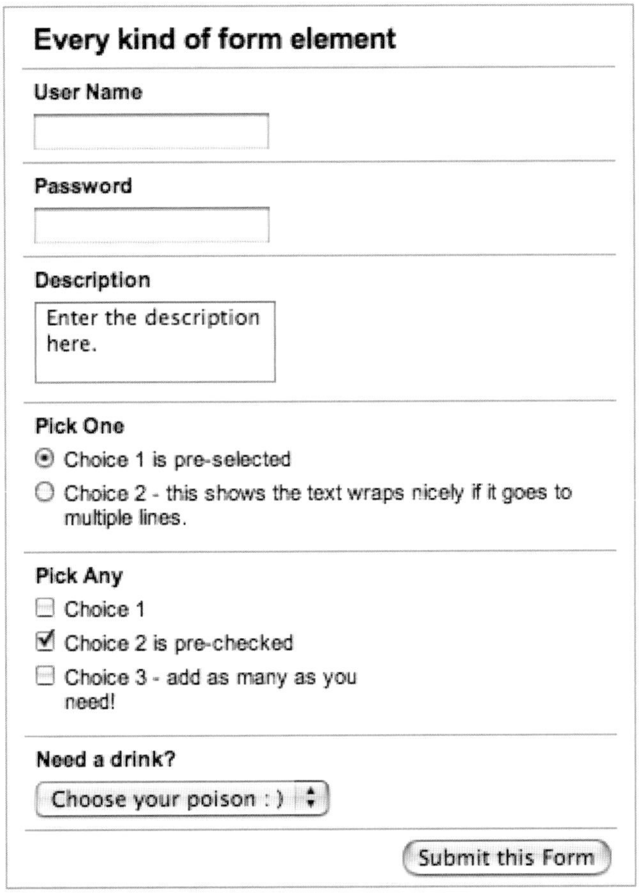

FIGURE 6.13 This example uses each of the different types of form elements.

Here's the code for this form

```
<body>

<!-- FORM WIITH LABELS ABOVE INPUT FIELDS -->

<div class="two_col_form">
```

```
<form action="process_form.php" method="post">

<div class="formsection">

  <h3>Every kind of form element</h3>

  <ul class="">

    <li>This list can be used to provide general info about
    filling the form</li>

    <li>Use this list also to display errors in the form.
    Adding an "error" class to the ul will turn the text
    red.</li>

    <li>You can cut and paste the form elements to create
    a form for your needs and it will automatically style
    itself to look like this one.</li>

  </ul>

</div>

<div class="formsection">

  <label for="user_name">User Name</label>

  <input type="text" id="user_name" name="user_name"
  size="18" maxlength="36" tabindex="1" />

</div>

<div class="formsection">

  <label for="password">Password</label>

  <input type="password" id="password" name="password"
  size="18" maxlength="20" tabindex="2" />

</div>

<div class="formsection">

  <label for="description">Description</label>

  <textarea id="description" name="description" rows="3"
  cols="14" tabindex="3">Enter the description here.
  </textarea>

</div>

<div class="formsection clearfix">

  <label for="radioset">Pick One</label>

    <div class="buttongroup" id="radioset">
```

add class="message" to display the list—for displaying errors etc.

a single line text field

end single line text field

a password field

end password field

a multi-line text field

end multi-line text field

radio buttons

```
                              <input checked="checked" id="radio1" name="radioset"
                              type="radio" value = "Choice_1" />

                                  <label for="radio1">Choice 1 is pre-selected</label>

                              <input id="radio2" name="radioset" type="radio"
                              value="Choice_2" />

                              <label for="radio2">Choice 2 - this shows the text wraps
                              nicely if it goes to multiple lines.</label>
```

| end buttongroup |⊢⊂ ` </div>`
| end radio buttons |⊢⊂ `</div>`
| checkboxes |⊢⊂ `<div class="formsection clearfix">`

```
                          <label for="checkset">Pick Any</label>

                            <div class="buttongroup clearfix" id="checkset">

                                <input type="checkbox" id="check1" name="checkset" value
                                = "1" tabindex="4" />

                              <label for="check1">Choice 1</label>

                              <input type="checkbox" checked="checked" id="check2"
                              name="checkset" value = "2" />

                                  <label for="check2">Choice 2 is pre-checked</label>

                              <input type="checkbox"  id="check3" name="checkset" value =
                              "3" />

                                  <label for="check3">Choice 3 - add as many as you
                                  need!</label>
```

| end buttongroup |⊢⊂ ` </div>`
| end checkboxes |⊢⊂ `</div>`
| the select, a.k.a. pop-up menu |⊢⊂ `<div class="formsection">`

```
                          <label>Need a drink?</label>

                              <select id="drink_choice" name="drink_choice">

                              <option value="0">Choose your poison : )</option>

                              <option value="tea">Tea</option>

                              <option value="coffee">Coffee</option>

                              <option value="water">Water</option>
```

```
                      <option value="beer">Beer</option>

                   </select>
```

end select — `</div>`

input must be wrapped in a block level element to validate — `<div>`

submit button — `<input type="submit" value="Submit this Form" />`

```
                   </div>

                </form>

             </div>

          </body>
```

Displaying a list of errors at the top of a form, after it is submitted and re-displayed to the user for corrections, is a common but rather basic way to handle errors. In many sites today, real-time validation using "no-page-refresh" Ajax techniques (if you don't know what Ajax is, see Jesse James Garrett's famous article which defined the Ajax term at http://www. adaptivepath.com/publications/ essays/archives/000385.php) enables any errors to be displayed right by the form fields as soon as the user finishes typing text into them. These kinds of interactions, while user-friendly, are somewhat complex to implement. I'll just illustrate the tried and tested methods of displaying errors at the top of the form and encourage you, for an example, to look at how the applications produced by 37signals.com do a great job of real-time Ajax-based form validation.

Let's look at the markup of each of the areas of this form in turn; each section is divided by a thin rule in the screenshot. In the markup, each section is contained in a div with the class `formsection`.

The first `formsection` div doesn't contain form elements, but a list. This list can be used to display instructions to the user, but its primary purpose is to display errors. As in **Figure 6.13,** this list is usually hidden (its display property is set to none). The server-side code (e.g., PHP) would add a customized version of this list, adding the class that makes it appear and the list items with error messages, into the page before re-presenting the page to the user so he can understand and correct the problems, and resubmit the form.

So even if you are not personally writing server-side code, you can set up the XHTML and CSS for a form so it is capable of displaying error messages and then work with the site's technical team to ensure that the server-side code adds the appropriate text and classes into the code to display errors as you intended.

Now let's look at the markup of the previous form in detail.

THE FORM ELEMENT

Every form is enclosed in a `form` element.

```
<form class="2_col_form" action="process_form.php"
method="post">
```

The class `two_col_form` associates the form with the CSS that styles it. The other two attributes of this form, `action` and `method`, are always required. `action` determines which page on the server holds the code that will process the form. (Often that processing code is placed in the same page of form itself, which, just like CSS, can be embedded in the head of a page. That code will run once the form is submitted by the user.) method determines how the data is passed to the server; post causes it to be passed invisibly in the HTTP header, and get causes it to be passed in the URL string.

FORM CONTROLS

Contained within the opening and closing form tags can be any number of form text fields, radio buttons, checkboxes, and selects, known collectively as form controls. (Form controls into which you can enter text are commonly known as *fields*.) Each control should have a label tag that associates the label with the control. The label tag is important if screen readers are going to make sense of your form, for reasons you will discover in a moment. Don't use a paragraph or a heading tag to label form controls.

The first three sections of this form illustrate the three types of text entry elements: text, password, and textarea.

THE TEXT INPUT CONTROL

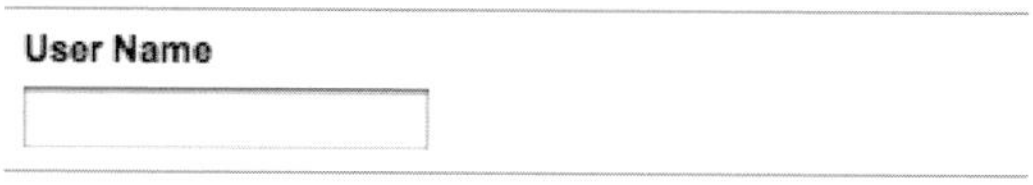

FIGURE 6.14 A single-line text field.

User Name

text is an input element for a single line of text, as shown in **Figure 6.14**, such as User Name. The basic format of a text field is

```
<label for="user_name">User Name</label>

  <input type="text" id="user_name" name="user_name"
  size="18" maxlength="36" tabindex="1" />
```

Forms controls are mostly based on the tag input, and the input's type attribute determines its appearance (a text field or radio button, for example). This input has the type text, which makes it appear as a single-line text field.

The control's id attribute associates it with the correct label tag; note how the label's for attribute and the control's id attribute match. The name attribute is used as the name part of the name/value pair passed to the server when the form is submitted; in this case, if the user enters the user name *css whiz*, then the name/value pair passed to the server from this control would be user_name=css whiz.

The size attribute determines how much text is visible in the control and therefore its width—in this case, 18 characters. The maxlength determines how many characters can be entered into the control, in this case, 36 characters.

THE PASSWORD INPUT CONTROL

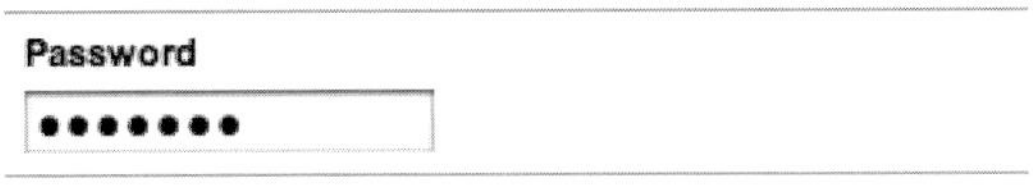

FIGURE 6.15 Although visually similar to the single line text field, text typed into a password field displays as a row of dots.

Password

••••••••

```
<input id="password" type="password" size="18" tabindex="2" />
```

An input with the type password is also a single-line field, as shown in **Figure 6.15**, and all the above applies to its markup too, but the user-typed text appears on-screen as a row of dots to prevent someone reading your password as you type it in. Note, however, the text typed is sent to the server as "clear text"; that is, it is not encrypted and is sent over the Internet to the server just like any other text from the form. If text is transmitted over a secure connection (look for https at the start of the page's URL), then it is encrypted as it sent between the browser and the server. E-commerce sites use this type of connection for payment transactions.

THE TEXTAREA INPUT CONTROL

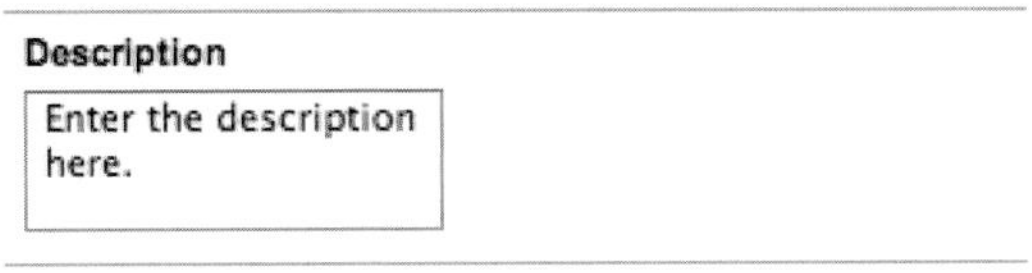

FIGURE 6.16 Whenever you want the user to be able to enter more than just a few words, use a multi-line Textarea field.

Description

Enter the description here.

```
<textarea id="description" name="description" rows="3"
cols="14" tabindex="3" >Enter the description here.
</textarea>
```

A textarea is a multi-line text field, as shown in **Figure 6.16**. Unlike the other text form elements, the text area's markup is an enclosing tag, and you can add text between the opening and closing tag to have default text display the field when the page loads, as illustrated by the highlighted text in the code above. The rows and cols attributes set the width and height respectively of the text area; if the user types more lines than defined by the rows attribute, a scroll bar appears so all the entered text can be reviewed.

THE RADIO BUTTON INPUT

Pick One

⦿ Choice 1 is pre-selected

○ Choice 2 - this shows the text wraps nicely if it goes to
  multiple lines.

```
<input checked="checked" id="radio1" name="radioset"
type="radio" value="Choice_1" />
```

Radio buttons , as shown in **Figure 6.17** , allow the user to indicate a choice; they are mutually exclusive, meaning the user can only pick one. If the user changes her mind and clicks another button, the first choice de-selects (just like the buttons on your car radio, hence the name). Use radio buttons for selections where there is only one possible choice from two or more selections. A group of radio buttons is created by giving each input in the group the same name attribute; then they interact correctly and only one can be selected at any time. Because there is no user-entered data associated with radio buttons, the value attribute determines the data to be passed if that particular radio button is selected. Note also you can add the checked attribute to one of the radio buttons in a set to have it pre-selected when the page loads.

THE CHECKBOX INPUT CONTROL

Pick Any

☐ Choice 1

☑ Choice 2 is pre-checked

☐ Choice 3 - add as many as you
  need!

```
<input name="checkset" id="check1" type="checkbox" size="35"
value = "Choice_1" tabindex="4" />
```

The only difference betweeen checkboxes and radio buttons as described above is that checkboxes, as shown in **Figure 6.18**, are not mutually exclusive and the user can check as many in a group as he wishes. Use checkboxes where the user might select several or all of the choices—the tomato, lettuce, onion, and pickle fixins in that online sandwich order, for example.

THE SELECT CONTROL

FIGURE 6.19 A Select input allows the user to make a selection from a number of choices in a pop-up menu.

Need a drink?

Choose your poison :) ⬍

```
<select name="drink_choice">

    <option value="0">Choose your poison : )</option>

    <option value="tea">Tea</option>

    <option value="coffee">Coffee</option>

    <option value="water">Water</option>

    <option value="beer">Beer</option>

</select>
```

The next form element is the select, shown in **Figure 6.19**, which is better known by the term *pop-up menu*. I think it's pretty clear how a select works from the markup above; just note that the name/value pair passed to the server is the value of the name attribute of the select element and the value of the value attribute of the selected choice, drink_choice=tea, for example.

THE SUBMIT BUTTON INPUT CONTROL

FIGURE 6.20 Clicking the Submit button causes all the form data to be submitted to the URL specified in the action attribute of the form element.

Submit this Form

input must be wrapped in a block level element to validate

```
<div>

<input type="submit" value="Submit this Form" />

</div>
```

Finally, there is the Submit button, shown in **Figure 6.20**, which rather confusingly is an also an input element, just like a text field, but which magically becomes a button when its type attribute is submit. The value attribute simply determines the text that appears on the button. Note that you can't just drop inline elements into the page when the DOCTYPE is Strict—the immutable laws of XML demand that inline elements be enclosed in an appropriate block level element, and according to the W3C validator, form just doesn't cut it for an `input` element. So, just like all the other controls on this page, I give the Submit button `input` a div parent.

So now that you understand how a form is marked up, let's get stylin'.

Form Styling

Here's the CSS for the form shown in **Figure 6.12**. There is nothing here you haven't seen before. Most of the floating is used to wrap divs around inner floated elements. This saves me from having to resort to using the `clearfix` code I described in Chapter 4.

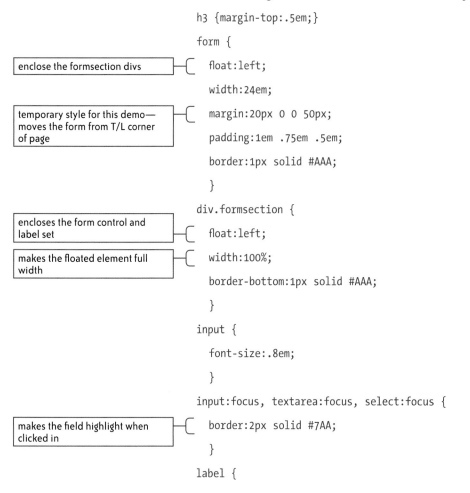

```
h3 {margin-top:.5em;}

form {

    float:left;

    width:24em;

    margin:20px 0 0 50px;

    padding:1em .75em .5em;

    border:1px solid #AAA;

    }

div.formsection {

    float:left;

    width:100%;

    border-bottom:1px solid #AAA;

    }

input {

    font-size:.8em;

    }

input:focus, textarea:focus, select:focus {

    border:2px solid #7AA;

    }

label {
```

enclose the formsection divs

temporary style for this demo—moves the form from T/L corner of page

encloses the form control and label set

makes the floated element full width

makes the field highlight when clicked in

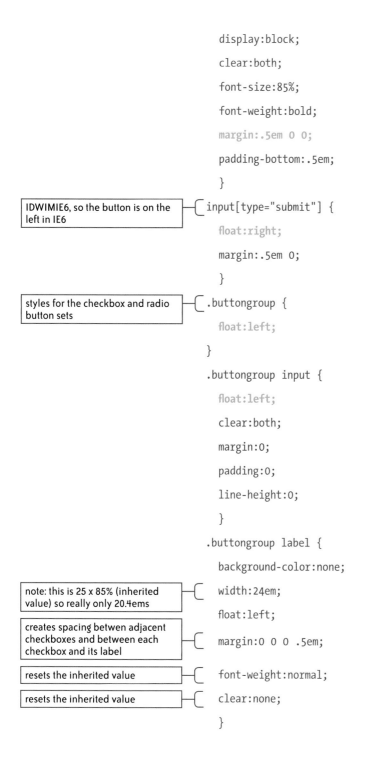

```
      display:block;

      clear:both;

      font-size:85%;

      font-weight:bold;

      margin:.5em 0 0;

      padding-bottom:.5em;

      }
```

IDWIMIE6, so the button is on the left in IE6
```
input[type="submit"] {

      float:right;

      margin:.5em 0;

      }
```

styles for the checkbox and radio button sets
```
.buttongroup {

      float:left;

      }

.buttongroup input {

      float:left;

      clear:both;

      margin:0;

      padding:0;

      line-height:0;

      }

.buttongroup label {

      background-color:none;
```

note: this is 25 x 85% (inherited value) so really only 20.4ems
```
      width:24em;

      float:left;
```

creates spacing betwen adjacent checkboxes and between each checkbox and its label
```
      margin:0 0 0 .5em;
```

resets the inherited value
```
      font-weight:normal;
```

resets the inherited value
```
      clear:none;

      }
```

The `form` element, which is the top level element of the rest of the form, is set to a width of 24 ems. The `formsection` divs around each label and control set is un-dimensioned, so each expands to the width of the form. By setting the label's display property to `block`, and removing its margins with the exception of a little space above it (first highlight in code above), the three text-entry fields and their labels stack nicely down the page. As long as we don't set the text-field widths (as determined by the `size` attribute in the XHTML) wider than the 24 ems of the form element, this is a pretty solid and simple layout.

Things are a little more complex when we get to the radio buttons and checkboxes. Not only do we need a label for each group of checkboxes or radio buttons, but a "sub-label" is needed for each individual element in the group. So I wrap up each set of radio buttons and their individual labels in a div with the class `buttongroup`. I float this div left to make it enclose the controls and their labels, which I also float (highlighted). By setting the width of these labels to be small enough to leave room for the little radio buttons and checkboxes, the labels float up beside them, and align nicely. Remember the example in Chapter 4 where the floated text block next to the floated image formed a column? That's exactly what happens here. If the label on an individual checkbox wraps to a second line, it perfectly aligns itself with the start of the line above, and all the following elements move down to make room for it.

Finally, I want to get the Submit button to sit to the right, where I believe it logically always belongs. I target just the Submit button input, (see `float:right;` highlighted above) and not all the other types of inputs in the form, by using an attribute selector, which defines that the `type` of the input must be `submit`. Of course, IDWIMIE6, in IE6 it's going to be on the left, but no biggie; I just think it is better usability to have it on the right.

And that's it. Forms are actually quite a lot of work as there are lots of important XHTML attributes that you need to get right for each control. However, the markup and styles here can help to speed things up. When you want to lay out forms for your own projects, by following the format of this markup (actually, by just cutting and pasting the appropriate `formsection` divs from the downloadable example), you can create the sequence of controls you need. Then you can modify the attributes of the individual elements to your specific requirements, and when you link this style sheet to the page, it will instantly style the form into this layout.

TINY SIGN-IN FORM

One of the toughest aspects of working with forms is getting them to sit in small spaces. A sign-in form on a sidebar column is a great example of what I mean (see **Figure 6.21**).

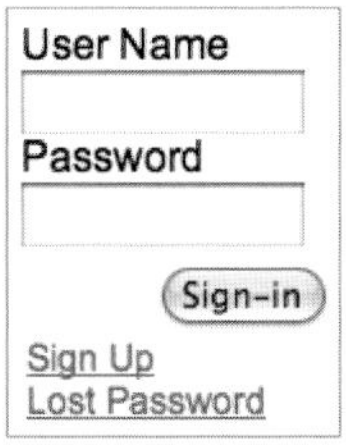

FIGURE 6.21 This sign-in form is neatly packed into a column that is only 128 pixels wide.

In this screenshot, the gray box is the border of a containing div that represents a narrow column—it's only 128 pixels wide.

Here is the markup

this div represents the column in which you might place this element	`<div id="column">`
tiny log-in form vertical	`<form id="tiny_form_vert" action="#" method="post">`

a single line text field	`<div class="formsection">`
	`    <label for="user_name">User Name</label>`
	`    <input id="user_name" type="text" size="10" />`

end single line text field	`</div>`

a password field	`<div class="formsection">`
	`    <label for="password">Password</label>`
	`    <input id="password" type="password" size="10" />`

end password field	`</div>`
submit button	`<div class="formsection">`
input must be wrapped in a block level element to validate	`<input type="submit" value="Sign-in" />`
end submit button	`</div>`
list for errors and links	`<div class="formsection">`
adding class 'error' displays error message paragraph	`<p class="">Problem with name or password</p>`

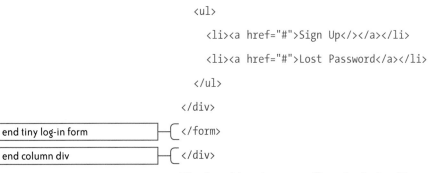

```
<ul>

    <li><a href="#">Sign Up</></a></li>

    <li><a href="#">Lost Password</a></li>

</ul>

</div>
```

end tiny log-in form ——(`</form>`

end column div ——(`</div>`

The first thing that you will notice is that I have marked-up this form by copying elements of the larger generic form above (which is part of the *Stylib* library), so it only took a few minutes to put it together.

Note at the end of this markup, I have a paragraph (highlighted) that will normally be hidden but which will be displayed if the user makes an error such as entering an invalid password and needs to be prompted to try again (**Figure 6.22**). Right now the class attribute has no value, but if we set that value to error, the paragraph will appear on the page. We'll see how this works in a moment.

FIGURE 6.22 An error message can be displayed if the username or password is incorrect.

The actual testing of the validity of the submitted data, and the adding of the class to make it display, must be done using server-side middleware such as PHP. You can learn how to do this by reading my book Codin' for the Web.

There is also an unordered list that holds two links that are always needed with this type of sign-in component. The Sign Up link would take a nonmember to a page (not shown) to sign up and create a username and password if he hasn't done so before. For a current member, there is a Lost Password link to a page (not shown) where he can request his lost password be sent to his registered email address.

I start the related CSS by removing the margins from every element and setting a small overall size for the text. Note all the sizes are set in ems so that this layout scales perfectly if the user changes the overall font size. This even includes the width of the containing element, whose 8 ems width equates to 128 (16 times 8) pixels.

Here is the CSS:

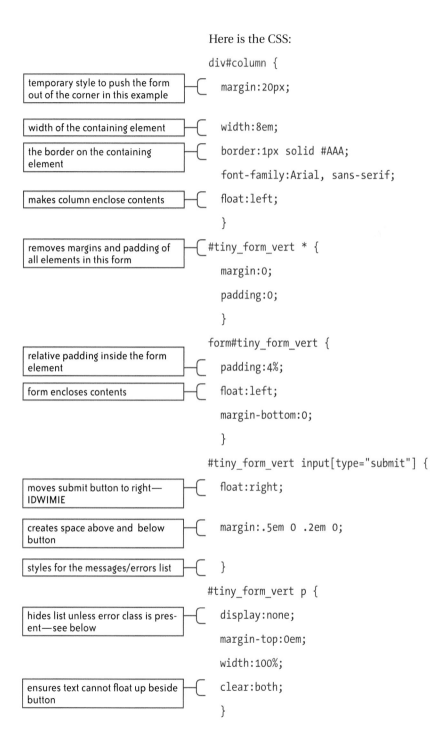

```
div#column {

    margin:20px;

    width:8em;

    border:1px solid #AAA;

    font-family:Arial, sans-serif;

    float:left;

}
#tiny_form_vert * {

    margin:0;

    padding:0;

}
form#tiny_form_vert {

    padding:4%;

    float:left;

    margin-bottom:0;

}
#tiny_form_vert input[type="submit"] {

    float:right;

    margin:.5em 0 .2em 0;

}
#tiny_form_vert p {

    display:none;

    margin-top:0em;

    width:100%;

    clear:both;

}
```

Annotations:

- temporary style to push the form out of the corner in this example
- width of the containing element
- the border on the containing element
- makes column enclose contents
- removes margins and padding of all elements in this form
- relative padding inside the form element
- form encloses contents
- moves submit button to right— IDWIMIE
- creates space above and below button
- styles for the messages/errors list
- hides list unless error class is present—see below
- ensures text cannot float up beside button

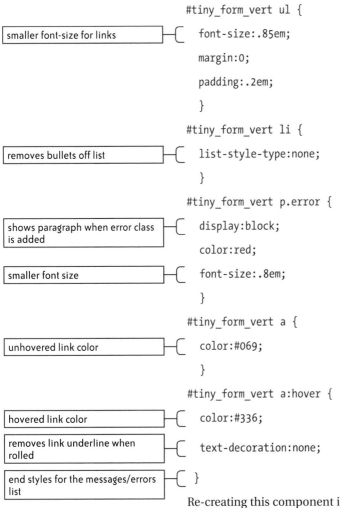

```
#tiny_form_vert ul {

    font-size:.85em;

    margin:0;

    padding:.2em;

}

#tiny_form_vert li {

    list-style-type:none;

}

#tiny_form_vert p.error {

    display:block;

    color:red;

    font-size:.8em;

}

#tiny_form_vert a {

    color:#069;

}

#tiny_form_vert a:hover {

    color:#336;

    text-decoration:none;

}
```

- smaller font-size for links
- removes bullets off list
- shows paragraph when error class is added
- smaller font size
- unhovered link color
- hovered link color
- removes link underline when rolled
- end styles for the messages/errors list

Re-creating this component is a good exercise to help develop your skills. Its markup and CSS are relatively short and straightforward, it illustrates how to organize nested elements with very tight tolerances, and you end up with a compact and useful element.

Let's now take a look a lists and menus.

Styling Lists and Menus

A list is simply a group of related text items: the names of some related objects or the steps in a process, for example. Lists can simply be a series of items that are displayed together, or can also be links that enable the user to navigate to other locations in your site.

A menu is a list that offers navigation choices—the text can be clicked. In this section, we'll first create a list, then turn it into a clickable menu. Finally, we'll create a multi-level menu with a top level of choices that reveals subchoices when a top-level choice is hovered. Let's start by looking at lists.

Lists

There are three types of lists: unordered, ordered, and definition lists. They have similar markup but should be used based on their content.

- **Unordered lists** are bulleted by default. You can change this bullet to a hollow circle or a square, or you can even replace the bullet with a graphic or an entity such as ~ (tilde).

- **Ordered lists** are numbered by default. You can change the numbers to letters of the alphabet or to Roman numerals.

- **Definition lists (or nested lists)** contain subitems; you might use this type of list for a glossary of terms.

The markup for lists is very simple. Here's the code for an unordered list

```
<ul>
<li>Gibson</li>
<li>Fender</li>
<li>Rickenbacker</li>
<li>Ibanez</li>
</ul>
```

This unordered list opens with an unordered list (ul) tag, contains a number of list items (li), and then closes with another ul tag.

An ordered list is very similar except the list tag is ol instead of ul.

```
<ol>

<li>Gibson</li>

<li>Fender</li>

<li>Rickenbacker</li>

<li>Ibanez</li>

</ol>
```

FIGURE 6.23 XHTML provides many options for formatting lists.

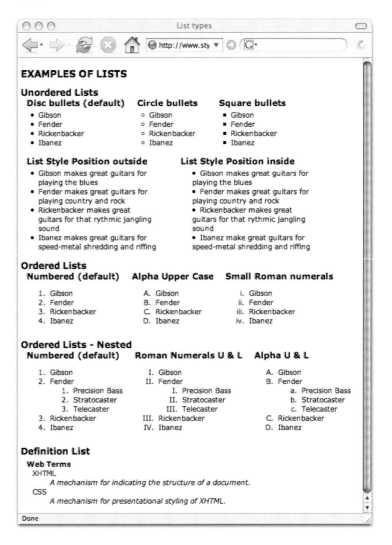

In an ordered list, each item is sequentially labeled using numbers, letters, or Roman numerals, depending on the value of the `list-style-type` property. You can place the label either outside of the list or within in it using the `list-style-position` property.

A definition list has three elements:

```
<dl>Web Terms

  <dt>XHTML</dt>

    <dd>A mechanism for indicating the structure of a
    document.</dd>

  <dt>CSS</dt>

    <dd>A mechanism for presentational styling of XHTML.</dd>

</dl>
```

It opens with a definition list tag (`dl`) and then has any number of definition terms (`dt`) and their associated definition descriptions (`dd`).

Figure 6.23 shows unordered, ordered, and definition lists, using only the markup shown previously, but with variations of `list-style-type` and `list-style-position` properties.

STYLING LISTS

Lists are the basis for navigation and menus; after all, navigation elements, such as links in a sidebar, usually consist of a list of pages you can visit, so a menu is really a list of choices. This is why it's considered good practice to style navigation and menus as lists. One very important advantage of this thinking is that if the user is viewing the page in a user agent—perhaps a mobile phone—that cannot apply the CSS styles, the XHTML list markup will at least present the navigation or menus as a neat stack of links. Let's begin by styling a set of navigation links that you might find on the left sidebar of almost any site.

Here's the markup for an unordered list inside of a div, so you can see it in relation to a containing element (in the context of left navigation, the container would be the left column):

```
<div class="listcontainer">

  <ul>

    <li>Gibson</li>

    <li>Fender</li>

    <li>Rickenbacker</li>
```

```
            <li>Ibanez</li>

        </ul>

</div>
```

First, let's display the div so we can see our unstyled list inside it
(**Figure 6.24**).

```
body {font: 1.0em verdana, arial, sans-serif;}

div#listcontainer {border:1px solid #000; width:160px;
font-size:.75em; margin:20px;}
```

FIGURE 6.24 An unstyled, unordered list.

Second, let's turn on the borders of the `ul` and the `li` elements so
that we can see the position of the individual elements of the list.

```
ul {border:1px solid red;}

li {border:1px solid green;}
```

FIGURE 6.25 The list and the list element borders displayed in Firefox.

FIGURE 6.26 The list and the list element borders displayed in IE7. Clearly, there is a difference in the default padding and margins between IE7 and Firefox.

In **Figures 6.25 and 6.26**, the ul has a red border and each li has a green border. As you can see, Firefox (**Figure 6.25**) uses padding on the ul to indent the list (the green li elements are pushed away from the red ul container) and also adds small top and bottom margins to separate the list from surrounding items. Internet Explorer (**Figure 6.26**) uses a margin on the ul to indent the list (note the ul is wrapped tight around the li elements and both are moved away from the div), and Internet Explorer only adds a bottom margin, not a top one. These differences can make it hard to have lists look the same across browsers. The only way to overcome these discrepancies is first to reset the default margin and padding values to zero and then restyle them.

So let's set the ul and li margins and padding on both types of list elements to zero.

```
ul {border:1px solid red; margin:0; padding:0;}

li {border:1px solid green; margin:0; padding:0;}
```

Now the margins and padding look the same in both Firefox and Internet Explorer (**Figures 6.27 and 6.28**).

*Using the universal selector to set the margins and padding of all elements to zero (with * {margin:0; padding:0;}) at the top of your style sheet will have the same effect, so if you do that, you don't need to do it again in the list styling.*

FIGURE 6.27 The list and the list element borders displayed in Firefox with the margins and padding set to zero. Now the bullets hang outside the unordered list element.

FIGURE 6.28 The list and the list element borders displayed in IE7 with the margins and padding set to zero. The bullets hang outside the unordered list element so, unlike Firefox, IE does not display them.

Note that the bullets, which belong to the li elements, are now hanging outside of the div. If the div were right against the edge of the browser window, the bullets wouldn't even be visible. So you always have to apply some minimal amount of left margin to the li, or padding to the ul. This ensures that the bullets are within the div, so that they won't overlap other elements on the page, and that

Internet Explorer 6 & 7 will actually display them. So let's now set the left margin (**Figures 6.29 and 6.30**).

```
div#listcontainer {border:1px solid #000; width:160px;
font-size:.75em; margin:20px;}

ul {border:1px solid red; margin:0 0 0 1.25em; padding:0;}

li {border:1px solid green; margin:0;}
```

FIGURES 6.29 AND 6.30 Now Firefox and IE display the list identically.

Note that I used the shorthand style to set *all* the margins (highlighted), not just the left margin. If you don't keep the others explicitly set at zero, the default top and bottom margins, which are different for each browser, will reappear. Also, now we have placeholders ready for the other three values in case we want to change them later.

Let's change the space between the list items since they're a little too close together

```
div#listcontainer {border:1px solid #000; width:160px;
font-size:.75em; margin:20px;}

ul {border:1px solid red; margin:0 0 0 1.25em; padding:0;}

li {border:1px solid green; border-bottom:2px solid #069;
margin:0; padding:.3em 0;}
```

The obvious way to do this is to set the `margin-top` or `margin-bottom` on the `li` elements, but I prefer to use identical top and bottom padding. This keeps the borders of the `li` elements touching instead of creating space between them, which gives us some more options for styling. To show you why it's better to increase the padding than to change the margin, I've replaced the boxes around the elements with neat horizontal lines between each item (**Figure 6.31**).

FIGURE 6.31 By adding vertical padding, the borders of each list item are exactly halfway between each line of text, and we get a nicely positioned dividing line when we style the list item's bottom border.

By adding the top and bottom padding to increase the height of the li elements instead of creating space between them, the top and bottom edges of the li elements are exactly halfway between each line of type. Now when you style either their top or bottom edges, you get a line exactly halfway between them.

Now let's do some more cleanup on this list (**Figure 6.32**).

1. Remove the bullets.

2. Set the margins on the ul element so that the list is better positioned within the div.

3. Indent the list items so they are not flush with the edge of the rules.

FIGURE 6.32 Now we pad the list elements, remove the bullets, and indent the text with respect to the dividing lines.

Here are the changes to the markup:

```
body {font:1em verdana, arial, sans-serif;}
```

```
div#listcontainer {border:1px solid #000; width:160px;
font-size:.75em; margin:20px;}
```

```
ul {border:0; margin:10px 30px 10px 1.25em; padding:0;
list-style-type:none;}
```

```
li {border-bottom:2px solid #069; margin:0; padding:.3em 0;
text-indent:.5em}
```

The most notable modification made at this step is using the
list-style-type property, with a value of none, to remove the bullets. The text-indent property moves the text in slightly from the
left edge of the line, and the new margins on the ul position the list
nicely within the container.

The list would certainly look better if we added a line across the top
of the first item. The ideal solution is to add a border-top to just
the first list item. There is a simple way to do that—using the CSS
pseudo-class :first-child. Sadly, IDWIMIE—Internet Explorer 6
does not understand that pseudo-class.

This means that we either add the line with the :first-child
pseudo-class and accept, zen-like, that it will not appear in Internet
Explorer, or we come up with a work-around. Let's use the pseudo-
class first, and then think about a work-around for our less-compliant but popular friend, Internet Explorer 6. Here's the code:

```
body {font:1em verdana, arial, sans-serif;}
```

```
div#listcontainer {border:1px solid #000; width:150px;
font-size:.75em; margin:20px;}
```

```
ul {border:0; margin:12px 20px 10px 1.25em; padding:0;
list-style-type:none;}
```

```
li {border-bottom:2px solid #069; margin:0; padding:.3em 0;
text-indent:.5em;}
```

```
li:first-child {border-top:2px solid #069;}
```

FIGURE 6.33 Here we use the
:first-child pseudo element as it
is intended to be used, to create a
needed difference between the first
element in a group and the other elements; in this case, to add a fifth line
to our set of four list items.

Now let's take a look at a simple fix for Internet Explorer 6 & 7. When the bullets were removed, the ul element shrank down to the same width as the list items. We can now create our top line by applying the style to the top border of the ul, which contains all the list items. Instead of using the markup I just listed, you could use the following, which makes the top line appear in Internet Explorer too.

```
body {font:1em verdana, arial, sans-serif;}

div#listcontainer {border:1px solid #000; width:150px;
font-size:.75em; margin:20px;}

ul {border:0; margin:12px 20px 10px 1.25em; padding:0;
list-style-type:none; border-top: 2px solid #069}

li {border-bottom:2px solid #069; margin:0; padding:.3em 0;
text-indent:.5em}
```

The visual outcome is identical to **Figure 6.33**. Sometimes you can find an easy work-around like this for Internet Explorer, and sometimes you have to accept that not everyone is going to get the same experience. As long as everyone gets an acceptable experience, that's OK.

CONVERTING THE LIST INTO A MENU

We now have something that looks a lot like a set of navigation links. All we need to do is turn what are now lines of text into a menu—clickable links—and we'll have an attractive and functional navigation component (**Figure 6.34**). This is quite simple using this code:

```
<div id="listcontainer">

<ul>

<li><a href="gibson.htm">Gibson</a></li>

<li><a href="fender.htm">Fender</a></li>

<li><a href="rickenbacker.htm">Rickenbacker</a></li>

<li><a href="inbanez.htm">Ibanez</a></li>

</ul>

</div>
```

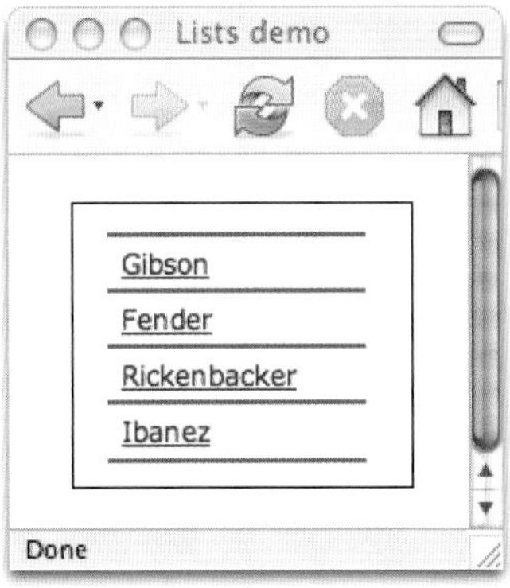

FIGURE 6.34 Adding anchor tags around the text of the list items turns them into clickable links.

Note in the code above how the link tags are closest to the content and nested inside the list items.

BASIC LINK STYLING

Now let's give these links some style. First, let's remove the under-lining from them in their normal, "sitting-there-waiting-for-some-thing-to-happen" state, and then, when the users rolls the cursor over the link, let's make it change color.

Also, since this is the last step to complete our navigation compo-nent, we'll do some cleanup: We need to adjust the ul bottom mar-gin and add context (the id of the containing div) to the selectors so that only the elements within our listcontainer div are affected by the styles. To show you how to use the pseudo-class, as you would if IE were able to understand it, and still have the top line display, I've reinstated it into the code and added a star hack, as described in the sidebar "The Star Hack and Backslash Hack," to make the line above the first list item appear in Internet Explorer 6 & 7.

If you are building a site for long-term use, it's good practice to put hacks for IE6 into their own style sheet, and then later, when IE6 finally shuffles off to the place where browsers go to die, you can simply remove that "hack sheet."

Here's the final code for our list-based navigation component, and you can see the finished result in **Figure 6.35**.

```
body {font:1em verdana, arial, sans-serif;}

div#listcontainer {border:1px solid #000; width:150px;
font-size:.75em; margin:20px;}

div#listcontainer ul {border:0; margin:12px 20px 12px 1.25em;
padding:0; list-style-type:none;}

div#listcontainer li {border-bottom:2px solid #069; margin:0;
padding:.3em 0; text-indent:.5em}

div#listcontainer li:first-child {border-top:2px solid #069;}
```

```
div#listcontainer a {text-decoration:none; color:#069;}

div#listcontainer a:hover {color: #00;}

* html div#listcontainer ul {border-top:2px solid #069;}
```

star hack for IE6 only - IE7 understands the :first-child pseudo class and ignores the star hack

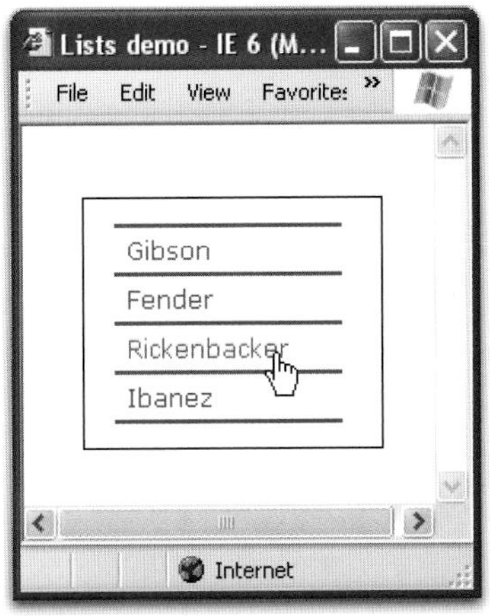

FIGURE 6.35 The completed menu, with the rollover effect on the link, shown in IE6.

The Star Hack and the Backslash Hack

A *hack* is the term for using CSS in ways other than the way it was intended to be used. Hacks enable CSS to be targeted to, or hidden from, specific browsers. A very common use of a hack is to provide alternate code for Internet Explorer 6.

The Star Hack

You have seen that the great-granddaddy of all ancestor elements is the `html` element; all elements are its descendants. However, Internet Explorer 6 is unique in that it has an unnamed element that is a parent of the `html` element, so by referencing this element in a selector, you create a rule that is only read by Internet Explorer 6 (and earlier). Because this element has no name, you reference it with * (known as star), the universal CSS selector, which effectively means "any element." As an example, a common way to use the star selector is like this

```
div * ul {…CSS declarations here…}
```

Here, the `ul` is not selected if it is a child of the div, but it is if it is a grand-child. You use the * to say that it doesn't matter what the in-between child element is.

(continued on next page)

The Star Hack and the Backslash Hack *(continued)*

So, using this same selector to create a rule that is only read by Internet Explorer 6, you write

```
* html …more specific selectors… {…CSS declarations here…}
```

For example

```
div#box {border:1px solid blue;}
```

```
* html div#box {border:1px solid red;}
```

In this example, all browsers set the border to blue, except Internet Explorer 6 for Windows and Internet Explorer for Mac, which read the second rule also and display the box border in red.

However, the more compliant Internet Explorer for Mac can interpret both the * selector and some CSS that Internet Explorer 6 for Windows cannot interpret. So you need some way to ensure that only Internet Explorer for Windows reads the star hack rule. You do this by putting the star hack rule inside a pair of comments, which are written in a special way to take advantage of a strange, unique behavior of Internet Explorer for Mac.

The Backslash-Comment Hack

If you write a comment with a backslash right before the closing *, highlighted in this line of code,

```
/* this a comment \*/
```

then Internet Explorer for Mac does not think the comment has ended and ignores all the CSS that follows until it encounters a comment that is closed in a normal way. (If you like to add comments after, or on the same line as, your selectors, don't do it here, since the positioning of the comments is what makes this hack work.)

For example,

```
/* a hack for IE Win only \*/
```

```
* html div#listcontainer ul {border-top:2px solid #069;}
```

```
/*end of hack */
```

Here, Internet Explorer for Mac ignores the line with the * html selector, even though it is perfectly capable of reading it; it thinks the first comment doesn't close until the end of the second one, so the * html selector is hidden from it. The combination of the star and backslash hacks gives you a rule that is only read by Internet Explorer 6 for Windows. However, with Internet Explorer for Mac now almost obsolete, I tend to use the star hack without wrapping it in the backslash hack. It's your choice.

I've included a couple of variations of styling for this menu in the download for this chapter on www.stylinwithcss.com.

Now let's take what we have learned about lists to the next level and create a multi-level menu.

Creating CSS-Based Menus

Drop-down menus allow you to offer your users a large number of navigation options using very little screen estate, while providing an insight into your site's structure. The menus illustrated here, which you can find in the *Stylib* library files, could provide links to dozens of pages, although only the top level choices are visible until the user hovers over the menu.

Here is what these menus look like (**Figure 6.36**):

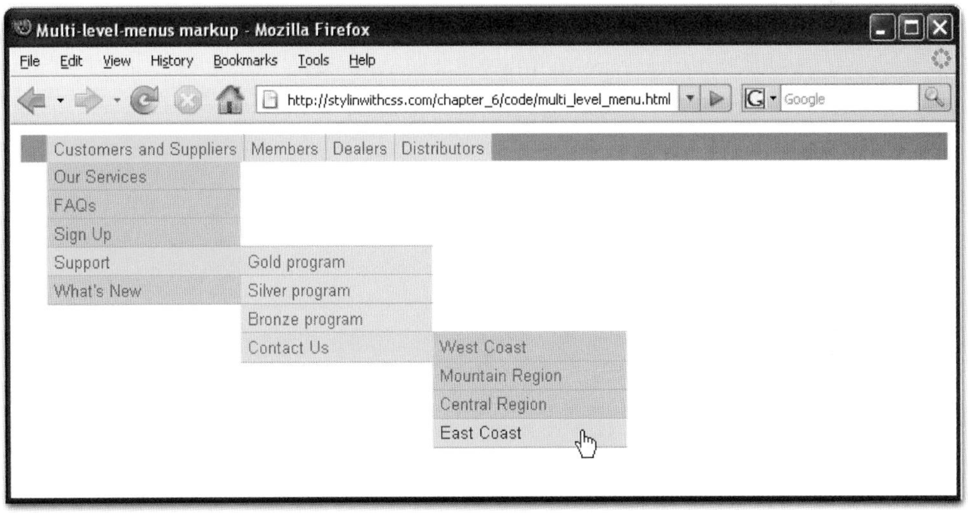

FIGURE 6.36 A multi-level menu written in CSS.

Anyone who read the original edition of *Stylin' with CSS* might think they have seen these menus in **Figure 6.36** before, but I have entirely rewritten the CSS to make them lighter (less code), and optimized them for the new breed of browsers that has emerged since *Stylin'* was written way back in 2004. The user-modifiable CSS, such as colors, line weights, and font sizes, is separated from the more complex code that makes the menus work, so you can dive in and make stylistic changes confidently, knowing you will not break the underlying "mechanics." These menus also now work better in IE6, as I have hacked the bugs that prevented the backgrounds of the menu items from responding to clicks in that browser. So

As shown in Figure 6.36, the multi-level menu in the Stylib library can support up to four menu levels. Although more levels could be easily added, beyond four levels becomes a bit cumbersome for the user to navigate.

while they are visually similar (the XHTML markup I use to demo them here is unchanged from the original *Stylin'* version), the CSS is greatly improved.

If my email is anything to go by, drop-down menus like these appear to be one of the most sought-after pieces of CCS code, and I wrote my original version of them back in 2003 after I became tired of dealing with the complexities of making menus work with JavaScript. As you can see from **Figure 6.36**, this menu can be up to four levels deep, and it is very easy to implement in your site. All you need to do is write a simple set of unordered lists, just like the ones we saw in the navigation element we made previously, and nest them inside each other to create the various levels of the menu, as I will show you shortly. Then wrap the whole thing in a div that has a class to associate the menu with the related CSS (`multi_level_menus_class.css` in the *Stylib* library), and you are done. If you plan to generate the menu choices from items in your site's database, the programmers on your team will love the simplicity of the code (just nested unordered lists) that their middleware has to generate to populate these menus.

Other CSS-based menus that I saw before I wrote these required different classes for every level of the menu to be present on every list item, which I felt made them unnecessarily complex. So when I originally approached the problem of creating a menu from nested list markup, I wanted to have it work without needing to add any additional markup—just vanilla XHTML list markup and the CSS. What follows is an exercise that will teach you how to create CSS drop-down menus from "ID-and-class-free" lists. All that's required is context—a surrounding div with a class, so the correct CSS styles are applied to the list within. The biggest benefit of this all-CSS based approach is that it scales to a limitless number of choices at every level, simply by adding more items to the nested lists, without any modifications to the CSS.

A DROP-DOWN MENU TUTORIAL

Rather than take you through the lengthy and complex CSS of the multi-level menu, let's look at a more simple example to help you understand the concepts behind it. This is a fun exercise to write for yourself from scratch. It's not too complex, but it incorporates just about every CSS technique that we have seen so far. So once you can successfully write the CSS for this menu, you will feel more confident in tackling all kinds of CSS development problems.

In this exercise, we will create a two-level menu: a horizontal row of choices and a menu that drops from each one when hovered. Let's start with the markup for the top level.

```
<div id="multi_drop_menus">

  <ul>

    <li><a href="#">Item 1</a></li>

    <li><a href="#">Item 2</a></li>

  </ul>

</div>
```

As you can see, this is the same markup structure as the navigation component from earlier: a div that contains an unordered list element that contains two list items that each contains a link. Getting these elements styled into the finished menu so they are accurately aligned inside one another like little Russian dolls is key to getting the menu styled correctly. Let's start by applying a different colored border or background to each of the four element types (div, ul, li, and a) so that we can keep an eye on their relationship to one another as we work.

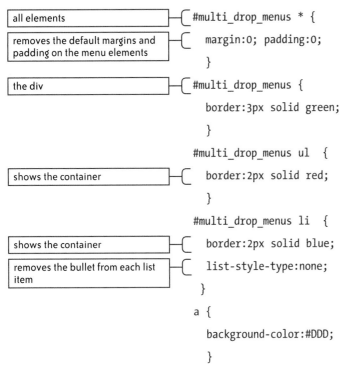

all elements	`#multi_drop_menus * {`
removes the default margins and padding on the menu elements	`  margin:0; padding:0;`
	`}`
the div	`#multi_drop_menus {`
	`    border:3px solid green;`
	`    }`
	`#multi_drop_menus ul  {`
shows the container	`    border:2px solid red;`
	`    }`
	`#multi_drop_menus li  {`
shows the container	`    border:2px solid blue;`
removes the bullet from each list item	`    list-style-type:none;`
	`    }`
	`a {`
	`    background-color:#DDD;`
	`    }`

I first use the universal selector * to remove the default margins and padding of all the elements. Then I style the border of the div green, the ul red, and the li blue. Finally, I make the background of the innermost element, the link (a), a pale gray—that is going to be the background color of the menu choices for now.

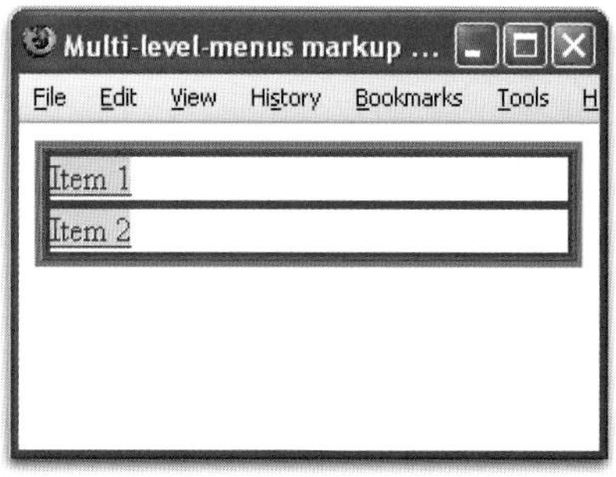

FIGURE 6.37 The four types of elements that will make up our menu are displayed with their default positioning.

As **Figure 6.37** shows (thanks to the borders and background we added), the block level elements fill the width of the browser window and the link, which as an inline element, shrink-wraps its content. The list items (li) are presently stacked above each other, which is perfectly correct because they are block level elements. Of course, for a horizontal menu, we need them to sit side-by-side, so let's float them, so that they do that (**Figure 6.38**). We modify the li rule so it looks like this

```
#multi_drop_menus li  {

border:2px solid blue;

  list-style-type:none;

  float:left;

  }
```

makes the list items sit side by side

FIGURE 6.38 Once we float the list items, the div and the ul snap closed.

Hmm, what happened to our boxes? Well, once we float the list items, there is no un-floated content in the ul (and therefore the parent div) so both close up, and the list items hang down. We really want those elements to enclose the list items, so what's to be done? If you said "Float them, too!" then you obviously were paying attention in the Floating and Clearing section of Chapter 4, as this simple step solves the problem nicely (**Figure 6.39**).

```
#multi_drop_menus {

    border:3px solid green

    float:left;

}
```

makes the div enclose the ul

```
#multi_drop_menus ul  {

    border:2px solid red;

    float:left;

}
```

makes the ul enclose the li's

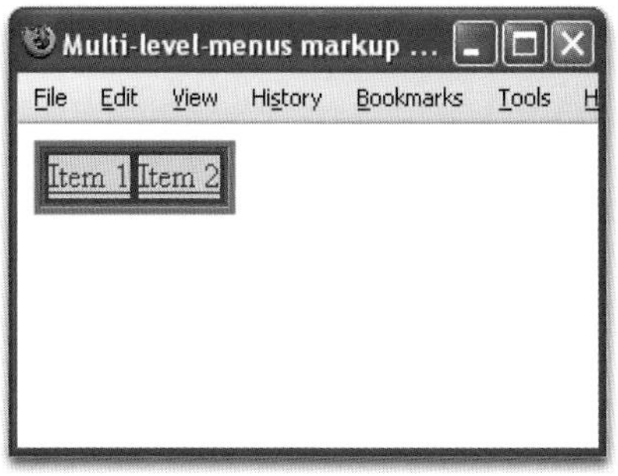

FIGURE 6.39 With the div and ul floated too, the floated list items are enclosed again.

Now we're getting somewhere. These floated elements now nicely shrink-wrap the li elements and our horizontal menu is starting to take shape. Let's next make some space around the text—it's really jammed in there and actually touches the containing element on the sides—by adding some padding around the link's text. I am going to temporarily put a rather excessive amount of vertical padding here (1 em) to illustrate a key aspect of making these menus work correctly.

```
#multi_drop_menus a {

    background-color:#DDD;

    padding:1em 6px;

}
```

FIGURE 6.40 The gray background of the link is clearly larger, but it has spread out to vertically cover the containing elements' borders.

As you can see in **Figure 6.40**, something isn't right here. The link's background has become larger, but has spread itself vertically over the containing elements, instead of pushing outward on them and resizing them. The fact is that inline elements don't interact with their containing elements in the way you might expect when you apply padding and borders to them. Information about the vertical padding of inline elements isn't passed up the hierarchy to the containing elements in the same way as block level elements, so the containing elements don't know that they should resize themselves to accommodate the larger area now occupied by the link. The simple remedy is to convert the links to block elements also.

```
#multi_drop_menus a {

    display:block;

    background-color:#DDD;

    padding:1em 6px;

        }
```

makes the link's container element size correctly

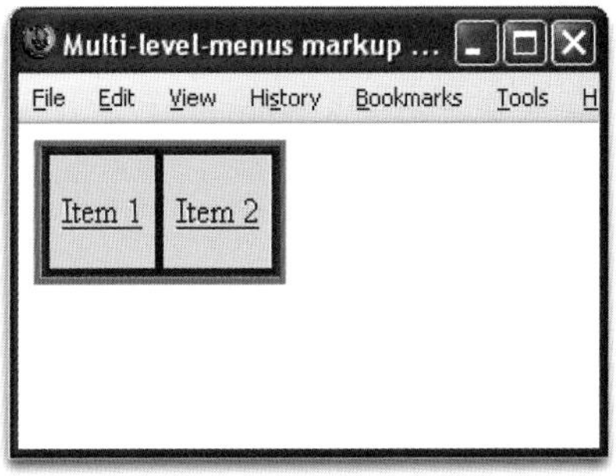

FIGURE 6.41 With the links converted to block elements, the containing elements correctly size themselves to enclose the links.

Once the links are block level elements, the containers are passed the information they need to resize correctly, as you can see in **Figure 6.41**. The next step is to make the links produce some kind of visual response when hovered (and now that I've made my point, we'll set that vertical padding to a more sensible amount at the same time).

```
#multi_drop_menus a {

    display:block;

    background-color:#DDD;

    padding:.3em 6px;

        }
```

a realistic amount of vertical padding for the link

```
#multi_drop_menus a:hover {

    color:#CCC;

    background-color:#666;

    }
```

the hovered text color

the hovered background color

FIGURE 6.42 The link background and type color now change color when the link is hovered.

With the hover now working, as **Figure 6.42** illustrates, a little styling of the borders and colors would give us a nice functional horizontal menu. However, I want to leave these borders on for now so you can clearly see what's happening while we look at the next step—adding the drop-downs. After we've done that, then we'll make our menu look more attractive.

CREATING THE DROP-DOWNS ON THE MENU

The various levels of the menu are created by nesting lists inside of lists. Take a very close look at this markup:

```
<div id="multi_drop_menus">

    <ul>

    <li><a href="#">Item 1</a>

        <ul>

            <li><a href="#">Item 1a</a></li>
```

```
            <li><a href="#">Item 1b</a></li>
          </ul>
        </li>
        <li><a href="#">Item 2</a></li>
      </ul>
    </div>
```

I have added a second unordered list inside the first list item, which is highlighted; this is the drop-down menu. Note exactly where it is placed—right before its parent list item closes. Observe how the closing element of the top-level list item follows the entire second-level list. You have to get this organization right or your menu won't drop down. Let's take a look at how this arrangement displays.

FIGURE 6.43 At this point, the only styling on the drop-down is inherited from the horizontal top level menu, so the drop-down's list items line up horizontally, too.

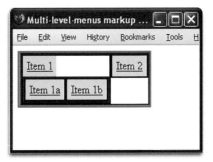

Because we haven't written any specific styles for the drop-down yet, the drop-down, simply inherits the styles from the top level and aligns itself horizontally, as you can see from **Figure 6.43**. Of course, in order for it to be a drop-down menu, we need it to stack vertically instead. The way to do this is to create the absolute/relative positioning relationship between the two levels of the menu that we have seen several times by now.

```
#multi_drop_menus li  {
    border:2px solid blue;
    list-style-type:none;
    float:left;
    position:relative;
}
```

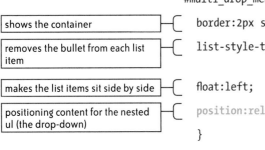

shows the container	`border:2px solid blue;`
removes the bullet from each list item	`list-style-type:none;`
makes the list items sit side by side	`float:left;`
positioning content for the nested ul (the drop-down)	`position:relative;`

```
#multi_drop_menus li ul {

    position:absolute;

    width:7em;

}

#multi_drop_menus li ul li{

    width:100%;

}
```

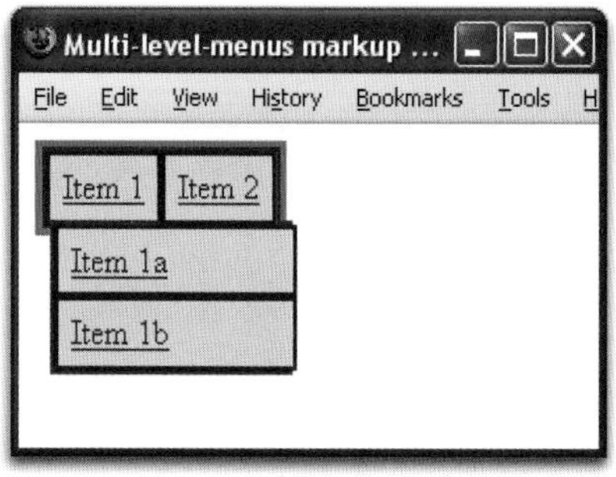

FIGURE 6.44 With the positioning relationship created between the list and the sublist, and the li elements forced to fill the dimensioned ul element, the sublist elements stack to create the drop-down menu.

If you try to get the drop-down to stack by unfloating the li elements, you will discover what I discovered—IE 6 and 7 leave gaps between the menu items. That's why I adopted the approach of making the li elements fill the ul element, which is actually a more robust solution. There, I saved you another three hours.

linking to this file makes the drop-downs work in IE6

Once we tell the drop-down that its positioning context is the outer list, it positions itself nicely, as shown in **Figure 6.44**, right below the top level of the menu, just where we want it. Now, we set a width for the drop-down's ul element—I chose 7 ems, and you can make it as wide as you want—and then set its child li elements to width:100% to force each one to fill the width of ul. With room for only one li across the width of the ul, they stack one under the next, which is just what we want. We didn't even have to unfloat them.

Now we get to the fun bit where we bring our menu to life, so that the drop-down only appears when we hover over the related top-level element.

```
#multi_drop_menus {

    behavior:url(../../lib/js_tools/csshover.htc);

    font-family:lucida, arial, sans-serif;

    border:1px solid #686;

    float:left;

}
```

```
#multi_drop_menus li ul {

    position:absolute;

    width:7em;

    display:none;

}
```

hides the drop-down (revealed when hovered—see below)

```
#multi_drop_menus li:hover ul {

    display:block;

}
```

reveals the drop-down when the parent li is hovered

FIGURES 6.45A & B Two simple rules hide the drop-down menu and reveal it when the associated menu element is hovered. The csshover.htc file is added to enable IE6 to respond to the hover on the li elements.

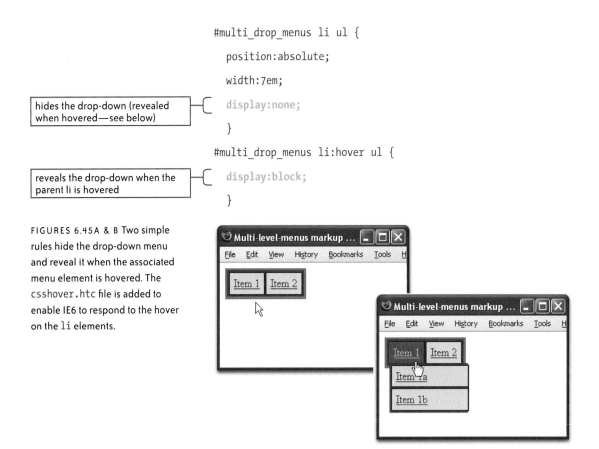

The first step is to add display:none to the ul of the drop-down to hide it. Then we add a rule with this interesting little selector

```
#multi_drop_menus li:hover ul {display:block;}
```

The highlighted part means apply this rule to the ul when its parent li is hovered. Bingo! As soon as the top-level choice of the menu is hovered (**Figure 645B**), the associated drop-down appears. When the menu is unhovered, this rule no longer applies, and the drop-down is hidden again (**Figure 6.45A**).

Note, highlighted in the code block above, the use of an Internet Explorer behavior that invokes a piece of JavaScript code called csshover.htc to allow Internet Explorer 6 to respond to hovers on all elements, not just links, which is essential for this menu to work. Remember that the path for the file is relative to the page, not to the CSS. This is relevant if the CSS is in a separate file and location from the XHTML. See the sidebar "The Hover Behavior for Internet Explorer" in Chapter 4 for more details.

All that is left is a bit of cleanup to get rid of the colored guide borders that have been so helpful while we were going through this section, and replace them with some more appropriate and attractive styles. I'll also modify the markup (not shown, but in the downloadable file) to add a third top-level menu choice and add drop-downs to all three of them. Here's the CSS code for the completed menu, with the cosmetic additions highlighted, which gives the result shown in **Figure 6.46**.

FIGURE 6.46 The complete menu, all styled up and ready to launch your Web career into the stratosphere.

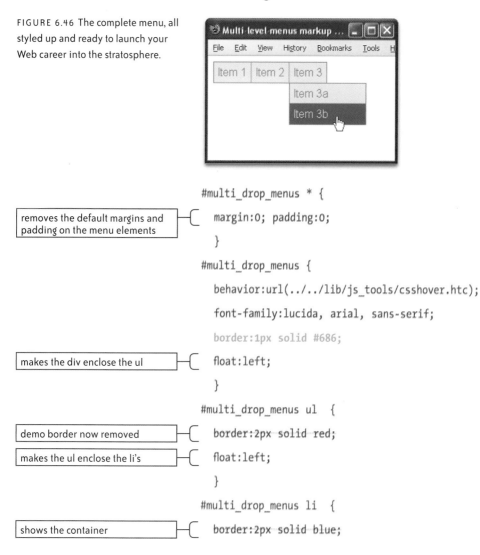

```
#multi_drop_menus * {
```
removes the default margins and padding on the menu elements
```
    margin:0; padding:0;

}

#multi_drop_menus {

    behavior:url(../../lib/js_tools/csshover.htc);

    font-family:lucida, arial, sans-serif;

    border:1px solid #686;
```
makes the div enclose the ul
```
    float:left;

}

#multi_drop_menus ul  {
```
demo border now removed
```
    border:2px solid red;
```
makes the ul enclose the li's
```
    float:left;

}

#multi_drop_menus li  {
```
shows the container
```
    border:2px solid blue;
```

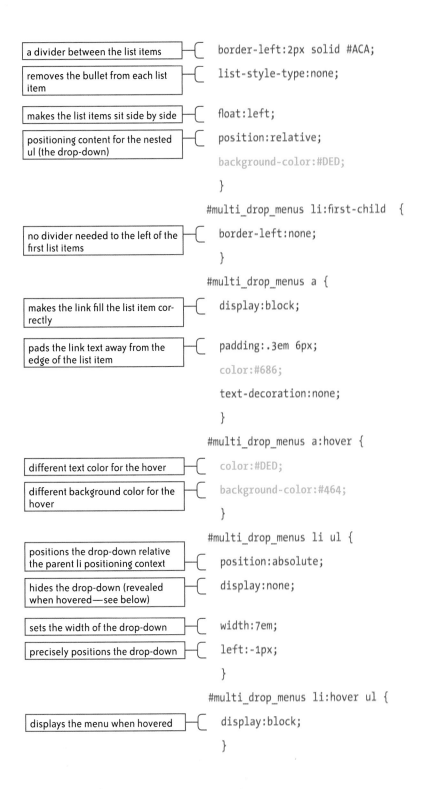

a divider between the list items —⊂ `border-left:2px solid #ACA;`

removes the bullet from each list item —⊂ `list-style-type:none;`

makes the list items sit side by side —⊂ `float:left;`

positioning content for the nested ul (the drop-down) —⊂ `position:relative;`

`background-color:#DED;`

`}`

`#multi_drop_menus li:first-child  {`

no divider needed to the left of the first list items —⊂ `border-left:none;`

`}`

`#multi_drop_menus a {`

makes the link fill the list item correctly —⊂ `display:block;`

pads the link text away from the edge of the list item —⊂ `padding:.3em 6px;`

`color:#686;`

`text-decoration:none;`

`}`

`#multi_drop_menus a:hover {`

different text color for the hover —⊂ `color:#DED;`

different background color for the hover —⊂ `background-color:#464;`

`}`

`#multi_drop_menus li ul {`

positions the drop-down relative the parent li positioning context —⊂ `position:absolute;`

hides the drop-down (revealed when hovered—see below) —⊂ `display:none;`

sets the width of the drop-down —⊂ `width:7em;`

precisely positions the drop-down —⊂ `left:-1px;`

`}`

`#multi_drop_menus li:hover ul {`

displays the menu when hovered —⊂ `display:block;`

`}`

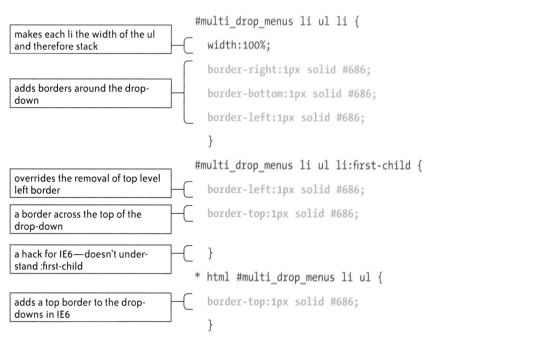

```
#multi_drop_menus li ul li {
```

makes each li the width of the ul and therefore stack
```
    width:100%;
```

adds borders around the drop-down
```
    border-right:1px solid #686;

    border-bottom:1px solid #686;

    border-left:1px solid #686;

}
```

```
#multi_drop_menus li ul li:first-child {
```

overrides the removal of top level left border
```
    border-left:1px solid #686;
```

a border across the top of the drop-down
```
    border-top:1px solid #686;
```

a hack for IE6—doesn't understand :first-child
```
}
```

```
* html #multi_drop_menus li ul {
```

adds a top border to the drop-downs in IE6
```
    border-top:1px solid #686;

}
```

This little demo menu works well in all the *Stylin'* browsers, including IE6. However, the *Stylib* file `multi_level_menu_class.css` is the drop-down menu file I recommend, as that code has been through more use on real sites, supports more levels, and with the addition of a second class to the container, can stack the top level of the menu vertically for use in a navigation sidebar. While the code for these menus is fairly complex, once it's written (which, in your case, it is), it's fairly easy to implement drop-down menus in a dynamic site. The back-end system only needs to write out the XHTML list structure, and as is typical when using JavaScript, not custom code for each element of the menu.

And that brings us to the end of this long chapter. I hope these examples inspire you to create your own versions of elements like these for yourself, or at least to take and modify the ones that I have shown here. In the final chapter, we will use our new CSS skills to assemble the layouts and components we have seen so far into finished Web pages.

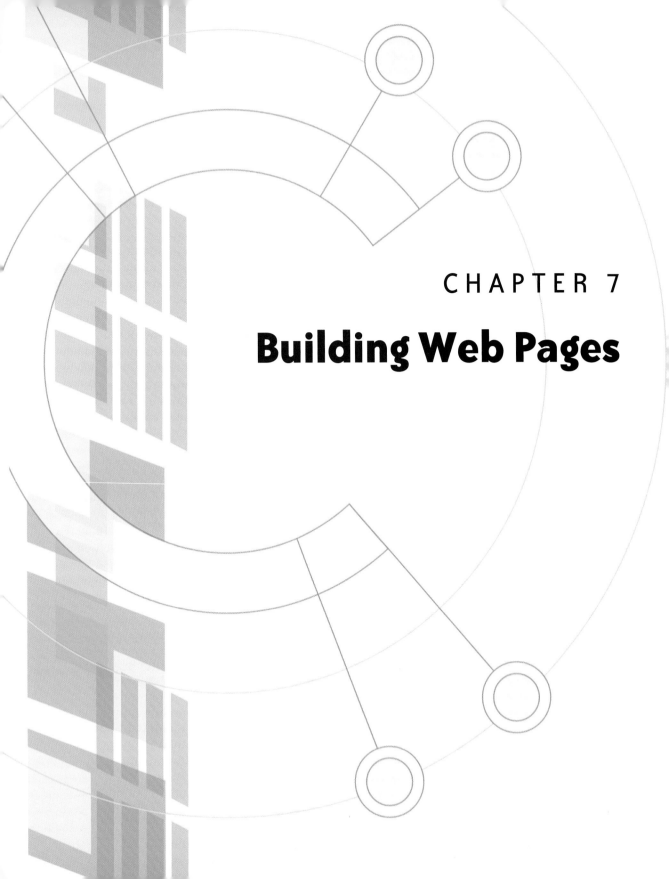

CHAPTER 7

Building Web Pages

IN THIS FINAL CHAPTER, we'll bring together everything you have learned in the preceding chapters and look at how to organize pages into a complete site. I'll show you how to set up the folder structure so you can organize your XHTML, CSS, and JavaScript files, and demonstrate some other options for linking your CSS files to the pages. I'll show you how to add different types of interface components into the pages and to structure the related CSS. We'll see techniques that minimize the amount of code you need so it's easy to write, and to later find and edit, the CSS that styles each element of the markup.

It's not necessary to have access to the Stylib *library to create this or any other page. You can copy the styles from the book or simply invent your own. However, it's always better to use code from the* Stylib *library than copy it from the book, as any issues found with book's code will be fixed in the library.*

I'll show all this by creating the Web site for this book, *Stylin' with CSS*. The site will have a home page that will provide an overview of the book and describe what's available on the site, and various other pages that include the Table of Contents, CSS-related links, and a sign-up form.

The focus of this chapter will be the home page. We'll see how we can use a page template from the *Stylib* library and easily add to it various other *Stylib* components, such as the form layout styles, drop-down menus, and the text and color styles that we have seen earlier, to minimize the amount of custom coding required to complete these pages. We'll also see methods of sharing styles between the pages and some background image techniques that help visually break up the underlying grid of the layout.

The *Stylin'* Site

Here is the completed home page at its maximum and minimum browser window widths (**Figures 7.1** and **7.2**).

FIGURE 7.1 The finished *Stylin'* home page at maximum width.

FIGURE 7.2 The finished *Stylin'* home page at minimum width.

This page is built on the three-column liquid layout we saw in Chapter 5. Before seeing in detail how it is put together, let's look at the key features of this page. There are four background images. The header and the footer each have a dark graphic with large lettering, and the NiftyCorners code (see Chapter 5) is used to round off the corners of the header and the footer.

The circle graphic on the left side of the page goes into the `two_column` div that encloses two left columns, so it can appear across both of them, while the large graphic based on the cover of the book goes into the `main_wrapper` div that encloses the entire layout. I've moved this background graphic to the right, away from the navigation column, to have it appear behind the center and right columns. The placement of these two graphics in divs that span the columns enables them to visually unite the side columns and the content area.

Note the two text headings in the header. One is positioned to the left and the other to the right. Their relationship changes as the page width varies, as you can see by comparing **Figures 7.1** and **7.2**. You can see a similar effect provided by right-positioned elements when you size the liquid pages of both the Amazon and Jing sites that I featured in Chapter 5.

The menu bar under the header is styled with the `multi_level_menu.css` style sheet from the *Stylib* library, and you will notice if you visit the *Stylin'* Web site that the drop-downs of this menu are transparent and the underlying page is visible through them. This transparency is created programmatically using the various CSS opacity options of the different browsers.

On the left navigation bar is a transparent round-cornered box that can increase in height as more content is added. The transparency here is created not programmatically but graphically, by using three .png background images with their transparency levels set in Adobe Fireworks. The center area of the box can expand as content is added, through the use of a repeat setting on the CSS for the background of the element. I also added the small sign-in form that we saw in Chapter 6 inside this area.

In the content column, the text wraps itself around a floated image, followed by an unordered list. On the right sidebar is an image of the book cover with a drop shadow (the shadow was created in Adobe Photoshop), with a simple unordered list of links below.

Setting Up the Folder Structure

When you start building a Web site, you first set up a folder, usually referred to as the *local folder,* on your computer. This folder ultimately contains an exact copy of the finished Web site that will be located in the *root folder* on your Web server (see "The Root Directory" sidebar). When you are ready to upload your site to your Web server, you use an FTP client to move the contents of the local folder, but not the folder itself, into the root directory on the Web server.

If you are using Adobe Dreamweaver, then this is the folder that you select as the Local Root Folder when you set up the FTP information for the site.

The Root Directory

The root directory is the one to which the root URL for your Web site points. A URL provides a unique address for every document on the Internet.

Every domain, such as stylinwithcss.com, is associated via the Domain Name System (DNS, a kind of phone book for the Web) with an IP address (Internet Protocol address, the unique numerical name of every server on the Internet). When you type a URL in your browser, the DNS looks up the domain name, finds the IP address of the associated server, and forwards the request to that server.

When the server receives the request for the page, it uses the domain name associated with the request to route the request to a specific folder on the server that relates to that domain: the root folder. If the URL contains a path directly to a specific page, that page is served to the requesting Web browser. If the requested URL is simply www.stylinwithcss.com, with no file name specified, the root folder is searched, and if it contains a page called default. html (or .htm), home.html, or index.html, that page is automatically served.

In short, the root folder is the top folder in the hierarchy of your Web site, and thanks to your ISP or network administrator, it is associated with your Web address. Learn more about the DNS system on the InterNIC site (www. internic.net/faqs/authoritative-dns.html).

If you are not using Dreamweaver or another editor with a built-in FTP client, you will need a separate FTP (File Transfer Protocol) client. Either way, in order to log in, you will need to enter the host name, user name, and password. Then you can upload your files and folders from the local folder on your computer to the root folder of your site's server. You can obtain the FTP log-in information from your ISP (Internet Service Provider) or, if you are in a corporate environment, your network administrator.

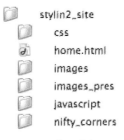

FIGURE 7.3 The Adobe Dreamweaver local folder set-up for the *Stylin'* site.

The only page you absolutely need in the root level folder (my local version of this folder is called stylin2_site in **Figure 7.3**) is the home page, which is the `3_col_liquid_faux.html` file, renamed to home.html so it loads automatically. See the sidebar called "The Root Directory" for details on this. Although you can put all the XHTML pages at this top level, it's good practice to organize them into subfolders.

A note on how sites get built in the corporate world…

Development of large sites is almost always driven by a business requirements document, which describes the user needs for the site and the functionality that must be provided to meet those needs. In order to end up with a site that meets these requirements, the next step is to create a content list that describes what content is going into the site, and a functional specification that describes the features that need to be programmed and how they will work. Next comes site architecture, which is where the real design work begins.

When I set up the folder structure of a new site, I always create four folders first, inside the root folder, called `css`, `javascript`, `images`, and `images_pres`. The first two contain the CSS and JavaScript files, respectively. The `images` folder holds all the images that relate to the content—the photograph and the image of the book, in the case of this page. The `images_pres` folder contains all the presentational images, such as backgrounds, that are part of the visual design rather than the content.

Organizing the images across two folders in this way makes it much easier to update the design of your site; you could update the images in the `images_pres` folder but leave the content-related images in the `images` folder as is. Alternatively, if you want to syndicate your content, you would only need to provide the XHTML markup and images from the `images` folder—believe me, no one wants your site's background images when displaying your content on their own site. As a rule of thumb, if an image is part of the structure of the page and is therefore referenced from the XHTML, that image belongs in the `images` folder. If an image is referenced from the CSS, and is therefore part of the page's presentation, it belongs in the `images_pres` folder.

Creating the Site Architecture

Even for a simple site like this one, it's worth drawing an *architecture diagram* to make you plan out the site's structure before you start creating graphics and code. An architecture diagram also lets you see the balance of content between the various areas of the site, and forces you to consider what the pages will be called and the kinds of logical groups into which they are organized. This is very important work in the development of a large site, and worth doing even for this site, which will be only a few pages. **Figure 7.4** shows the architectural diagram for the *Stylin'* site.

Some presentational aspects of the site are suggested by **Figure 7.4**, although its primary purpose is to indicate site structure. You can see in the screenshot above that at the top of the architecture diagram I've dropped in the wireframe layout of the page (see **Figure 7.5**), which began as a hand-drawn sketch and then was refined on the computer. A wireframe represents a page layout as simple boxes with black-and-white text and gray rectangles for images. There is no effort at this point to represent the visual look of the site, and this

FIGURE 7.4 A simple architecture diagram for the *Stylin'* site.

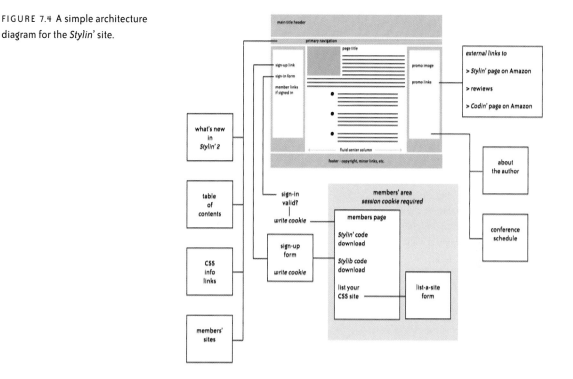

allows the focus to be on issues of organization, hierarchy, and overall balance of the layout, without getting sidetracked by determining the right shade of blue or the precise cropping of graphics. There's a time for such work, but it's too distracting right now.

Web Design Is Not Just Visual Design

At the *Voices that Matter Conference* in San Francisco in October 2007, I heard several designers ask if this structure-driven approach could work for them, as they always start from the visual design of the page and then build from there. First, I think the structural and presentational aspects of the design can develop together, but when coding begins, the structure has to lead, as it's the framework on which the presentation hangs. So I think it's fine, and even desirable, to have a visual design in front of you as you start to code. Often, I will take a printout of the page design, and start drawing the boxes that represent divs around the elements, grouping related areas of content together. I will give each of those boxes a name that I will later use as a div ID. If you do this, you can treat those boxes as the basis of your wireframe, then you can lead with the structure and let the visual design be added in as you develop the page's markup.

For this site, the home page wireframe looks like **Figure 7.5**.

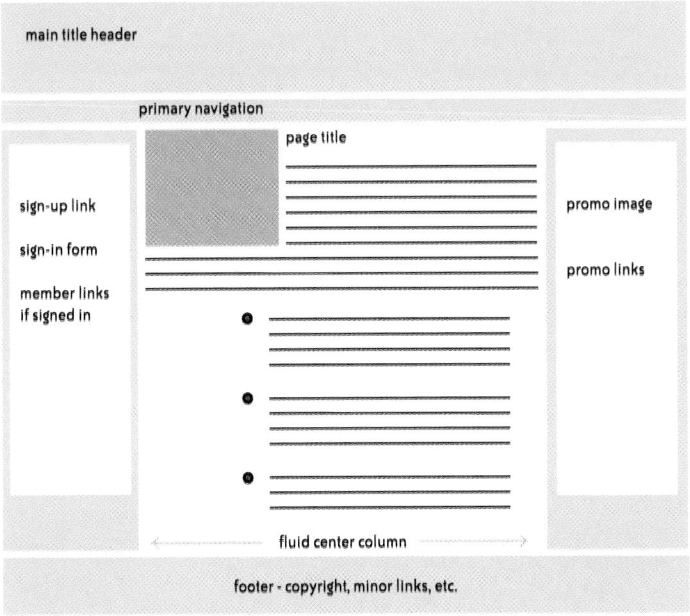

FIGURE 7.5 This simple wireframe provides a basis for coding the CSS for the page.

The nature of developing with CSS means that we can turn a wireframe into a working prototype Web page without the visual design being completed. In the case of icyou.com, which we saw in Chapter 4, I first coded a CSS prototype with the basic layout of the key pages, but focused only on the content organization and user interactions and didn't worry about visual issues such as coloring type and adding background graphics. Of course, there were numerous minor modifications and additions to the CSS as the final visual design took shape. My point is that by escaping from the "slice the finished graphics and drop them into a table" development methodology of yore, and moving to a structure-driven CSS approach, the interface coding and visual design can happen as a collaborative and iterative process, rather than one or the other driving the development process by being completed entirely before the other starts.

So let's begin by laying out the content of the page without worrying too much about colors and graphics in this first pass. Our focus will be on the layout of the content to show its hierarchy and relationships.

In order to create this three-column liquid-center page, we need the same markup and CSS for this layout that we developed in Chapter 5. Because we have the *Stylib* library to call on, we don't need to write this code again—we can get it from the library. The markup is called `3_col_liquid_faux.html`. I copy this file from the Layout folder of the library into the root folder and rename it as `home.html`—this will make it automatically load when someone enters only www.stylinwithcss.com as the URL. I won't bother copying the faux graphics we used in Chapter 5, as I will make new graphics for this site.

Copy the Required CSS Files from the Library

Now I copy the associated CSS file, `3_col_liquid_faux.css`, into the CSS folder—no need to change its name. I'll also copy over some other style sheets I know we will need in this site, `text_n_colors.css`, `multi_level_menus.css`, and two style sheets for forms, `form_layout_2_col.css` and `sign_in_form.css`.

Also, because the `3_col_liquid_faux.html` template uses the NiftyCorners code to round the corners of the header and footer, and I want to retain that effect in this design, I've copied over the NiftyCorners folder and put it at the top level next to the CSS and JavaScript folders.

I also need a JavaScript file, `minmax.js`, to control the layout width in IE6, so I copy it from the library's JavaScript folder into the site's JavaScript folder.

In the next step, we will associate the CSS files with the XHTML file in a way we have not looked at so far, which provides some advantages when a site starts to grow to a large number of pages.

The @import Rule

Up to now we have used the `link` element to associate external CSS files with our XHTML pages. However, this can also be done with the `@import` rule. The `@import` rule is a CSS rule, not an XHTML element, like link. In order to use it in our XHTML pages, we need to wrap it in a `style` element; this makes it an embedded style of the kind we saw in Chapter 2. We might add this code into the head of our document:

```
<style type="text/css">

  @import url(css/mystylesheet.css);

</style>
```

which is the equivalent of

```
<link href="css/mystylesheet.css" rel="stylesheet" />
```

Both of these methods associate the style sheet with the page. `@import` is useful because, being CSS, it can be used in a style sheet. In other words, you can link your page to one style sheet that contains a list of `@import` rules, each of which loads a style sheet.

So, rather than dumping the hundreds of lines of styles needed for a typical site into a single style sheet, I can organize my CSS into a number of separate style sheets and load them using a single link tag in the XHTML page. Typically, I use one style sheet for the layout, one for text, and others for large components such as the forms and menus that might appear in some pages but not others. As you will see, this allows me to load only the style sheets that any given page actually needs.

To do this, I add a listing of a set of style sheets to an "import" (my term) style sheet, and then associate just this import style sheet with all the pages that need those style sheets. This import style sheet, which lives in the CSS folder along with all the other style sheets, effectively acts as a pointer to a set of style sheets. By organizing different combinations of the site's style sheets in multiple import sheets, I can then, with a simple style tag in each page, associate a particular set of style sheets with any page that needs them.

For example, in the home page for the *Stylin'* site you'll find

```
<link href="import_3liq_txt_signin_menu.css" media="all"
rel="stylesheet" />
```

This, of course, associates the page with the style sheet `import_3liq_txt_signin_menu.css`.

In that style sheet, as its name suggests, is

```
@import url(3_col_liquid_faux.css);

@import url(text_n_colors.css);

@import url(sign_in_form.css);

@import url(multi_drop_menus_class.css);
```

Now all the style sheets I need for the home page are associated with the home page. I can now add and drop style sheets without having to modify the home page itself.

While this is a useful technique, note that a large number of style sheets for a single page are a factor that can affect site performance—see the sidebar "Site Performance."

Beware the FOUC!

Although you can use @import rules in an XHTML page to import style sheets, there is a problem that can occur. With only @import commands in the page and no link or script tags, IE6 can sometimes display the page content without CSS formatting momentarily as the page loads, which is not a very pleasant effect. This problem is known as a FOUC (meaning Flash Of Un-styled Content, not named after one's reaction upon seeing it). Using a link tag instead of an @import style in the XHTML to associate the import style sheet will fix this problem. As long as you have at least one link tag in your XHTML page, you will not see a FOUC. So, if you want to prevent the possibility of this problem, you can link the page to the import style sheet with a regular link tag, as I do in the examples in this chapter. If a link tag, or a script tag (used to associate JavaScript with your page) is present in the head of the page, your page won't trigger a FOUC. Learn more about the FOUC problem at http://bluerobot.com/web/css/fouc.asp/.

For the Registration page, which will have a full-size form in the content area but doesn't need the small sign-in form on the sidebar, I might create an import sheet called `import_3liq_txt_form_menu.css`, which contains this:

```
@import url(3_col_liquid_faux.css);

@import url(text_n_colors.css);

@import url(form_layout_2_col.css);

@import url(multi_drop_menus_class.css);
```

which I associate with the Registration page with

```
<link href="import_3liq_txt_form_menu.css" media="all" rel="stylesheet" />
```

Note I always start the import sheet names with `import_` so I know they are the pointers to the actual style sheets.

You can improve on the naming of these import sheets by relating them to the sections of your site—`import_product_listings.css`, for example.

Although @import rules can appear in any style sheet, they must appear at the very top of a style sheet, before any other CSS rules, or they are ignored.

Site Performance

Organizing your styles across multiple style sheets can really help you manage the numerous styles for your sites. However, don't split up your CSS for any given page into a very large number of style sheets. If you load more than say, five style sheets per page, even if they are not very big in kilobytes individually, you may start to see a slower page load performance. Often, more time is required to send the request and establish the connection for each file transfer than the time spent actually moving the data itself from server to browser. If you think this is happening, baseline the download speed with the multiple style sheets using Firebug (a debugging add-on for your Firefox browser—search www.getfirefox.com > Add-ons). Then copy all the styles into one style sheet, link your page to only that one style sheet, and measure again. If you see a noticeable difference, then you might want to start consolidating your styles into fewer style sheets.

However, there are a number of other factors that affect page rendering times—that is, the time between pressing the Enter key or clicking a link, and the page being fully displayed in the browser. These factors include network latency, server speeds, number of requests required (each image, external style sheet, and JavaScript file is a separate request), and the complexity of the CSS and any JavaScript that renders content to the screen. Some of these things are within your control, and some not. Yahoo!'s Yslow is a Firefox add-on that extends Firebug's capability and can help you further understand what is affecting your pages' performance. If you run a large Web site, I recommend you run your pages through Firebug and look at the Yslow tab also. Discussion around site performance and links to these and other tools can be found at http://davidherron.com/book-page/190-measuring-website-speed.

So now I have the three-column page template called home.html with four style sheets linked to it via the import sheet. It looks like **Figure 7.6**.

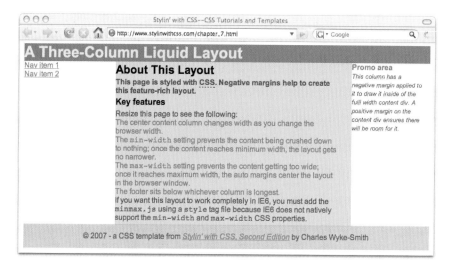

FIGURE 7.6 With the 3_col_liquid_faux template linked to its associated CSS file and the text_n_colors CSS file, I get this as the starting point for the site.

Only 3_col_liquid_faux.css and text_n_colors.css are actually affecting the page at this time. There is no associated markup for sign_in_form.css and multi_drop_menus_class.css yet, even though they are linked to the page. We'll look at markup for the form and menus shortly.

The Text and Colors Style Sheet

The `text_n_colors.css` style sheet is one that I wrote for a project a while ago and have since found very useful as a starting point for developing sites. Its purpose is to assign some overall styles for the most commonly used XHTML elements that are more to my taste than the default browser styles. This idea of creating style sheets that express one's personal design preferences as a starting point for each site is an interesting concept, and the `text_n_colors.css` style sheet is an evolving example of it. To make this set of "starter styles" as useful as possible, I've started to standardize the names of the main divs in my page layouts (`header`, `navigation`, `content`, `promo`, and `footer`, for example), as you have seen throughout this book. If those names don't make sense for the IDs of divs of a specific project, I just use names that are more relevant, and then do a quick search-and-replace on ID and class names in the style sheets to match up the style sheet with the "improved" names in the markup.

In the `text_n_colors.css` style sheet, I have created sets of colors and text sizes organized by a descriptive class name (e.g., `lime`, `olive`). Each style in each set has a contextual selector that uses one of these descriptive class names and a div ID (for example, `.lime #nav p {color:#444;}`). I can then easily select text styles for each of the main divs by simply adding a class name (`lime`, in this example) to the body tag of the page. (Take a look at the section of this style sheet I show below if this explanation is confusing to you.) I always seem to end up tweaking these styles for each specific project, but this style sheet makes a great starting point. I get an acceptable and harmonious look to my text and element backgrounds from the get-go, and it has already saved me hours of work.

I usually make a copy of the `text_n_colors.css` style sheet in the CSS folder of the project, and then, so I don't have to modify those styles directly, I add the styles specific to the site at the end of this style sheet, allowing me to override the preceding styles that I want to change. I will do this in the example that follows.

The `text_n_colors.css` style sheet which I copy from the library into each site's CSS folder, as I did previously, is currently a few hundred lines long as a I have a number of color schemes set up in it. At the end of the styling process, I tend to go back into this style sheet and remove all the sets of styles I didn't need—if I based my design on the set of color styles with the `lime` class, I might as well strip out the other color sets. To save space here, I won't show all the styles in this style sheet; I'll just show you the styles I kept from the original `text_n_colors.css` after completing the design for this site. Here they are, broken into sections with my comments between each section.

```css
* {
  margin:0;
  padding:0;
}
body {
  font: 1em Lucida, Arial, sans-serif;
}
h1, h2, h3, h4, h5, h6, ul, ol, dl {
  font-family: 'Trebuchet MS', Arial, serif;
}
```

I start by setting all the elements' margins to zero, set one font family for all the elements, and then set a second font family for headings and lists. Next, I deal with the heading sizes:

```css
h1 {font-size:2em;
}
h2 {font-size:1.5em;
  line-height:1.25;
  padding: 0 0 0 0;
}
h3 {font-size:1.25em;
  line-height:1.5;
}
h4 {font-size:1.125em;
}
h5 {font-size:1em;
}
h6 {font-size:.875em;
}
```

This resets the relative sizes of the headings. The default browser style sheet sizes for the large headings are too big, and the difference between the largest and smallest heading is extreme. My styles above make the smaller heading larger to produce a tighter range of heading sizes—even the smallest one now is bigger than the paragraph size. It doesn't make sense to me for headings to be smaller than regular text. Next, I set some basic styles for the most commonly used XHTML elements.

```
p {font-size:1em;}
```

```
code {font-size:1.25em;}
* html code {font-size:1.1em;}
```

a hack for IE6, because default size is larger in IE6

```
cite {
    font-size:.85em;
    font-style:italic;
    }
blockquote {
    width:30%;
    font-size:.7em;
    margin:0 0 1em 1em;
    padding:.3em .4em;
    border-top:2px solid;
    border-bottom:2px solid;
    }
blockquote cite {
    display:block;
    font-size:.85em;
    }
abbr, acronym {
    border-bottom:1px dashed #000;
    cursor:default;
```

```
    }
address {

    margin:0 1em .75em 1em;

    }
img {

    border:0;

    }
a:hover {

    text-decoration:none;

    }
```

Above are examples of some basic styles for some of the most common XHTML elements. Note these are element selectors without context, so they affect all elements of that type, wherever they appear on the page.

Next, lets look at some background colors for the main divs and type colors for the most common XHTML elements. I have several different color variations of these styles in the text_n_colors.css style sheet, but I will just illustrate the version that works with the class lime here.

```
.lime #main_wrapper {background-color:#FFF;}

.lime #header {background-color:#507EA1;}

.lime #nav {background-color:transparent;}

.lime #content {background-color:#CFE673;}

.lime #promo {background-color:transparent;}

.lime #footer {background-color:#BFCCD6;}


.lime h1 {

    color:#D6E2EC;

    }
.lime h2 {

    color:#000;

    }
```

```
.lime h3, .lime h5 {

  color:#000;

  }

.lime h4 {

  color:#507EA1;

  }

.lime h6 {

  color:#507EA1;

  }

.lime p {

  color:#555;

  }

.lime ul, .lime ol, .lime dl, .lime cite {

  color:#507EA1;

  }

.lime blockquote {

  color:#738040;

  }

.lime cite {

  color:#555;

  }

.lime table, .lime form {

  color: #507EA1;

  }

.lime a {

  color:#507EA1;

  }

.lime a:hover {

  color:#738040;

  }
```

```
.lime #nav a:hover, .lime #promo a:hover {

  color:#507EA1;

  }

.lime #nav a:hover, .lime #promo a:hover {

  color:#666;

  }
```

By adding the `lime` class to the body, these styles are applied to elements within a div with the specified ID. Let's next see what the markup, with the new content, looks like with these styles.

The Page Markup

Here's the XHTML markup for the home page:

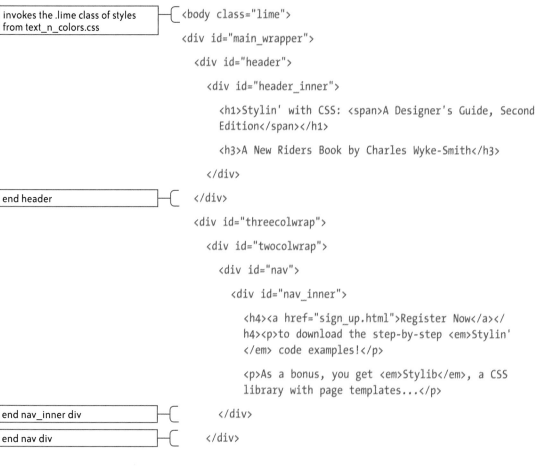

invokes the .lime class of styles from text_n_colors.css

```
<body class="lime">
<div id="main_wrapper">
  <div id="header">
    <div id="header_inner">
      <h1>Stylin' with CSS: <span>A Designer's Guide, Second
      Edition</span></h1>
      <h3>A New Riders Book by Charles Wyke-Smith</h3>
    </div>
```

end header

```
  </div>
  <div id="threecolwrap">
    <div id="twocolwrap">
      <div id="nav">
        <div id="nav_inner">
          <h4><a href="sign_up.html">Register Now</a></
          h4><p>to download the step-by-step <em>Stylin'
          </em> code examples!</p>
          <p>As a bonus, you get <em>Stylib</em>, a CSS
          library with page templates...</p>
```

end nav_inner div

```
        </div>
```

end nav div

```
      </div>
```

the center column

```
<div id="content">

    <div id="content_inner">

        <img src="images/cws_cropped_bw_170px.jpg" alt=
        "Charles Wyke-Smith - author of Styin' with CSS" />

        <p>In <em>Stylin' with CSS</em>, Charles Wyke-
        Smith takes you......examples and techniques.</p>

        <h4><strong><em>Stylin' with CSS</em> shows you
        how to:</strong></h4>

        <ul>

            <li>Create fixed-width....</li>

            <li>Create your own drop-down menus...</li>

            <li>Write for today's browsers...</li>

            <li>Accelerate site development...</li>

            <li>Use CSS like a pro...</li>

        </ul>

    </div>
```

end content inner

```
    </div>
```

end of content div

```
</div>
```

end of twocolwrap

```
</div>

<div id="promo">

    <div id="promo_inner"> <img src="images/book_cover.
    jpg" alt="Stylin' with CSS - second edition by Charles
    Wyke-Smith" />

        <ul>

            <li><a href="#">Buy

                this Book</a></li>

            <li><a href="#">Read

                Reviews of this Book</a></li>

            <li><a href="#">Other

                Books by this Author</a></li>

            <li><a href="#">About the Author</a></li>

            <li><a href="#">The Author's Conference Schedule
            </a></li>
```

```
                          <li><a href="#">Other Books We Recommend</a></li>

                            </ul>
```

end of inner promo div ──[
```
                            </div>
```
end of promo div ──[
```
                          </div>
```
end of threecolwrap div ──[
```
                        </div>

                      <div id="footer">

                        <div id="footer_inner">

                          <p>&copy; 2007 - Stylin' with CSS: A Designer's Guide,
                          Second Edition by Charles Wyke-Smith</p>
```
end of footer inner div ──[
```
                          </div>
```
end footer ──[
```
                        </div>
```
end main_wrapper ──[
```
                      </div>

                      </body>
```

This gives us **Figure 7.7**.

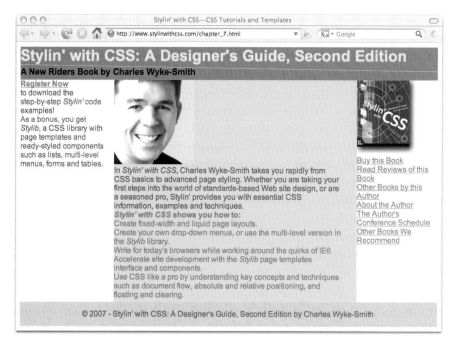

FIGURE 7.7 The placeholder content is replaced with the actual content for the site.

At this point, we have added the marked-up content into a pre-existing XHTML layout and styled it with the pre-existing `3_col_liquid_faux.css` and `text_n_colors.css` style sheets. This has got us quite a long way (**Figure 7.7**), but now it's time to start adding some styles to give this page its own unique look.

The Background Images

We'll first add some background graphics. There are four of them, one for the header, one for the footer, and two in the main area of the page. Let's start with the header and footer graphics (**Figures 7.8a and b**). They were created in Adobe Photoshop by simply putting huge gray type on a darker gray background and then exporting them in `.gif` format. They are each 880 pixels wide, which is the maximum width I plan for this liquid layout.

FIGURES 7.8A AND 7.8B The header and footer background graphics are both 880-pixel-wide .gif images.

Once these graphics are in the images folder, making them appear in the background of the header and footer simply requires opening the `3_col_liquid.css` file and adding the following CSS:

```
div#header {

    background:url(../images/gray_header.gif) repeat-y #383838;

}

#footer {

    clear:both;

    background:url(../images/gray_footer.gif) repeat-y #383838;

}
```

Note the use of `repeat-y` (repeat vertically) for both graphics, even though in normal circumstances, neither will actually visibly repeat. I do this because if either the header or footer becomes taller than its background graphic (which shouldn't happen but might if someone inadvertently adds too much text, or if the user sizes up the layout to a really large size from the View menu), then there won't be a gap below the background graphic—instead, it will repeat vertically. Also, in case the graphic doesn't load at all, I've added a gray background color. A background graphic is always displayed on top of a

The backgrounds of the header and footer were initially colored by the text_n_colors.css *style sheet, so I removed those styles from that style sheet.*

background color, so the color doesn't normally show if the graphic fills the background, as it does here. While always stating a background color along with any background image is good practice, it is especially important in this case, as the light-colored text I will have to use over these dark background graphics will barely show on the default white background color of the page if the background graphic doesn't load for some reason.

I also added a graphic of overlapping circles into the twocolwrap div that encloses the left and center columns, and added another larger graphic based on the cover of the book into the main_wrapper div.

```
div#main_wrapper {
```

[additional styles here not shown]

```
    background:url(../images/cover_circles.jpg) no-repeat
    300px 0;

}
```

```
#twocolwrap {
```

[additional styles here not shown]

```
    background:url(../images/full_arc.gif) no-repeat;

}
```

FIGURES 7.9A AND 7.9B These are the two graphics, full_arc.gif and cover_circles.jpg, that go behind the left and center, and center and right columns, respectively. Their borders are added here in the book for clarity and don't exist on the actual artwork.

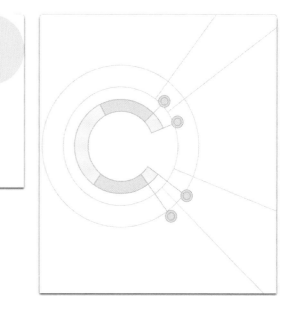

Note the use of the positioning units (highlighted). The main_wrappper div encloses the entire layout, so in order to have cover_circles.jpg (**Figure 7.9B**) nicely positioned behind the content area, I have to move it 300 pixels to the right. The default positioning of full_arc.gif (**Figure 7.9A**) puts it where it needs to be, so no additional positioning is required for that element.

One other small step I took at this point was to find the style that colored the background of the content area in the text_n_colors. css file and modify it so the background color is transparent, not lime green. Otherwise, this background image in the main_wrapper div would not show through the content div which overlays it. If two elements overlap, as the main_wrapper and content divs do, the child element appears on top of the parent element.

```
.lime #content {background-color:#FFF #CFE673;}
```

Now we are at this point (**Figure 7.10**).

FIGURE 7.10 The four background images are added to the layout.

The text styles in the header and footer could use some work, and we will change them when we deal with all the other text later. Meantime, let's add the drop-down menus.

The Drop-Down Menus

It is quite simple to make this menu work, as the markup is just a nested list structure. Once written, all you have to do is associate that markup with the already-written CSS and then style the colors to your liking. We previously associated the menu's style sheet with the page, so if we add some markup, the menu should be good to go.

```
</div>
    <div class="multi_drop_menus">
    <ul>
        <li><a href="#">What's New</a></li>
        <li><a href="#">Table of Contents</a></li>
        <li><a href="#">CSS Links</a>
          <ul>
            <li><a href="#">Link 1</a></li>
            <li><a href="#">Link 2</a></li>
            <li><a href="#">Link 3</a></li>
            <li><a href="#">Link 4</a></li>
          </ul>
        </li>
        <li><a href="#">Contact Us</a></li>
    </ul>
    </div>
    <div id="threecolwrap">
```

- end header → `</div>`
- ends multi-drop menus → `</div>`
- (etc) → `<div id="threecolwrap">`

Note the class on the div that associates the markup with the menu styles. You can see I dropped this div into the markup between the header and the wrappers that surround the column. This will allow it to sit nice and tight under the header, as **Figure 7.11** shows.

FIGURE 7.11 Because the `multi_level_menu.css` file is already associated with the page, the menu markup is instantly styled, although it still needs work for use in this page,.

The benefit of working with the preprogrammed library components is that you get a fairly satisfactory result first time. In this case, all we need to do is tweak the colors and create some space below the menu. A few minor changes to the menu's style sheet will do the job. All the user-modifiable styles for these menus are grouped at the top of the style sheet in the same order as the markup, and each style has a comment that explains its purpose, so it's easy to find and change the styles we need to adjust.

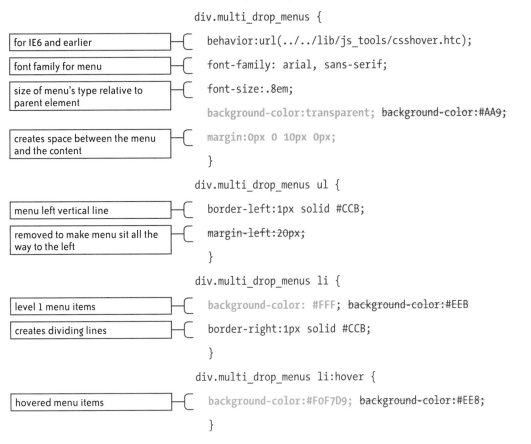

```
div.multi_drop_menus {
    behavior:url(../../lib/js_tools/csshover.htc);
    font-family: arial, sans-serif;
    font-size:.8em;
    background-color:transparent; background-color:#AA9;
    margin:0px 0 10px 0px;
}
div.multi_drop_menus ul {
    border-left:1px solid #CCB;
    margin-left:20px;
}
div.multi_drop_menus li {
    background-color: #FFF; background-color:#EEB
    border-right:1px solid #CCB;
}
div.multi_drop_menus li:hover {
    background-color:#F0F7D9; background-color:#EE8;
}
```

for IE6 and earlier

font family for menu

size of menu's type relative to parent element

creates space between the menu and the content

menu left vertical line

removed to make menu sit all the way to the left

level 1 menu items

creates dividing lines

hovered menu items

This gives the result shown in **Figure 7.12**.

FIGURE 7.12 The improved menu styling.

The menu's div that extended across the page before is actually still there but now is transparent. The left margin on the ul is removed, which moves the menu all the way to the left, and a small bottom margin creates space between the menu and the content area.

TRANSPARENCY ON THE DROP-DOWNS

The multi_level_menu.css file also has a capability to add transparency to the drop-down part of the menu. I've coded the style sheet so all you need to do is add the class transparent to the menu's containing div like this:

```
<div class="multi_drop_menus transparent">
```

and the menu immediately becomes transparent (**Figure 7.13**).

FIGURE 7.13 Simply adding the transparent class to the menu's div renders all the menu's drop-downs with a nice see-through effect.

Actually, the CSS specification uses the term *opacity*, which is, of course, the antonym of *transparency*—as something gets more transparent, it becomes less opaque.

Confusingly, there are three different ways of creating opacity between the various browsers.

values 0 to 100

1. **The IE method**: filter:alpha(opacity=90);

values 0 to 1

2. **The Mozilla (Firefox) method**: -moz-opacity:0.9;

3. **The CSS3 Standards method** (Safari and other SBCs): opacity:0.9;

values 0 to 1

So the transparency rule in the menu style sheet looks like this:

```
div.multi_drop_menus.transparent ul ul li {
```

| CSS3—values 0 to 1 |
| Firefox—values 0 to 1 |
| IE—values 0 to 100 |

```
  opacity:0.9;

  -moz-opacity:0.9;

  filter:alpha(opacity=90);

}
```

When you use the menus in your own projects, you can go into the style sheet and adjust the transparency level, but remember to do it in all three places.

The Transparent Sidebar Panel

As you can see if you look back at the finished page (**Figure 7.1**), the left sidebar has a gray box with rounded corners that is also transparent. However, the transparency here is not produced programmatically through the code, but in the way the graphics are created.

Rounded-corner boxes are the calling card of the Web 2.0 design movement, and it should be really easy to create them—after all, the capability to round the corners of divs is a feature of CCS3. However, with the exception of Mozilla-based browsers such as Firefox, which use a proprietary method of doing this, no browsers currently support this feature. Except for some efforts to simulate this effect with JavaScript, such as the NiftyCorners code we saw in Chapter 5, rounded-corner boxes have been created with graphics.

Creating Rounded Corners with JavaScript

Seeing as rounded boxes are so popular right now, here are some programmatic rounded boxes solutions:

Rounded Corners fromEditsite.net
  http://www.editsite.net/blog/rounded_corners.html

Spiffy Corners from Spiffy Corners.com
  http://www.spiffycorners.com/

Nifty Corners by Alessandro Fulciniti
  http://www.html.it/articoli/niftycube/index.html

Thrash Box from VertexWorks
  http://www.vertexwerks.com/tests/sidebox/

Although you can add rounded corners to divs using JavaScript (see the sidebar "Creating Rounded Corners with JavaScript"), I will now show you how to create rounded boxes with artwork. Creating a box with a fixed size is as simple as making the artwork and adding it to the page, but the trick is to create such boxes so that they expand to accommodate whatever content is chucked into them. If you want a fixed-width graphical box to expand vertically (which is what I want here), the easiest way is to create three pieces of artwork that go into the background of three containing elements.

How this actually works is easier to demonstrate than explain, so let's start by looking at the artwork. Here are three pieces of artwork I need: the top graphic with the curved top edge of the box, the middle graphic that repeats as many times as needed to fill the center of the box, and the bottom graphic with the curved bottom of the box (**Figure 7.14**).

FIGURE 7.14 Here are the three pieces of pale gray artwork that make up the box. All are 170 pixels wide. They each have a transparency of 37%.

I created these graphics in Adobe Fireworks by first drawing a 60-pixel-high pale gray box (hex color:#CCCCCC;). I then set its corner roundness to 16 and its transparency to 37% in the Properties palette. In the Modify menu, I set the Canvas Color to transparent to ensure the area removed by rounding the corners would reveal whatever background the box appeared on. Then I cropped the canvas using the Canvas Size window in the Modify menu to get the piece (top, middle, or bottom) I needed and exported it as a .png graphic. Then I used Undo to get back the original box and cropped it again to get the next bit I wanted, and exported that piece. Total time to create all three pieces of artwork: about seven minutes.

ADJUSTING THE LEFT COLUMN WIDTH

Before I add these pieces of artwork to the left column, I want to make the left column wider to create some space around the background box. Currently, the column is 170 pixels wide, and I want it to be 200 pixels—this will give me 15 pixels of margin each side of the 170 pixel wide box. It's easy to adjust the column widths in this liquid layout, as long as you remember that for each column's width setting there is a corresponding margin on the adjacent column.

```
#nav {
  float:left;
  width:150px;
  width:200px;
  }
#content {
  width:auto;
  margin-left:150px;
  margin-left:200px;
  margin-right:170px;
  padding:0;
  }
```

Because this layout is liquid, no adjustment is needed to the outer wrapper around the layout. This would be the case if we were working with one of the fixed-width templates.

Note that we are now putting background images over background images. We earlier added a background graphic, `full_arc.gif`, into the `two_col_wrap` div, which visually appears as the background for the `nav` div. Now, we are about to add the three pieces of artwork for the transparent box into divs inside the `nav` div. These pieces of artwork will appear over the artwork in the `two_col_wrap` div because their divs are descendants of `two_col_wrap` and therefore appear on top of it. This will mean that the furthest-back image in `two_col_wrap`, which is the circles, will show through the transparent box in the `nav` column—a nice visual effect.

ADDING THE TRANSPARENT BACKGROUND GRAPHIC TO THE COLUMN

So the next question is: Where do we add these background box graphics? Here is the plan: I am going to add the center background graphic into the `nav_inner` div. I'll add two more divs into the markup, one immediately before the inner div starts to hold the top curve of the box, and one right after the inner div to hold the curved bottom of the box. In this way, the curved pieces of the top and bottom of the box will sit directly above and below the center of the box, and look like part of it.

Let's add the extra divs into the markup.

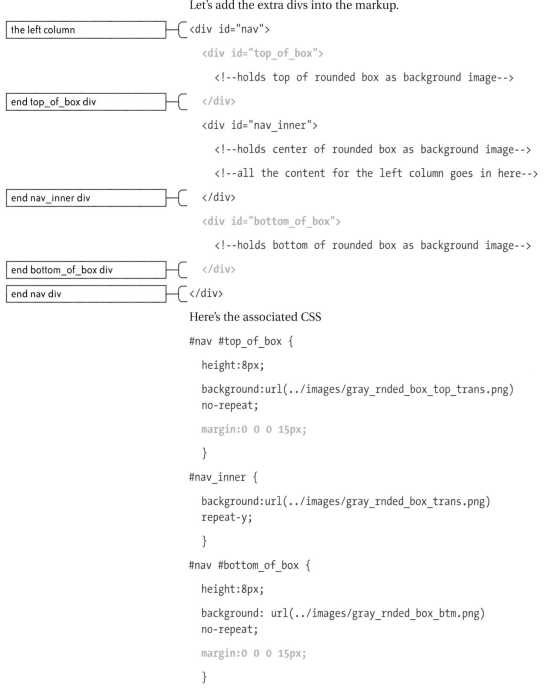

the left column

```
<div id="nav">

    <div id="top_of_box">

        <!--holds top of rounded box as background image-->
```

end top_of_box div

```
    </div>

    <div id="nav_inner">

        <!--holds center of rounded box as background image-->

        <!--all the content for the left column goes in here-->
```

end nav_inner div

```
    </div>

    <div id="bottom_of_box">

        <!--holds bottom of rounded box as background image-->
```

end bottom_of_box div

```
    </div>
```

end nav div

```
</div>
```

Here's the associated CSS

```
#nav #top_of_box {

    height:8px;

    background:url(../images/gray_rnded_box_top_trans.png)
    no-repeat;

    margin:0 0 0 15px;

    }

#nav_inner {

    background:url(../images/gray_rnded_box_trans.png)
    repeat-y;

    }

#nav #bottom_of_box {

    height:8px;

    background: url(../images/gray_rnded_box_btm.png)
    no-repeat;

    margin:0 0 0 15px;

    }
```

Even though the CSS for the nav_inner div is in the 3_col_liquid. ccs file, I put this particular nav_inner style in the text_n_colors.css style sheet (where I am adding all the CSS I am writing especially for this page, additional to the library CSS), as it makes sense that it lives with the div style for the other parts of the box. However, I also need to make one small adjustment to the nav_inner div's styling in the 3_col_liquid.css style sheet. Here's what was originally there:

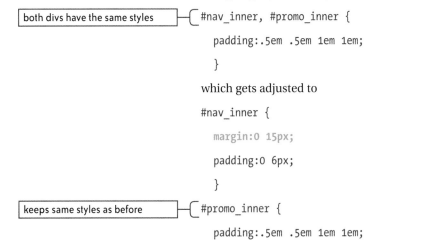

both divs have the same styles

```
#nav_inner, #promo_inner {

    padding:.5em .5em 1em 1em;

}
```

which gets adjusted to

```
#nav_inner {

    margin:0 15px;

    padding:0 6px;

}
```

keeps same styles as before

```
#promo_inner {

    padding:.5em .5em 1em 1em;

}
```

What I have done in the last two pieces of code is add 15 pixel margins to each side of the three divs that contain the graphics for the rounded box (highlights). This centers the composited box in the 200 pixel wide column—the box is 170 pixels wide and there are 15 pixels of margins each side. So now the inner div is exactly the same width as the rounded box in its background, and I can add 6 pixels of horizontal padding to each side of the innerdiv to ensure the content does not extend out to the edge of the box.

Now as we add content to the inner div, its background repeats to fill it, and the bottom curve of the box gets pushed down to always snugly sit below it. As the second graphic shows, no matter how much content we add to the inner div, the box expands to accommodate it (**Figures 7.15A** and **B**). The key to this effect is the repeat-y on the CSS of the background graphic for the inner div, which causes the background graphic to repeat as many times as needed, and the top and bottom graphic elements sandwich it snugly to form the rounded corners.

FIGURES 7.15A AND 7.15B The top, middle, and bottom graphic elements now touch and appear to be one graphic. In the right screenshot, I temporarily duplicated the content to show how the box expands as the content increases.

If you really want .png transparency in IE6, you can find an Internet Explorer behavior that will enable this at http://www.twinhelix.com/css/iepngfix/.

I will say it is a little tedious to create transparent boxes this way, and I wish that there were easier ways than resorting to using either JavaScript or the graphics approach I used in this example. Also, IDWIMIE—IE6 can't display repeating transparent background .png images, so I simply used the star-html hack to turn off these background elements in IE6, like this:

```
* html #nav #top_of_box, * html #nav_inner, * html #nav
#bottom_of_box {background:none;}
```

As the box serves only to enhance readability and the visual look of the page, it's not a major problem if it's not present.

Adding the Registration Form

Let's now add the Registration form into the nav_inner div so it appears below the text that is already there. Because we already have the XHTML and CSS for the sign-up form we created in Chapter 6 (which is exactly what we need here), this step goes very quickly. We drop in the markup that appears right after **Figure 6.21** in Chapter 6, which I won't repeat here. (You can also find the same markup in the *Stylib* library in a file called sign_up.html.) This markup goes right before the close of the inner_nav div.

```
<div id="nav_inner">
```
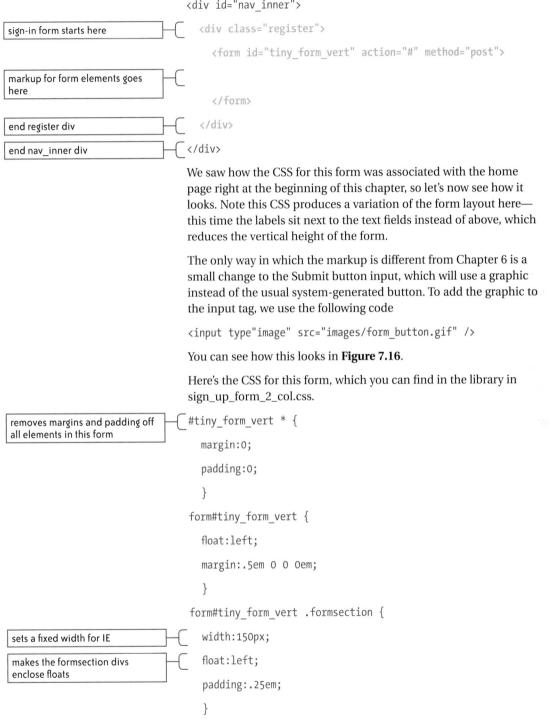

sign-in form starts here
```
  <div class="register">
    <form id="tiny_form_vert" action="#" method="post">
```

markup for form elements goes here
```
    </form>
```

end register div
```
  </div>
```
end nav_inner div
```
</div>
```

We saw how the CSS for this form was associated with the home page right at the beginning of this chapter, so let's now see how it looks. Note this CSS produces a variation of the form layout here—this time the labels sit next to the text fields instead of above, which reduces the vertical height of the form.

The only way in which the markup is different from Chapter 6 is a small change to the Submit button input, which will use a graphic instead of the usual system-generated button. To add the graphic to the input tag, we use the following code

```
<input type"image" src="images/form_button.gif" />
```

You can see how this looks in **Figure 7.16**.

Here's the CSS for this form, which you can find in the library in sign_up_form_2_col.css.

removes margins and padding off all elements in this form
```
#tiny_form_vert * {
    margin:0;
    padding:0;
}
form#tiny_form_vert {
    float:left;
    margin:.5em 0 0 0em;
}
form#tiny_form_vert .formsection {
```

sets a fixed width for IE
```
    width:150px;
```
makes the formsection divs enclose floats
```
    float:left;
    padding:.25em;
}
```

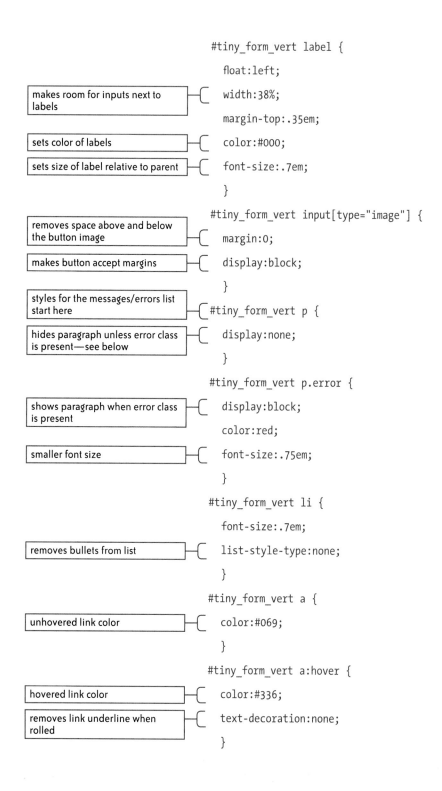

```
#tiny_form_vert label {

    float:left;

    width:38%;

    margin-top:.35em;

    color:#000;

    font-size:.7em;

}

#tiny_form_vert input[type="image"] {

    margin:0;

    display:block;

}

#tiny_form_vert p {

    display:none;

}

#tiny_form_vert p.error {

    display:block;

    color:red;

    font-size:.75em;

}

#tiny_form_vert li {

    font-size:.7em;

    list-style-type:none;

}

#tiny_form_vert a {

    color:#069;

}

#tiny_form_vert a:hover {

    color:#336;

    text-decoration:none;

}
```

makes room for inputs next to labels

sets color of labels

sets size of label relative to parent

removes space above and below the button image

makes button accept margins

styles for the messages/errors list start here

hides paragraph unless error class is present—see below

shows paragraph when error class is present

smaller font size

removes bullets from list

unhovered link color

hovered link color

removes link underline when rolled

The form element and its child elements can be dropped into a containing element, and it immediately styles itself, as shown in **Figure 7.16**, if you have the right class added to the `form` div and the CSS is associated with the page.

FIGURE 7.16 The sign-up form is now styled below the text. Note how the transparent box expands vertically to accommodate it.

What's New | Table of Contents

Register Now
to download the step-by-step
Stylin' code examples!
As a bonus, you get *Stylib*, a
CSS library with page
templates and ready-styled
components such as lists,
multi-level menus, forms and
tables.

Sign In
User Name
Password
Sign In
Lost Password?

Styling the Text

All that is left to do is style the text in the header content area, promo area (right column), and footer.

THE HEADER

The effect I want in the header is that the headline text touches the left edge of the header and the subhead text touches the right edge. Normally, I would pad content away from the edge of its containing element, as I did with text in the box on the left navigation, but I want to create a dramatic look for the header to go with the black and gray look, and the visual tension caused by the text going right out to the edges is just what I want.

To further play up this effect, I have floated one heading one way and one the other. As the liquid layout is resized, the two elements change their relative position, adding to the overall effect. Also, the header needs to be opened up vertically. Some margins on the elements will take care of that.

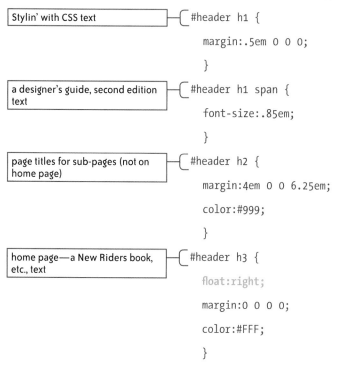

Stylin' with CSS text

```
#header h1 {

    margin:.5em 0 0 0;

}
```

a designer's guide, second edition text

```
#header h1 span {

    font-size:.85em;

}
```

page titles for sub-pages (not on home page)

```
#header h2 {

    margin:4em 0 0 6.25em;

    color:#999;

}
```

home page—a New Riders book, etc., text

```
#header h3 {

    float:right;

    margin:0 0 0 0;

    color:#FFF;

}
```

These simple styles give this visual effect in **Figures 7.17A** and **B**.

FIGURES 7.17A AND 7.17B The right-floated subhead moves under the left-aligned main head as the page is resized.

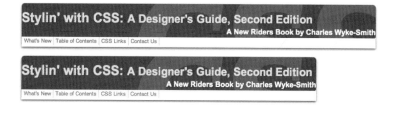

THE CONTENT AREA

The main adjustment needed for the center-column content area is to get the text to move up next to the photograph. This is achieved by floating the photograph left. Whenever I do this, I always add a right and bottom margin of perhaps .5 em to the floated image to ensure the text doesn't touch it.

```
#content img {

  float:left;

  margin:0 10px 5px 0;

}
```

Next, I add some styles for the paragraph next to the picture. I don't want too much text here, and I also want the list that follows to start below the image, so this is a chance to make a feature of this text and make it fairly large with plenty of line spacing.

```
#content p {

  font-size:1em;

  line-height:140%;

  margin-bottom:.75em;

}
```

Finally, a few small tweaks to the default list styling complete the content area for this page (**Figure 7.18**).

```
#content ul li {

  margin: 0 0 0 16px;

  padding:.3em 0;

  font-size:.8em;

}
```

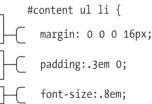

ensures the bullets aren't hanging left out of the containing ul

vertical space between the list items

smaller text size for the bullets

I mentioned back in Chapter 4 the importance of applying a width to floated elements, but this is not necessary with images; they are already inherently fixed width, so they can be floated without a corresponding width rule.

FIGURE 7.18 The styled content area. The floated image has small right and bottom margins so the text does not touch it.

In *Stylin' with CSS*, Charles Wyke-Smith takes you rapidly from CSS basics to advanced page styling. Whether you are taking your first steps into the world of standards-based Web site design, or are a seasoned pro, *Stylin'* provides you with essential CSS information, examples and techniques.

Stylin' with CSS shows you how to:

- Create fixed-width and liquid page layouts.
- Create your own drop-down menus, or use the multi-level version in the *Stylib* library.
- Write for today's browsers while working around the quirks of IE6.
- Accelerate site development with the *Stylib* page templates interface and components.
- Use CSS like a pro by understanding key concepts and techniques such as document flow, absolute and relative positioning, and floating and clearing.

THE RIGHT PROMO COLUMN

All I have in this column is the image of the book cover and a list of links. With the padding on the container provided by the `3_col_liquid_faux.css` style sheet, I don't need to do anything to the image. The list requires just a few styles to remove the bullets, reduce the type size, and better space the type. I also add a class to the first list item so I can bold it. (I would prefer to use a `:firstchild` style and avoid adding the class, but you guessed it, IDWIMIE6.) Here's the CSS, which gives the result shown in **Figure 7.19**.

FIGURE 7.19 Some simple styles on the list complete the right column.

Buy this Book
Read Reviews of this Book
Other Books by this Author
About the Author
The Author's Conference Schedule
Other Books We Recommend

```
#promo li {

  list-style-type:none;

  font-size:.8em;

  line-height:120%;

  padding:.3em 0;

  }

#promo li.big_link {

  font-weight:bold;

  }
```

All that's left is to style the footer.

THE FOOTER

Not much to do here, except make the type a little smaller and color it white.

```
#footer p {

  font-size:.75em;

  color:#FFF;

  }
```

As part of this final step, I will repair the path to the NiftyCorners file so the header and footer have rounded corners as in the original template. I will also take advantage of NiftyCorners' capability to set which corners on a box are rounded, and not round the bottom left corner of the header so the menu fits perfectly against it. I'll also fix the path to `minmax.js` file so that IE6 can apply the minimum and maximum widths specified in the CSS to the layout.

This code in the head of your page should look like this; you must ensure that your path names actually link to the files, and this code matches the file structure I showed at the start of the chapter.

```
<script type="text/javascript" src="js_tools/minmax.js">
</script>
```

load and use NiftyCorners

```
<script type="text/javascript" src="nifty_corners/javascript/
niftycube.js"></script>

<script type="text/javascript">
```

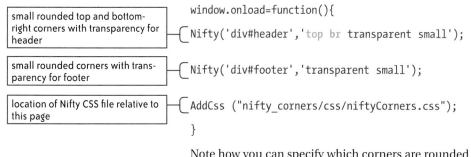

small rounded top and bottom-right corners with transparency for header

small rounded corners with transparency for footer

location of Nifty CSS file relative to this page

```
window.onload=function(){
  Nifty('div#header','top br transparent small');
  Nifty('div#footer','transparent small');
  AddCss ("nifty_corners/css/niftyCorners.css");
}
```

Note how you can specify which corners are rounded in the Nifty Corners JavaScript code (highlighted)—in this case, the top edge corners and the bottom right. This leaves the bottom-left corner with the usual squared-off corner. The transparency setting ensures the background graphic is visible.

And that's it—our page is complete (**Figure 7.20**).

FIGURE 7.20 The finished page.

Conclusion

CSS is a powerful mechanism for styling Web pages. Having a deep understanding of its workings gives you, the designer, the best chance of having your designs render accurately on the largest possible number of browsers. I have tried to include in this book the most useful techniques and insights that I know, and I encourage you to build on the *Stylib* library and the book's sample files here to create your own collection of page layouts and interface components.

As you can probably tell, I love working in CSS, and I hope this book has given you that same enthusiasm for its wonderful capabilities and provides you with the knowledge you need to realize your creative visions. Now it's your turn to start stylin', too.

APPENDIX A

XHTML Tags

The third column of this table indicates the DTD (Document Type Definition) required in the DOCTYPE for this tag to be useable: Strict, Transitional, or Frameset. See page 10 for more information about DTDs.

***Deprecated** means that this tag is useable but is being phased out, and therefore it is best not to use it. Often, a tag will have been deprecated because there is now a CSS alternative; for example, instead of using the XHTML* <center> *tag to center text, use the CSS property* text-align:center. *Note that deprecated tags fail validation in a document with a Strict DOCTYPE.*

XHTML TAGS

TAG	DESCRIPTION	DTD
<!--...-->	Defines a comment	STF
<!DOCTYPE>	Defines the document type	STF
<a>	Defines an anchor	STF
<abbr>	Defines an abbreviation	STF
<acronym>	Defines an acronym	STF
<address>	Defines an address element	STF
<applet>	*(Deprecated.)* Defines an applet	TF
<area>	Defines an area inside an image map	STF
<b>	Defines bold text	STF
<base>	Defines a base URL for all the links in a page	STF
<basefont>	*(Deprecated.)* Defines a base font	TF
<bdo>	Defines the direction of text display	STF
<big>	Defines big text	STF
<blockquote>	Defines a long quotation	STF
<body>	Defines the body element	STF
 	Inserts a single line break	STF
<button>	Defines a push button	STF
<caption>	Defines a table caption	STF
<center>	*(Deprecated.)* Defines centered text	TF
<cite>	Defines a citation	STF
<code>	Defines computer code text	STF
<col>	Defines attributes for table columns	STF
<colgroup>	Defines groups of table columns	STF
<dd>	Defines a definition description	STF
<del>	Defines deleted text	STF
<dir>	*(Deprecated.)* Defines a directory list	TF
<div>	Defines a section in a document	STF
<dfn>	Defines a definition term	STF
<dl>	Defines a definition list	STF
<dt>	Defines a definition term	STF
<em>	Defines emphasized text	STF
<fieldset>	Defines a fieldset	STF
<font>	*(Deprecated.)* Defines text font, size, and color	TF
<form>	Defines a form	STF

XHTML TAGS (continued)

TAG	DESCRIPTION	DTD
<frame>	Defines a sub window (a frame)	F
<frameset>	Defines a set of frames	F
<h1> to <h6>	Defines header 1 to header 6	STF
<head>	Defines information about the document	STF
<hr>	Defines a horizontal rule	STF
<html>	Defines an html document	STF
<i>	Defines italic text	STF
<iframe>	Defines an inline sub window (frame)	TF
<img>	Defines an image	STF
<input>	Defines an input field	STF
<ins>	Defines inserted text	STF
<isindex>	(Deprecated.) Defines a single-line input field	TF
<kbd>	Defines keyboard text	STF
<label>	Defines a label for a form control	STF
<legend>	Defines a title in a fieldset	STF
<li>	Defines a list item	STF
<link>	Defines a resource reference	STF
<map>	Defines an image map	STF
<menu>	(Deprecated.) Defines a menu list	TF
<meta>	Defines meta information	STF
<noframes>	Defines a noframe section	TF
<noscript>	Defines a noscript section	STF
<object>	Defines an embedded object	STF
<ol>	Defines an ordered list	STF
<optgroup>	Defines an option group	STF
<option>	Defines an option in a drop-down list	STF
<p>	Defines a paragraph	STF
<param>	Defines a parameter for an object	STF
<pre>	Defines preformatted text	STF
<q>	Defines a short quotation	STF
<s>	(Deprecated.) Defines strikethrough text	TF
<samp>	Defines sample computer code	STF
<script>	Defines a script	STF
<select>	Defines a selectable list	STF

XHTML TAGS (continued)

TAG	DESCRIPTION	DTD
<small>	Defines small text	STF
<span>	Defines a section in a document	STF
<strike>	*(Deprecated.)* Defines strikethrough text	TF
<strong>	Defines strong text	STF
<style>	Defines a style definition	STF
<sub>	Defines subscripted text	STF
<sup>	Defines superscripted text	STF
<table>	Defines a table	STF
<tbody>	Defines a table body	STF
<td>	Defines a table cell	STF
<textarea>	Defines a text area	STF
<tfoot>	Defines a table footer	STF
<th>	Defines a table header	STF
<thead>	Defines a table header	STF
<title>	Defines the document title	STF
<tr>	Defines a table row	STF
<tt>	Defines teletype text	STF
<u>	*(Deprecated.)* Defines underlined text	TF
<ul>	Defines an unordered list	STF
<var>	Defines a variable	STF
<xmp>	*(Deprecated.)* Defines preformatted text	

APPENDIX B

CSS Properties

BACKGROUND

PROPERTY	DESCRIPTION	VALUES	IE	F	N	W3C
background	A shorthand property for setting all background properties in one declaration	*background-color* *background-image* *background-repeat* *background-attachment* *background-position*	4	1	6	1
background-attachment	Sets whether a background image is fixed or scrolls with the rest of the page	scroll fixed	4	1	6	1
background-color	Sets the background color of an element	*color-rgb* *color-hex* *color-name* transparent	4	1	4	1
background-image	Sets an image as the background	url(*URL*) none	4	1	4	1
background-position	Sets the starting position of a background image	top left top center top right center left center center center right bottom left bottom center bottom right *x% y%* *xpos ypos*	4	1	6	1
background-repeat	Sets if/how a background image will be repeated	repeat repeat-x repeat-y no-repeat	4	1	4	1

Browser support: IE: Internet Explorer, F: Firefox, N: Netscape. Numbers indicate earliest browser version supporting this property.

W3C: The number in the "W3C" column indicates in which CSS recommendation the property is defined (CSS1 or CSS2).

BORDER

PROPERTY	DESCRIPTION	VALUES	IE	F	N	W3C
border	A shorthand property for setting all of the properties for the four borders in one declaration	*border-width* *border-style* *border-color*	4	1	4	1
border-bottom	A shorthand property for setting all of the properties for the bottom border in one declaration	*border-bottom-width* *border-style* *border-color*	4	1	6	1
border-bottom-color	Sets the color of the bottom border	*border-color*	4	1	6	2
border-bottom-style	Sets the style of the bottom border	*border-style*	4	1	6	2
border-bottom-width	Sets the width of the bottom border	thin medium thick *length*	4	1	4	1
border-color	Sets the color of the four borders, can have from one to four colors	*color*	4	1	6	1
border-left	A shorthand property for setting all of the properties for the left border in one declaration	*border-left-width* *border-style* *border-color*	4	1	6	1
border-left-color	Sets the color of the left border	*border-color*	4	1	6	2
border-left-style	Sets the style of the left border	*border-style*	4	1	6	2
border-left-width	Sets the width of the left border	thin medium thick *length*	4	1	4	1
border-right	A shorthand property for setting all of the properties for the right border in one declaration	*border-right-width* *border-style* *border-color*	4	1	6	1
border-right-color	Sets the color of the right border	*border-color*	4	1	6	2
border-right-style	Sets the style of the right border	*border-style*	4	1	6	2
border-right-width	Sets the width of the right border	thin medium thick *length*	4	1	4	1
border-style	Sets the style of the four borders, can have from one to four styles	none hidden dotted dashed solid double groove ridge inset outset	4	1	6	1

(continued on next page)

BORDER (continued)

PROPERTY	DESCRIPTION	VALUES	IE	F	N	W3C
border-top	A shorthand property for setting all of the properties for the top border in one declaration	*border-top-width* *border-style* *border-color*	4	1	6	1
border-top-color	Sets the color of the top border	*border-color*	4	1	6	2
border-top-style	Sets the style of the top border	*border-style*	4	1	6	2
border-top-width	Sets the width of the top border	thin medium thick *length*	4	1	4	1
border-width	A shorthand property for setting the width of the four borders in one declaration, can have from one to four values	thin medium thick *length*	4	1	4	1

CLASSIFICATION

PROPERTY	DESCRIPTION	VALUES	IE	F	N	W3C
clear	Sets the sides of an element where other floating elements are not allowed	left right both none	4	1	4	1
cursor	Specifies the type of cursor to be displayed	*url* auto crosshair default pointer move e-resize ne-resize nw-resize n-resize se-resize sw-resize s-resize w-resize text wait help	4	1	6	2

(continued on next page)

CLASSIFICATION (continued)

PROPERTY	DESCRIPTION	VALUES	IE	F	N	W3C
display	Sets how/if an element is displayed	none inline block list-item run-in compact marker table inline-table table-row-group table-header-group table-footer-group table-row table-column-group table-column table-cell table-caption	4	1	4	1
float	Sets where an image or a text will appear in another element	left right none	4	1	4	1
position	Places an element in a static, relative, absolute, or fixed position	static relative absolute fixed	4	1	4	2
visibility	Sets if an element should be visible or invisible	visible hidden collapse	4	1	6	2

DIMENSION

PROPERTY	DESCRIPTION	VALUES	IE	F	N	W3C
height	Sets the height of an element	auto *length* %	4	1	6	1
line-height	Sets the distance between lines	normal *number* *length* %	4	1	4	1
max-height	Sets the maximum height of an element	none *length* %	-	1	6	2

(continued on next page)

DIMENSION (continued)

PROPERTY	DESCRIPTION	VALUES	IE	F	N	W3C
max-width	Sets the maximum width of an element	none *length* %	-	1	6	2
min-height	Sets the minimum height of an element	*length* %	-	1	6	2
min-width	Sets the minimum width of an element	*length* %	-	1	6	2
width	Sets the width of an element	auto % *length*	4	1	4	1

FONT

PROPERTY	DESCRIPTION	VALUES	IE	F	N	W3C
font	A shorthand property for setting all of the properties for a font in one declaration	*font-style* *font-variant* *font-weight* *font-size/line-height* *font-family* caption icon menu message-box small-caption status-bar	4	1	4	1
font-family	A prioritized list of font family names and/or generic family names for an element	*family-name* *generic-family*	3	1	4	1
font-size	Sets the size of a font	xx-small x-small small medium large x-large xx-large smaller larger *length* %	3	1	4	1
font-size-adjust	Specifies an aspect value for an element that will preserve the x-height of the first-choice font	none *number*	-	-	-	2

(continued on next page)

FONT (continued)

PROPERTY	DESCRIPTION	VALUES	IE	F	N	W3C
font-stretch	Condenses or expands the current font-family	normal wider narrower ultra-condensed extra-condensed condensed semi-condensed semi-expanded expanded extra-expanded ultra-expanded	-	-	-	2
font-style	Sets the style of the font	normal italic oblique	4	1	4	1
font-variant	Displays text in a small-caps font or a normal font	normal small-caps	4	1	6	1
font-weight	Sets the weight of a font	normal bold bolder lighter 100 200 300 400 500 600 700 800 900	4	1	4	1

GENERATED CONTENT

PROPERTY	DESCRIPTION	VALUES	IE	F	N	W3C
content	Generates content in a document. Used with the :before and :after pseudo-elements	*string* *url* counter(*name*) counter(*name, list-style-type*) counters(*name, string*) counters(*name, string, list-style-type*) attr(*X*) open-quote close-quote no-open-quote no-close-quote	1		6	2

(continued on next page)

GENERATED CONTENT (continued)

PROPERTY	DESCRIPTION	VALUES	IE	F	N	W3C
counter-increment	Sets how much the counter increments on each occurrence of a selector	none *identifier number*				2
counter-reset	Sets the value the counter is set to on each occurrence of a selector	none *identifier number*				2
quotes	Sets the type of quotation marks	none *string string*	-	1	6	2

LIST AND MARKER

PROPERTY	DESCRIPTION	VALUES	IE	F	N	W3C
list-style	A shorthand property for setting all of the properties for a list in one declaration	*list-style-type* *list-style-position* *list-style-image*	4	1	6	1
list-style-image	Sets an image as the list-item marker	none *url*	4	1	6	1
list-style-position	Sets where the list-item marker is placed in the list	inside outside	4	1	6	1
list-style-type	Sets the type of the list-item marker	none disc circle square decimal decimal-leading-zero lower-roman upper-roman lower-alpha upper-alpha lower-greek lower-latin upper-latin hebrew armenian georgian cjk-ideographic hiragana katakana hiragana-iroha katakana-iroha	4	1	4	1
marker-offset		auto *length*		1	7	2

MARGIN

PROPERTY	DESCRIPTION	VALUES	IE	F	N	W3C
margin	A shorthand property for setting the margin properties in one declaration	*margin-top* *margin-right* *margin-bottom* *margin-left*	4	1	4	1
margin-bottom	Sets the bottom margin of an element	auto *length* %	4	1	4	1
margin-left	Sets the left margin of an element	auto *length* %	3	1	4	1
margin-right	Sets the right margin of an element	auto *length* %	3	1	4	1
margin-top	Sets the top margin of an element	auto *length* %	3	1	4	1

OUTLINES

PROPERTY	DESCRIPTION	VALUES	IE	F	N	W3C
outline	A shorthand property for setting all the outline properties in one declaration	*outline-color* *outline-style* *outline-width*	-	1.5	-	2
outline-color	Sets the color of the outline around an element	*color* invert	-	1.5	-	2
outline-style	Sets the style of the outline around an element	none dotted dashed solid double groove ridge inset outset	-	1.5	-	2
outline-width	Sets the width of the outline around an element	thin medium thick *length*	-	1.5	-	2

PADDING

PROPERTY	DESCRIPTION	VALUES	IE	F	N	W3C
padding	A shorthand property for setting all of the padding properties in one declaration	*padding-top* *padding-right* *padding-bottom* *padding-left*	4	1	4	1
padding-bottom	Sets the bottom padding of an element	*length* *%*	4	1	4	1
padding-left	Sets the left padding of an element	*length* *%*	4	1	4	1
padding-right	Sets the right padding of an element	*length* *%*	4	1	4	1
padding-top	Sets the top padding of an element	*length* *%*	4	1	4	1

POSITIONING

PROPERTY	DESCRIPTION	VALUES	IE	F	N	W3C
bottom	Sets how far the bottom edge of an element is above/below the bottom edge of the parent element	auto % *length*	5	1	6	2
clip	Sets the shape of an element. The element is clipped into this shape, and displayed	shape auto	4	1	6	2
left	Sets how far the left edge of an element is to the right/left of the left edge of the parent element	auto % *length*	4	1	4	2
overflow	Sets what happens if the content of an element overflow its area	visible hidden scroll auto	4	1	6	2
position	Places an element in a static, relative, absolute, or fixed position	static relative absolute fixed	4	1	4	2
right	Sets how far the right edge of an element is to the left/right of the right edge of the parent element	auto % *length*	5	1	6	2
top	Sets how far the top edge of an element is above/below the top edge of the parent element	auto % *length*	4	1	4	2

(continued on next page)

POSITIONING (continued)

PROPERTY	DESCRIPTION	VALUES	IE	F	N	W3C
vertical-align	Sets the vertical alignment of an element	baseline sub super top text-top middle bottom text-bottom *length* %	4	1	4	1
z-index	Sets the stack order of an element	auto *number*	4	1	6	2

TABLE

PROPERTY	DESCRIPTION	VALUES	IE	F	N	W3C
border-collapse	Sets whether the table borders are collapsed into a single border or detached as in standard HTML	collapse separate	5	1	7	2
border-spacing	Sets the distance that separates cell borders (only for the "separated borders" model)	*length length*	5M	1	6	2
caption-side	Sets the position of the table caption	top bottom left right	5M	1	6	2
empty-cells	Sets whether or not to show empty cells in a table (only for the "separated borders" model)	show hide	5M	1	6	2
table-layout	Sets the algorithm used to display the table cells, rows, and columns	auto fixed	5	1	6	2

TEXT

PROPERTY	DESCRIPTION	VALUES	IE	F	N	W3C
color	Sets the color of a text	*color*	3	1	4	1
direction	Sets the text direction	ltr rtl	6	1	6	2
line-height	Sets the distance between lines	normal *number* *length* %	4	1	4	1
letter-spacing	Increase or decrease the space between characters	normal *length*	4	1	6	1
text-align	Aligns the text in an element	left right center justify	4	1	4	1
text-decoration	Adds decoration to text	none underline overline line-through blink	4	1	4	1
text-indent	Indents the first line of text in an element	*length* %	4	1	4	1
text-shadow		none *color* *length*				
text-transform	Controls the letters in an element	none capitalize uppercase lowercase	4	1	4	1
unicode-bidi		normal embed bidi-override	5			2
white-space	Sets how white space inside an element is handled	normal pre nowrap	5	1	4	1
word-spacing	Increases or decreases the space between words	normal *length*	6	1	6	1

PSEUDO-CLASSES

PSEUDO-CLASS	PURPOSE	IE	F	N	W3C
:active	Adds special style to an activated element	4	1	8	1
:focus	Adds special style to an element while the element has focus	-	1.5	8	2
:hover	Adds special style to an element when you mouse over it	4	1	7	1
:link	Adds special style to an unvisited link	3	1	4	1
:visited	Adds special style to a visited link	3	1	4	1
:first-child	Adds special style to an element that is the first child of some other element	-	1	7	2
:lang	Allows the author to specify a language to use in a specified element	-	1	8	2

PSEUDO-ELEMENTS

PSEUDO-ELEMENT	PURPOSE	IE	F	N	W3C
:first-letter	Adds special style to the first letter of a text	5	1	8	1
:first-line	Adds special style to the first line of a text	5	1	8	1
:before	Inserts some content before an element		1.5	8	2
:after	Inserts some content after an element		1.5	8	2

MEDIA TYPES

MEDIA TYPE*	DESCRIPTION
all	Used for all media type devices
aural	Used for speech and sound synthesizers
braille	Used for Braille tactile feedback devices
embossed	Used for paged Braille printers
handheld	Used for small or handheld devices
print	Used for printers
projection	Used for projected presentations, like slides
screen	Used for computer screens
tty	Used for media using a fixed-pitch character grid, like teletypes and terminals
tv	Used for television-type devices

* Used as the media attribute of the link tag or with the @media attribute. See @media examples at:
   http://w3schools.com/css/css_mediatypes.asp

The tables in these Appendices were reproduced by permission from W3 Schools, an award-winning and free e-learning site for Web developers (www.w3schools.com). These tables can be found on the W3 Schools site, where every section has links to examples and detailed explanations of each tag and property.

Index